A RODALE SEWING BOOK

SEWING SECRETS

FROM THE

FASHION INDUSTRY

· · · · · · · · ·

PROVEN METHODS TO HELP YOU
SEW LIKE THE PROS

Edited by
Susan Huxley

Rodale Press, Emmaus, Pennsylvania

OUR MISSION

We publish books that empower people's lives.

RODALE BOOKS

Sewing Secrets from the Fashion Industry Editorial Staff

Editor: Susan Huxley
Cover and Interior Book Designer: Darlene Schneck
Illustrator: Barbara Field
Photographer: John Hamel
Interior Photo Stylists: John Hamel, Susan Huxley, and Darlene Schneck
Studio Manager: Leslie Keefe
Copy Editor: Carolyn Mandarano
Manufacturing Coordinator: Patrick T. Smith
Production Manager: Helen Clogston
Indexer: Nan N. Badgett
Editorial Assistance: Stephanie Wenner

Rodale Home and Garden Books

Vice President, Editorial Director: Margaret Lydic Balitas
Senior Editor, Craft Books: Cheryl Winters Tetreau
Art Director: Michael Mandarano
Copy Director: Dolores Plikaitis
Office Manager: Karen Earl-Braymer

If you have any questions or comments concerning this book, please write to:

Rodale Press, Inc.
Book Readers' Service
33 East Minor Street
Emmaus, PA 18098

Library of Congress Cataloging-in-Publication Data

Huxley, Susan.
    Sewing secrets from the fashion industry : proven methods to help you sew like the pros / edited by Susan Huxley.
        p.   cm.—(A Rodale sewing book)
    Includes index.
    ISBN 0–87596–719–1   (hc : alk. paper)
        1. Dressmaking.   2. Tailoring (Women's)   I. Title.   II. Series.
    TT515.H89   1996
        646.4'04—dc20   95–46499

**Distributed in the book trade
by St. Martin's Press**

2 4 6 8 10 9 7 5 3   hardcover

Contents

Meet the Authors vi   How to Use This Book viii

GETTING STARTED

TIPS AND TECHNIQUES

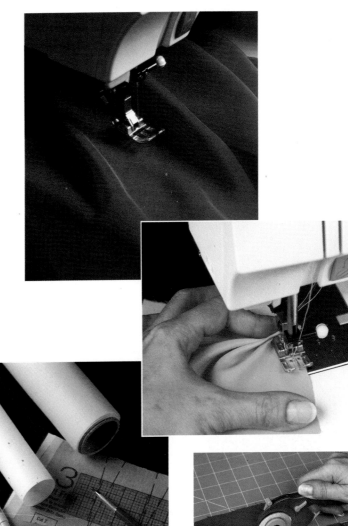

PUTTING IT ALL TOGETHER

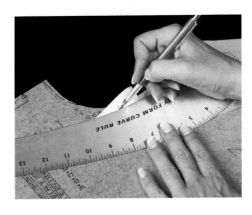

Meet the Authors

Laurel Hoffman

A former instructor at the Philadelphia College of Textiles and Science, Laurel began her career in custom couture in Philadelphia. She then worked in industrial bridal couture and later sportswear, making patterns and eventually supervising factory production. She is experienced in all phases of industrial manufacturing, including draping and design, cutting and sample making, patternmaking, grading, layouts, and factory production.

Barbara Kelly

Fit, fabric behavior, and construction techniques are the specialties of Barbara Kelly. For more than 30 years, she has taught home sewers the secrets of well-designed and beautifully constructed garments. While she continues to teach, Barbara also works as a freelance fit and sewing consultant for designers in San Francisco. She is a member of the Professional Association of Custom Clothiers. In addition, Barbara was a contributing writer and sample maker for the public television series "Sewing Today" and for the publication Vogue/Butterick's Designer Sewing Techniques. For this book, Barbara carefully researched industry techniques and modified or adapted procedures so that home sewers can achieve the ready-to-wear look and streamlined construction techniques of the garment industry.

Julia Reidy Linger

Julia has a degree in patternmaking from the Fashion Institute of Technology in New York City and is the chief executive officer of Patterns & Production, Ltd., in Oklahoma. Her company provides a full range of pattern services to ready-to-wear manufacturers on a global scale. Working hand in hand with production managers, she also consults on construction and production. Julia is nationally known for her seminars on fitting, industrial construction, and pattern drafting. Her involvement in the garment industry began when she was 12 years old. She brings to this book 25 years of experience in home sewing, custom clothing design, and commercial clothing construction.

Elissa Meyrich

A former instructor at Parsons School of Design in New York City, Elissa's expertise is based on a lifetime in the garment industry. As a designer in sample rooms, she works side by side with top professional sewers and patternmakers. Elissa owned a sportswear company, with her clothes retailing in Macy's, Ann Taylor, and other specialty stores. Today she is a consultant to fiber companies and manufacturers.

The owner of Sew Fast/Sew Easy on 57th Street in New York City, Elissa now teaches professional garment industry techniques and design sense to home sewers.

Lonny Noel

At age 16, Lonny Noel began her career of 20-plus years in the apparel industry. After earning a certificate for power sewing from the Community College and Technical Institute in Pennsylvania, she worked as a sewing machine operator. Eventually she was promoted to a section supervisor for 70 sewing and pressing operators on 20 operations. She was the quality assurance lab manager for the Greif Companies Inc., a leading manufacturer of tailored men's suits, sportcoats, career apparel, and formalwear. Lonny approves preproduction interfacings, develops ideal fusing condition specifications, and performs product testing on hundreds of fabrics.

You can find a listing of the topics associated with each author on page 242.

Special Thanks

The creation of a book of this nature involves the talents and resources of many. The following companies gave freely of their time, knowledge, and products.

Pfaff American Sales Corporation loaned both the sewing machine (model 7550) and the serger (Hobbylock 4870) that appear in almost every photograph in this book. The very heavy industrial machines shown on pages 4–5 were supplied and delivered to the photography studio by **Atlantic Sewing Machine and Leasing Company Inc.** of Nazareth, Pa.

A significant contribution was also made by **Fashion Fabrics** of St. Louis, Mo. A little over a year before this book was printed, this mail-order company agreed to supply almost all of the fabric that was used for the step-by-step photographs.

When it was time to create the contents page and the back cover, **The Souder Store,** in Souderton, Pa., let the photography team borrow more than 20 bolts of fabric. (They filled the entire back of the book designer's car, and the editor wanted to smuggle it all home to add to her stash!)

Other sources of wisdom and products include **Allentown Sewing Machine Outlet,** Allentown, Pa., **The Bon-Ton Department Store,** Allentown, Pa., **Freudenberg Nonwovens, Pellon Division,** Chelmsford, Mass., **HTC-Handler Textile Corporation,** Moonachie, N.J. (for fusibles and a Twin Fit dressform), and **June Tailor,** Richfield, Wis.

The authors would like to express their gratitude to the following people and companies:

Laura Hotchkiss Brown, couture sewing instructor, San Francisco, Calif.; Beth Grady Buckland, Allentown, Pa.; Butterick Pattern Service; and Professors Lana Colavita, Jane Likens, and Sylvia Rosen, Philadelphia College of Textiles and Science.

Reginald Fairchild, design director at Vogue Pattern Service, New York, N.Y.; May Fong, sample maker, New York, N.Y.; Hank Ford, designer, San Francisco, Calif.; Helen Griffin; Terry and John Kiskaddon, owners of the designer clothing company Harper Greer, San Francisco, Calif.; and Lee Louie, sample maker and patternmaker, New York, N.Y.; and McCall Pattern Company.

Carolyn Ramsey, a production patternmaker; Jacque Ross, designer and instructor at the Fashion Institute of Design and Merchandising, Los Angeles, Calif.; Lisa Shepard, creative director, HTC-Handler Textile Corporation, Consumer Products Division, Hillside, N.J.; Harry Shonteff, sewing equipment broker, San Francisco, Calif.; Simplicity Pattern Company Inc.; Alison Tucek, Bernina of America instructor, San Francisco, Calif.; Beverly Upton, production manager, Think Tank, San Francisco, Calif.; Vogue Pattern Service.

How to Use This Book

This book has changed the way I sew. When I began editing **Sewing Secrets from the Fashion Industry,** I was intrigued by the techniques and ideas. So I pulled out my fabric stash and started to play. First I added a false placket and the no-fail, perfectly shaped patch pocket to a jumper. Then I made a bagged lining for a vest and crowded a sleeve cap.

I kept adding new ideas to my repertoire until, one day, I realized that my skills had improved and I was using a technique from this book every time I sat down at my machine. And more people were asking me where I bought my clothes, rather than saying, "I see you've been sewing."

I hope that you try a technique that I mentioned above before you read this book from cover to cover. **Sewing Secrets from the Fashion Industry** is organized so that you can turn to any subject and head for your sewing machine. For additional information, refer to "Getting Started," beginning on page 1, and "Putting It All Together," beginning on page 207, to lead you through the assembly procedure for your garment.

In some cases, you have several options for construction and assembly techniques, so choose the method or treatment that feels right for you. By so doing, you will be practicing one of the guiding principles of the garment industry: There's no one "correct" way to make a garment. Selected techniques and treatments are based on available equipment, the machine operators' skill levels, and the garment's cost. Of course, all professionals have techniques to which they return again and again

and, perhaps, which they insist are better than others. The experts that I worked with didn't always agree. In these cases, I included the options so that you can decide what's right for you.

For Rodale, the creation of this book is a landmark; the editors always strive for clear, easy-to-follow instructions, but now hundreds of step-by-step photos are also included. It's our goal to give you all of the information you need to express your creativity and skill.

Susan

The team for *Sewing Secrets from the Fashion Industry* spent hundreds of hours in the studio creating more than 800 photographs. Photographer John Hamel, *left,* formerly a nonsewer, can now operate a serger. Book designer Darlene Schneck, *top rear,* learned to describe every imaginable construction detail...which she does over and over and over again. I'm at the *far right.* Melody D'Amico, *sitting,* thought I was joking when I insisted that, as the hand model, she should wear gloves when sunbathing.

Getting Started

Equipment

As many sewers know, it is possible to make a garment with very few tools. Scissors, a sewing machine, a few pins, plus a needle and thread are enough to get the job done. Yet such a limited sewing kit will slow down assembly and add layers of frustration to the process.

In the garment industry, sewing notions are kept to a minimum, and core equipment, like sewing machines and pressing tables, are highly specialized. Nevertheless, the following tools of the trade are considered indispensable.

AWLS are found next to the sewing machine bed of almost every sample maker and machine operator in the garment industry. This indispensable sewing aid functions like an extra finger to manipulate fabric near the presser foot.

FRENCH CURVES AND HIP CURVES are versatile metal or plastic rulers used to blend necklines, armhole lines, and hiplines when altering patterns.

L-SQUARES ensure that lines are perfectly perpendicular.

NOTCHERS are not necessary when working with pattern pieces. They are useful, however, when punching holes in patterns for notches and marking the placement for buttonholes and pockets.

PAPER, either tissue or drafting that's dotted at 1-inch increments (such as Alpha-Numeric Marking Paper), is helpful for making patterns. It also provides cutting control when laid under and cut with difficult fabrics. If you buy a 40-inch-wide roll of paper, consider having it mounted on a curtain rod under the cutting table because this paper tends to bruise along its edges if it is stood on end.

PERMANENT MARKERS are a good choice for placing lines and information on pattern pieces. It is important to use pens containing permanent, non-soluble ink so that the ink doesn't bleed onto fabric pattern pieces.

At-a-glance pattern identification, which will speed the sewing process, is possible by employing industrial coding. Most patterns for a garment's primary fashion fabric are drawn with black ink. Alterations, corrections, and patterns to be cut from secondary fabrics are marked in red ink. Blue may be used for further correcting and on pattern pieces to be cut from a third fabric. Trim placement is marked on patterns in green ink.

PINS are available in many sizes and shapes. This variety reflects their many uses and the personal preferences of sewers. Since industrial sewing requires few pins, a couple of containers of small- to medium-weight pins are all that is necessary.

ROTARY CUTTERS are controversial. Some experts shun the tool, saying it hampers precision cutting. Other sewers like it because the rotary blade quickly slices through fabric, and the blades are easily replaced. These sewers see a strong similarity between the rotary cutter and the "power saws" used in the industry. Although computerized cutting equipment is employed in cutting rooms, in many cases, it is still cost-effective for staff to cut multiple plies of fabric with hand-held tools that look similar to the saws found in woodworking shops.

Using a rotary cutter demands a high degree of control to avoid cutting on an angle into fabric plies, improper notch depth, messy corners, and overextended slash lines. The position of both hands and the tool, refined through constant use, can overcome these drawbacks. See "Rotary Cutting Techniques" on page 70.

A self-healing mat must be used with a rotary cutter.

SHEARS can last a lifetime and are an important investment. The popular choice among home sewers is a pair of 10-inch shears, but professionals prefer the longer blades on the 12-inch version. The larger scissors have a longer cut, can work through several plies at once, and because of the heavier weight, can build up momentum while cutting. Surprisingly, the 12-inch shears are extremely versatile and can cut very small, intricate pieces from even delicate fabric.

Shears should be sharpened by a professional. Be careful not to drop them because this may knock them out of alignment.

THIMBLES don't come in as many sizes as there are fingers. To make one "fit," gently step on it so that the sides are slightly flattened.

TRANSPARENT RULERS with grids printed on them are loved by both pattern drafters and quilters. Buy the 2-inch-wide × 18-inch-long ruler that is marked in inches and doesn't have a metal strip on one edge.

A CURVE RULE

8

SHOP TALK

Marks with Distinction

....

I DON'T RECOMMEND WATER- OR air-soluble pens because I haven't had consistent results with them, and I haven't found them in sample rooms. If you press as you sew, the chemical is set. I really like using a chalk wheel or a sharp fabric marking pencil.

Barbara Kelly

Why Buy an Industrial Sewing Machine?

Anyone who spends hours at a sewing machine, be it from 9 to 5 in a designer's studio or evenings and weekends in the home, values a sewing machine's quality of stitching, options, and durability. As you know, an almost personal relationship is established with a favorite machine. But at some point, most active home sewers wonder if they're ready for an industrial machine. The answer to this question isn't simple. Certainly an industrial machine is more durable, and the stitch quality is exceptional, but the sewer is often locked into very specialized functions.

A home-sewing machine is designed to simulate the operations of several industrial machines, accomplished by changing feet, inserting cams, changing boards, pushing buttons, moving levers, or turning dials. Of course, it cannot take the place of many intricate and powerful machines, but it does give the sewer flexibility.

There are many types of industrial-sewing machines. In the apparel industry, machines are selected, calibrated, and well maintained for optimum performance on a given fabric with a specified needle and thread combination for a particular application in the production of a garment. When the application is complete, the machine is reset by a technician or traded for another. These machines have durable metal parts,

whereas the same can't be said for all home-sewing machines.

An industrial machine must rest in a specially designed table that also accommodates the motor, foot pedals, knee lift, and switch. The entire apparatus is heavy and not as aesthetically appealing as a home-sewing machine and cabinet. It also isn't as portable.

The single-needle lockstitch, also called a single needle or high-speed oiler, is the most popular and versatile sewing machine in the industry. It is designed to produce consistent results in sample and production rooms. The lockstitch forms precise and secure straight stitches on the top and underside of the fabric as the needle thread and bobbin thread lock each

time the needle passes through the fabric. The lockstitch machine with a single needle and bobbin thread most resembles a home-sewing machine, but there are differences.

Home-sewing machines operate quietly at graduating

SHOP TALK

Exclusive Use

A SEWING MACHINE BECOMES finely attuned to an operator's touch and will break down less often when only one operator uses it.

Barbara Kelly

speeds, have a small motor, and are multifunctional. Industrial machines are stronger and noisier because they operate at one high speed from a powerful motor. They require controlled skill and coordination to operate.

The motor on the lockstitch and other industrial-sewing machines can be equipped to automate backstitching. Sewing can be repeated in various combinations when a machine is accessorized with a control panel and memory bank. In addition, a machine can be rigged with the following: handling equipment for manipulating the fabric; a laser light for reading a marker; a computer chip for controlling the length, direction, and number of stitches; multiple needles and bobbins for locking special threads; feed dogs for adjusting the top and bottom layers of fabric; and knives for clipping the threads after the sewing is completed.

Industrial-sewing machines without bobbins have loopers to form a chain of crochetlike stitches. An overlock, also called a serger by many people even though these machines are slightly different, is an example of one type. Not only does this machine look different from a lockstitch but it also operates differently. It cannot stitch in reverse, but it does several operations at once: sews the fabric, cuts the edges, and wraps the cut edges with thread.

Like the home-sewing machine, the home serger is designed to simulate the operations of several industrial machines, including

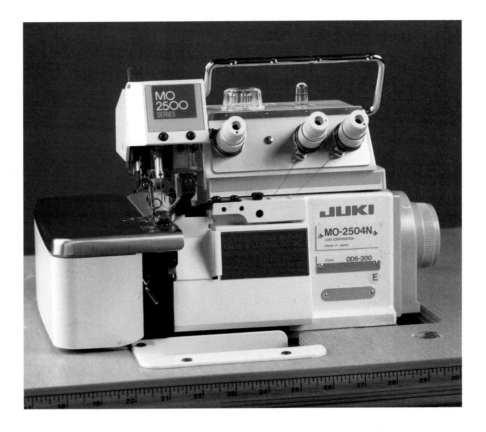

the overlock. The home serger offers flexibility and allows the home sewer to mimic combinations of stitches that look similar to those found in ready-to-wear.

All industrial machines take only industrial needles that come in boxes of 100, with a limited number of suppliers willing to break the boxes into quantities of 10. There is a wide range of thread types for industrial machines, but they must be purchased in large quantities.

To best utilize your home machine and its capabilities, you should become familiar with all of its operations. Knowing about your machine will allow you to make the changes you need to simulate an industrial operation.

Stitch Length

Before starting a sewing project, run your fabric through your machine to test the combination of needle size, thread type, tension, and stitch length. In general, the stitch length will depend upon the weight of the fabric; the heavier the fabric, the longer the stitch. Variations in weave, texture, and grainline may influence the results. The guidelines on these two pages show ranges of stitches along with their purpose. The imperial and metric measurements don't match exactly because sewing machines aren't matched for this comparison when they are tuned.

Fine stitching: 14 to 24 stitches per inch (spi) or 1 to 2 mm. Use this setting for seams in garments made from lightweight fabrics. This example is 24 spi.

Basting: 5 to 8 spi or 4 to 5 mm with an altered tension. Such large stitches are temporary because they are easy to remove. This example is 6 spi.

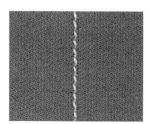

Reinforcing: 18 to 20 spi or 1½ mm. At points of strain or to prevent fraying when a seam allowance is clipped, choose this stitch length. This example is 18 spi.

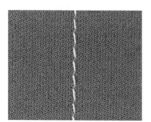

Regulation: 10 to 15 spi or 2 to 3 mm. This is the setting that is commonly used for sewing most seams, with 12 spi or 2.5 mm being the most common. This example is 12 spi.

Long stitching: 8 to 10 spi or 2 to 4 mm is used to ease in fullness. This example is 10 spi.

SPINNING YARNS

Pros Don't Always Use Industrial Machines

LINDA LORRAINE, WHO HAS HER OWN BUSINESS IN San Francisco and primarily makes fashion and therapeutic gloves, has an industrial lockstitch, a commercial and computerized home-sewing machines, and a home serger. Because the scale of her work is small, on knits, and mostly for custom orders, she prefers sewing on her computerized home machine. For constructing and finishing the short, curved seams, she feels less "in control" when she sews them on the other machines. She can quickly wind a bobbin and change thread for each pair of gloves. The home machine also gives her a range of practical stretch stitches, with her favorite being a serpentine, or sewn-out zigzag, and a stretch overlock. These stitches eliminate bulk and allow her to easily make any necessary alterations.

Barbara Kelly

FABRIC	STITCH LENGTH		THREAD	NEEDLE
Brocade, medium weight		12 spi or 2.5 mm	Molnlycke polyester	Medium jeans/denim sharp 90/14
Challis, medium weight		12 spi or 2.5 mm	Mettler mercerized cotton 50/3	Medium/fine universal 80/12
Lycra, two-way stretch		12 spi or 2.5 mm	Gutermann polyester	Medium/fine stretch 75/11
Shirting, lightweight		14 spi or 2 mm	Mettler polyester	Fine sharp 70/10
Ultrasuede		Near 10 spi or 3 mm	Molnlycke polyester	Medium stretch 75/11
Velvet		12 spi or 2.5 mm	Gutermann polyester	Medium-fine universal 80/12
Wool coating, heavy		9 spi or 3 mm	Gutermann polyester	Heavy universal 100/16

Presser Feet

Professional results are the product of precision sewing, and one of the most effective ways to maintain accuracy is by using the appropriate presser feet. Once you are accustomed to matching the presser foot to the procedure, garment construction will be easier, faster, and more satisfying.

There are hundreds of specialized presser feet on the market. Nevertheless, about a handful is all that is required to execute most sewing techniques.

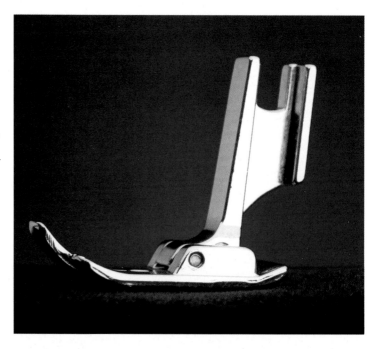

There's More!

INSERTING ELASTIC IN A WAIST-band casing is a simple process when a zipper foot is used. See "Allover Elastic Waistband" on page 191 for instructions.

The invisible zipper foot's appearance can vary between manufacturers. With the right presser foot, an invisible zipper is one of the easiest types of zippers to insert in a garment.

The blind hem foot has a special stitch pattern that works especially well on cotton knits, double knits, and loose weaves. Otherwise, it is best to hand sew a blind hem. In addition to its typical use, the blind hem foot is an effective topstitch guide.

The rolled hem foot, or baby hem foot as it's called in the garment industry, is essentially a "folder." It guides fabric and makes a fine hem that is no wider than ¼ inch.

SHOP TALK

Let Your Fingers Do the Walking

THE WALKING FOOT IS A PERFECT example of an accessory that gives home sewers an advantage over industrial machine operators. This attachment cannot be used in the industry because it does not work well on high-speed machines. Instead, sample makers use their fingertips to apply additional pressure to control fabric and ensure it is feeding evenly.

Elissa Meyrich

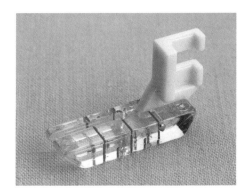

The Little Foot is relatively new to the home-sewing market, yet it is similar to a type of zipper foot found in the industry. Try using it for a lapped zipper insertion, as a seam guide, or for sewing seams with a ¼-inch seam allowance. Collars are also easier to attach with the Little Foot if the neckline seam allowance was previously trimmed to ¼ inch.

The roller foot is good for "sticky" fabrics. It's also especially effective on suede. A Teflon foot, named for the coating that allows it to glide over fabric, is commonly used in the industry for the same purpose.

There's More!

THE TRICK TO SUCCESSFULLY using a rolled hem presser foot is feeding the fabric at an angle. This method is descibed in "Hems" on page 119.

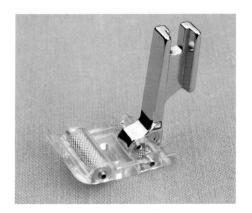

The topstitch foot helps sew an even ¼- or ⅜-inch row of straight stitches. The foot is so useful that even a busy sample maker will take the time to switch to one. Not all sewing machine manufacturers make a presser foot just for topstitching. Instead, they may recommend that an edge stitch foot, which may look like the one shown here, be used. Any foot that has a vertical line by which you can sight is suitable. Just as important as the presser foot is the topstitch needle. It should have a large eye and a groove on the back of the shank.

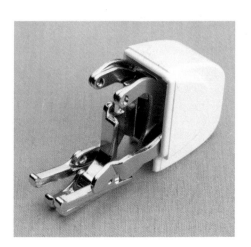

The walking foot, which is also called an even-feed foot, is effective for handling difficult or slippery fabrics and multiple plies. The foot works with the feed dogs to move, or evenly feed, fabric under the needle. Velvets made from either silk or rayon are some of the most difficult fabrics to sew. A walking foot will ensure that both layers of fabric match at the end of the seam. This presser foot will also help maintain the match points when sewing plaids and make sewing corduroy and thick layers of fabric much easier jobs.

Most presser feet work at a slower pace than the feed dogs. Industrial sewing machine operators use this to their advantage when joining a pattern piece with added ease to a smaller pattern piece. See "Feed Dogs" on page 10 for information on this technique.

Feed Dogs

Mastering the feed dogs will eliminate the use of pins and improve your ability to ease a garment pattern piece into a smaller one. The keys are the position of the fabric on the needle plate and the amount of tension applied to one or both pattern pieces as they are sewn together.

In any case, applying tension to a seam as it is sewn is a good habit to establish because it helps prevent ripples and puckers.

A simple way of remembering how to use those two rows of teeth under the presser foot is to think of the phrase "feed the dog." Just as most pet owners often feed their dogs excess food, placing the longer of the two pattern pieces on the feed dogs will "eat," or ease, the excess fabric into the seam. For example, when sewing sleeves into the armscye, place the sleeve side closest to the needle plate so that you can use the feed dogs to ease in the cap. Likewise, for neck edges and collars, the neck edge should always be nearest to the dogs. In this photo, the presser foot was removed, but in all but specialized stitching, it should remain in position.

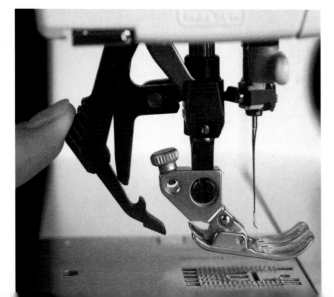

Some newer sewing machines have a differential, or dual, feed to ensure that the top layer of fabric moves under the presser foot at the same rate as the fabric next to the feed dogs. To use the easing ability of the feed dogs, you must disengage the differential feed.

Manually Adjusting Fabric Feed

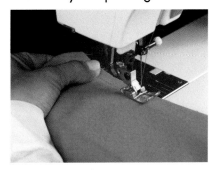

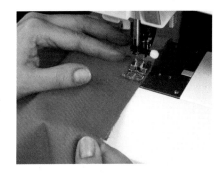

1 Sewers without a differential feed can manually simulate the effect. Hold the layers of fabric in front and behind the presser foot, and adjust the tension on the top layer of fabric with one of the methods described here.

2 Short fabric pieces are easier to handle. Position the matched raw edges on the needle plate. Lower the presser foot. Lift both pieces off the bed and match the raw edges at the far end. Hold the pattern pieces taut and sew.

3 To ease uneven, longer pattern pieces, pin mark one side of both the long and short lengths in quarters, pinning in the seam allowances. Match the raw edges at the start of the seam, match the notches as you sew, and hold the top fabric taut.

4 You can ease a long fabric length to a shorter piece without matching the pin marks. Match the raw edges at the start of the fabric lengths and position them on the needle plate. Lower the presser foot. Lift only the top fabric off the sewing machine bed. Hold it taut and let the longer fabric, which is closest to the feed dogs, rest on the bed. Sew the seam. During this process, hold both lengths of fabric feeding out from behind the presser foot taut.

Matching Plaids

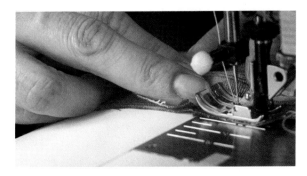

1 Feed dogs are also helpful for aligning plaids at the seams. Match the first dominant plaid line in the pattern repeat on both pattern pieces, place the pieces on the bed, and lower the presser foot.

2 Align the next dominant plaid line on the seamline. Place your hand between the two pattern pieces, gently holding the two layers together at the next plaid line. Place the first finger of your right hand on top of the seam, the second finger in between the two layers, and the rest of your hand underneath the top pattern piece. The fingers will guide the two layers of the seam together as your hand slides down the length of the seam. With your left hand, hold the pattern pieces beside or behind the presser foot. Sew.

3 As you sew, ensure that the approaching dominant plaid lines on both pattern pieces match, pulling each layer as necessary. Also reposition your hands as necessary.

Seam Guides

Sample makers frequently work with a magnetic seam guide. This is an additional tool placed or screwed on or near the needle plate of the machine. It creates a "wall" against which the edges of garment pieces can butt while being sewn. The guide ensures perfectly straight, accurate seamlines. Even curves and jacket fronts are easier to execute with a seam guide in position.

In addition, you will find that your sewing speed will improve with the use of a seam guide. Eyes can be trained to look at the guide and not at the machine's needle. This encourages you to concentrate on the seamline that is being created. A guide will also eliminate the need to trace sewing lines onto garment pattern pieces, also called cut components in the garment industry, prior to assembly.

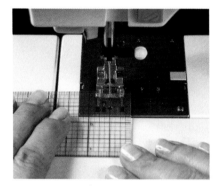

1 Place a clear ruler on the needle plate. Slide it underneath the presser foot, and lower the needle until the tip is almost touching the ruler. Shift the ruler until the right edge is the same distance from the needle as the desired seam allowance.

2 Place the seam guide on the needle plate, butting the left edge against the ruler. Remove the ruler.

SHOP TALK

Professional "Guide"ance

SOME HOME-SEWING MACHINES are sold with seam guide attachments. Yet there are manufacturers that do not recommend the use of a magnet on their computerized machines. Speak to your sewing machine dealer or call the manufactuer directly to find out if a magnet will damage your equipment.

Elissa Meyrich

Sewing Convex Curves

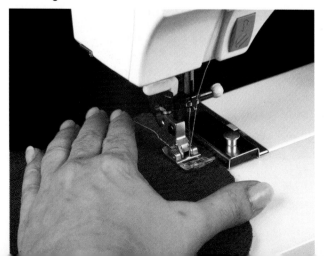

Convex curves, like the bottom of a pocket, are easy to sew with a seam guide. With the pocket under the presser foot, place your left hand on the fabric and sew. As you approach the curve, shift the fabric with a twist of the wrist, then reposition your left hand.

Sewing Concave Curves

1 Start sewing a seam on a concave curve at the straightest portion. A crotch seam, for example, is sewn from the waist down. As you enter the curve, make sure the fabric in front of the presser foot is relaxed.

2 Upon approaching the curve, pull the fabric to the left so that it moves away from the machine. The fabric feeding under the presser foot will continue to butt against the seam guide. The fabric will ruffle to the left of the presser foot. On sharp curves, the ruffle will be more pronounced.

3 Continue shifting the fabric to the left, so that the seam allowance at the presser foot is straight. At the most pronounced part of the curve, the raw edges of the seam allowance will still butt against the seam guide.

SHOP TALK

Substitutions Abound

AN ALTERNATIVE TO A MAG-netic seam guide is adhesive foam tape. Position a 1-inch-long piece of tape on the sewing machine bed, with the inner edge the desired distance from the machine's needle. In the industry, anything goes—you'll see pieces of masking tape and even Post-it notes stuck on a machine bed.

Laurel Hoffman

Sergers

Although overlock machines have been used in the garment industry for many years, they were only introduced to home sewers in the early 1970s. Now most sewers either own, or want to own, one. It's easy to see why. This is the quickest performing machine for today's sewer. Its speed far exceeds that of a sewing machine, plus it adds a nonfraying finish and sews seams at the same time.

There is a bit of confusion, however, about this machine. Whether a three-, four-, or five-thread version, the home-sewing industry usually calls them all sergers. Yet only a five-thread serger, which produces an overlocked edge accompanied by a chain stitched seam, can accurately be called a serger. The three- and four-thread machines produce only an overlock stitch.

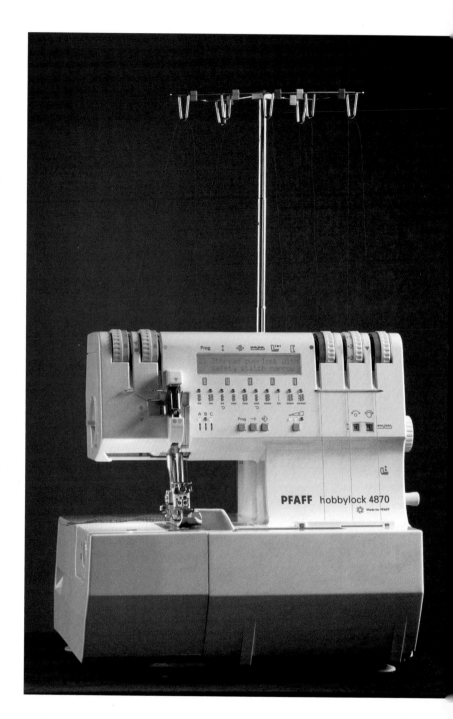

There's More!

SERGED AND OVERLOCKED SEAM finishes that are appropriate for certain fabrics are described in "Seam Finishes Using a Sewing Machine" on page 169.

1 This procedure is effective for all types of sergers. Raise the presser foot and pull the threads out of the tension disks. On some models, the tension releases automatically, so it is not necessary to pull the threads out of the tension disks.

2 Cut all of the threads above the tension disks or near the cones. Place the new thread on the spool rods and pull a few inches of thread from each. Tie each old thread to the corresponding new thread with a tight overhand knot. If desired, clip the thread ends.

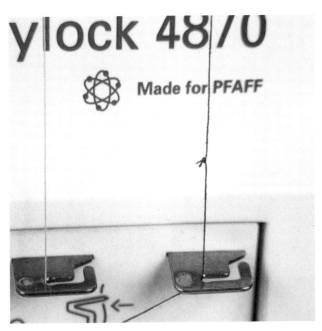

3 Grasp the thread in front of the needle's eye. Gently pull until the knot for the new thread is through all of the guides. Cut off the knot and insert the new thread through the needle. One by one pull the remaining old threads until the new threads have made their way through all of the guides.

4 Place the threads back in the tension disks, tugging them to ensure they are in position. Place all of the threads on the throat plate and lower the presser foot. Hold the end of the threads taut, and run the machine to create a tail chain about 3 inches long.

Fit

The part of the fashion industry that creates ready-to-wear (RTW) clothing bases the fit of its garments on standard pattern pieces, called slopers, that match the measurements of its target customers. Only custom clothiers and haute couture designers create patterns to fit specific clients. As a home sewer, you straddle these two extremes. You use pattern pieces that are designed to fit an "average" body, and you have the option of altering them to obtain a custom fit. By applying the RTW use of slopers with customized pattern alterations based on your measurements, you can sew garments that perfectly fit your client—you.

To determine which pattern company produces a sloper closely related to your figure and posture, note the differences within the patterns and review the information in "Key Questions to Ask When Selecting a Fitting Pattern" on page 24. You may also want to work through "Body Measurements Workshop," beginning on the opposite page, to obtain detailed information before selecting a fitting pattern.

SHOP TALK

Perfection Comes in Many Sizes

BUYING THE RIGHT SIZE, WHETHER IT BE FOR a fitting or a fashion garment pattern, is perplexing for two reasons. First, pattern sizes are so different from ready-to-wear (RTW) clothing sizes. There is no standard size 10 in RTW as there is on the Standard Body Measurement Chart published by the National Bureau of Standards (NBS) and used by a majority of the American pattern companies. Garment manufacturers periodically adjust the measurements on their specification sheets, since they find that consumers no longer reflect the statistics on that standardized chart. But the pattern companies agreed to use the measurement chart published by the NBS in the early '70s and for consistency, they have maintained its usage.

The second reason for confusion is that most women's measurements don't correspond with one size. All pattern companies now use multisize fashion patterns because they are aware of figure variations needing a range of sizes.

Barbara Kelly

Body Measurements Workshop

The key to good fit is selecting a fitting pattern that is suitable for your body's frame. And the first step in this process is taking comprehensive, accurate body measurements. The step-by-step photographs on the following pages will guide you through this process. For future reference, fill in your own measurements in the space provided.

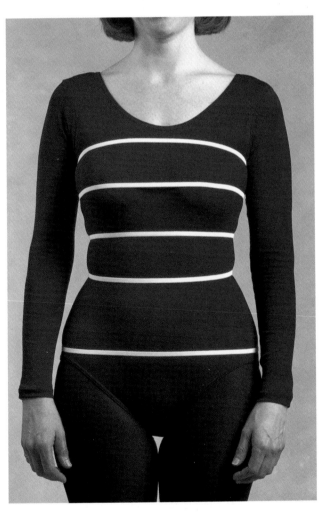

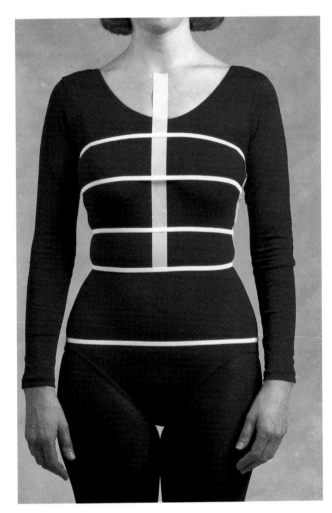

1 Ask a companion to help you take your body measurements while you are wearing foundation garments or form-fitting tights.

2 Place elastics around your hips, your waist, your rib cage directly under your bust, the fullest part of your bust, and under your arms above the fullest part of your bust. Mark the center front and center back with masking tape. Stand with a relaxed posture while your companion is taking your measurements.

Waist to the floor at center front:_____

Waist to the floor at center back:_____

Crotch to the floor at your inner leg:_____

Kneecap to the floor:_____

Bottom of your ankle to the floor:_____

Waist to the floor over your right hip:_____

Waist to the floor over your left hip:_____

Crotch length from your waist at center front to your waist at center back:_____

Waist from side to side through center front:_____

Waist from side to side through center back:_____

Hips at the fullest
part from side to
side through
center front:_____

Hips at the fullest
part from side to
side through
center back:_____

Thigh circumfer-
ence at the fullest
part above your
knees:_____

Waist to the fullest
part of your
thighs:_____

Calf circum-
ference:_____

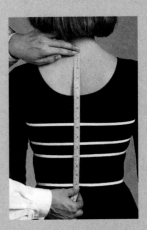

Prominent bone at
the base of the
back of your neck
to your waist at
center back;
masking tape posi-
tioned at center
back is
optional:_____

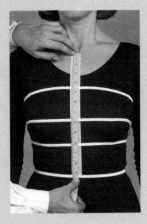

Center front at the
top of your col-
larbone to center
front at your
waist:_____

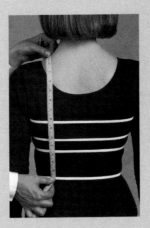

Right neck/shoulder
to your waist at
the back:_____

Left neck/shoulder
to your waist at
the back:_____

Right neck/shoulder,
  across your bust to
  your waist:_____

Left neck/shoulder,
  across your bust to
  your waist:_____

Waist to your bust
  tip:_____

Bust tip to bust
  tip:_____

Upper back from
  shoulder tip to
  shoulder tip:_____

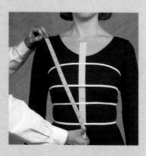

Right shoulder tip
  to your waist at
  center front:_____

Left shoulder tip to
  your waist at
  center front:_____

Right shoulder tip
  to your waist at
  center back:_____

Left shoulder tip to
  your waist at
  center back:_____

Midshoulder to rib
  cage directly
  under your right
  breast:_____

Midshoulder to rib
  cage directly
  under your left
  breast:_____

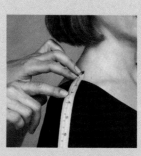

Right shoulder/neck
  to your shoulder
  tip:_____

Left shoulder/neck
  to your shoulder
  tip:_____

Shoulder blades from your right arm crease to your left arm crease 1 inch above your arm hinge:_____

Right underarm 1 inch below your arm hinge to your waist:_____

Left underarm 1 inch below your arm hinge to your waist:_____

Inside right arm 1 inch below your arm hinge to your wrist with your arm relaxed and slightly bent:_____

Inside left arm 1 inch below your arm hinge to your wrist with your arm re-laxed and slightly bent:_____

Right wrist to your elbow:_____

Left wrist to your elbow:_____

Right elbow circum-ference with your arm bent:_____

Left elbow circumfer-ence with your arm bent:_____

Right outer arm from your shoulder tip across your elbow to your wrist with your arm relaxed and slightly bent:_____

Left outer arm from your shoulder tip across your elbow to your wrist with your arm relaxed and slightly bent:_____

Right wrist cir-cumference:_____

Left wrist cir-cumference:_____

Fullest part of your right upper arm:_____

Fullest part of your left upper arm:_____

Slopers

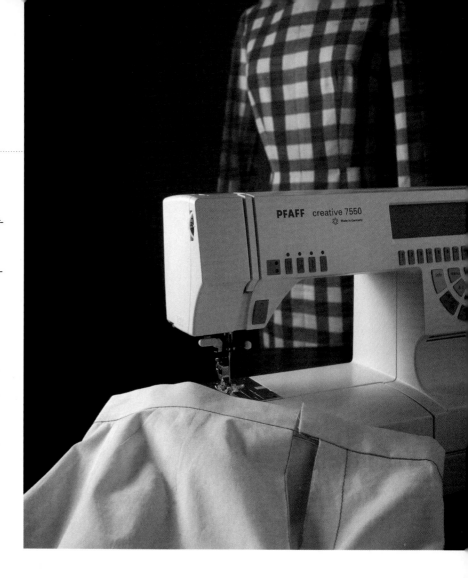

In design studios where flat patternmaking is used, the starting point for any garment is the creation of master blocks. A block set includes a bodice front, bodice back, skirt front, skirt back, and sleeve. This set is referred to as a sloper. A patternmaker drafts the sloper, using measurements from a standardized chart or a dress form having the proportions of a fit model who closely resembles the target customer.

Developing a personal sloper is like having a private label. You can use it to quickly determine whether it's necessary to alter a fashion pattern by laying it over the tissue of any fashion pattern to see how the pattern will relate to your body. See "The Sloper Shortcut to Fast Pattern Alterations" on page 39.

Your sloper contains minimal wearing ease and only structural details, while your fashion pattern contains design ease with design features. Generally, you will make the same adjustments on the fashion pattern that you made on the sloper. However, if you choose a pattern with loose styling and a minimum of fit, like an oversize shirt, you might decide that adjustments are unnecessary.

Patternmakers prefer to remove the dart interior and exclude the seam and hem allowances from slopers so that all of the cut edges of the pattern are either stitching lines or foldlines. This makes blocks easy to manipulate without the interference of the seam allowances and the hem. In this chapter, we have excluded the seam allowances and hems from the blocks to illustrate professional techniques.

SHOP TALK

Fit for You

IF YOU PREFER TO SEW FASHION patterns from one company more than from another, you should select the basic fitting pattern from that company. Base your selection of a single-size pants pattern on your hip measurement.

Barbara Kelly

Slopers for Home Sewers

Major commercial pattern companies offer home sewers patterns for basic blocks, or slopers. Called fitting patterns, they are listed in catalogs located in fabric stores. The basic pattern blocks and information about measuring, adjusting, sewing, fitting, and using the blocks are included in each pattern envelope, thus allowing you to customize the basic blocks without knowing how to draft a pattern.

Select a fitting pattern that best suits your body measurements, then fine-tune the fit by making flat pattern alterations. (See pages 28–38.) Finally, compare the blocks to the fashion patterns. See "The Sloper Shortcut to Fast Pattern Alterations" on page 39.

To determine which pattern company produces a block closely related to your figure and posture, note the differences within the patterns and consider the "Key Questions to Ask When Selecting a Fitting Pattern" on page 24. You may also want to work through the "Body Measurements Workshop" on pages 17–21 to obtain detailed information before selecting a fitting pattern.

Not all pattern companies have a basic pants fitting pattern, but most have a dart-fitted, slim-legged pattern that closely resembles their in-house pants sloper. Use this pattern to establish a pants sloper for yourself. To achieve consistent results with each pair of pants you construct, you need to know the shape of your body in two-dimensional terms and prepare each pants pattern to relate to your shape.

To select a fitting pattern similar to your body shape, ask yourself these questions. This chart is more subjective than "Body Measurements Workshop" on pages 17–21, but you can compare your body measurements, determined in the workshop, with the same locations on the pattern pieces. Consider it another approach to, or complementary information for, selecting your pattern. Trust your experience, intuition, and knowledge of your body as you work through this section.

PERSONAL CHARACTERISTIC	LOCATION TO EVALUATE ON THE PATTERN	CHARACTERISTICS OF RECOMMENDED SLOPER
Does my head tilt forward?	Center front at the top of collarbone to center front at waistline	New Look, Style, and Burda draft the lowest center front necklines
Do I have broad shoulders?	Right shoulder/neck to shoulder tip and left shoulder/neck to shoulder tip	New Look, Style, and Simplicity draft the longest shoulder seamline
Do I have a wide back?	Shoulder blades from right arm crease to left arm crease 1 inch above the arm hinge	New Look, Style, and Burda draft the widest back
Is my back more erect or more rounded?	Right shoulder tip to waist at center back and left shoulder tip to waistline at center back	Burda drafts the largest dart for contouring around the upper back
Is there more than a 2-inch difference between my chest and bust measurements?	Right shoulder tip to waist at center front and left shoulder tip to waist at center front	New Look and Style have built in the most fitting ease through the bust; McCall's offers the least
Is my bust apex high or low?	Midshoulder to rib cage directly under the right breast and midshoulder to rib cage directly under the left breast	Burda and Simplicity draft bust darts that radiate from a high bust point; New Look and Style bust darts radiate from a lower point
Does my bust have a wide or narrow spread?	Bust tip to bust tip	McCall's and Burda have darts that aim toward a narrow spread; New Look and Style have a wider spread
Do I have a full ribcage and waist?	Waist from side to side through center front plus waist from side to side through center back	New Look, Style, and Burda are fuller through the waist and have narrow waist darts
Am I full in the hip and thighs?	Hips at the fullest part from side to side through center front plus hips at the fullest part from side to side through center back	New Look, Style, and Simplicity draft the most here; Vogue and Butterick have the most slender drafts
Do I have full or thin arms?	Fullest part of the right upper arm and fullest part of the left upper arm	New Look and Simplicity draft the widest bicep; Burda drafts the least

Choosing the Right Size

Purchasing a multisize pattern allows you to compare and select measurements using the seamlines from all of the sizes. See the "Body Measurements Workshop" on pages 17–21 to obtain the measurements you need in order to develop your sloper. In the instructions, the fitting pattern pieces will be called blocks.

Bust circumference does not reveal cup size, nor does it describe bone structure or build around the shoulders and neck, which are difficult areas to fit. If you are an A or B cup and have a medium frame, base your pattern size selection on your bust measurement.

When you are a C cup or larger, base your pattern size choice on your chest measurement because that best describes your frame. Take your chest measurement around your body above the bust and include the shoulder blades and flesh in front of and behind your arm.

Adjusting Master Blocks

*C*AREFUL SELECTION OF A FITTING pattern size is a step toward ensuring nice-fitting garments. Nevertheless, you may need to further adjust your blocks to accommodate problem areas.

The instructions that accompany your fitting pattern offer suggestions. In addition, you can refer to "Alterations for Patterns and Blocks" on pages 28–38. If you choose to alter your blocks, you should also test fit the blocks in fabric, transfer any adjustments back to your blocks, and reinforce the blocks.

Barbara Kelly

Test Fitting a Sloper

Measurements and adjusted blocks can come close to creating your body shape for a garment, but they cannot completely duplicate the fabric's reaction as it drapes around your body. Therefore, you need to make a full muslin fitting shell from your blocks.

The term muslin originated with the type of fabric used to make a test garment. Muslin fabric is inexpensive and plain, allowing the eye to see the silhouette and structural lines. Gingham is another good choice because the horizontal and vertical lines are obvious and aid in identifying the test garment's fit and hang.

1 Cut the seam allowances and hems off your blocks. Adjust your blocks to fit your trouble spots. Straighten the gingham's cut edges along the weft. Steam press it to preshrink, smooth wrinkles, and square the grainlines.

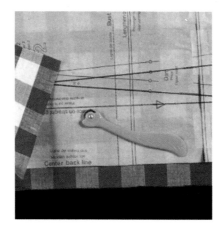

2 Fold the gingham in half along the warp, with the white and colored checks exactly aligned. Place your blocks on the fabric. Insert a piece of dressmaker's tracing paper, waxy side down, between a block and the top gingham layer. Place another piece, waxy side up, under both gingham layers.

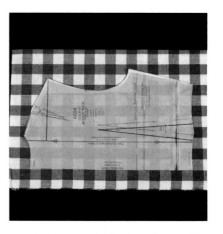

3 Outline each block and trace the darts with a tracing wheel. Draw a ½-inch seam allowance along the neckline, armholes, and waist, then draw a 1-inch seam allowance along the center, side, and shoulder. Allow for a 1-inch hem. On a pants sloper, draw a ½-inch seam allowance along the crotch seam and a 1-inch seam allowance along the zipper opening. Cut the blocks from the fabric.

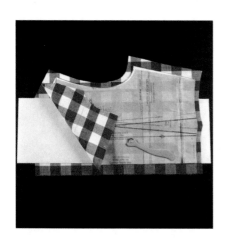

4 Insert dressmaker's tracing paper between the two layers of gingham, and use your tracing wheel to mark the grainline, bust line, hipline, crotch line, and bicep lines on the outside of all of the blocks. Construct and fit your fitting shell, following the instructions included with your fitting pattern.

5 When you are satisfied with the fit of your gingham, transfer all of the adjustment information back to your blocks. Rub a pen over the pins holding the adjustments, as well as the folded edges of the new stitching lines. Remove the pins, and measure the distance between the original seamlines and your new markings.

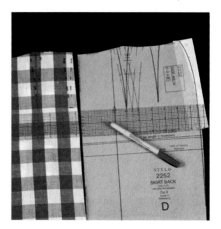

6 Draw new lines on your blocks to reflect the specific adjustments. Check that all of the corresponding seams and notches match. Compare these with your purchased fashion patterns to avoid guessing about their fit and feel.

Reinforcing Your Blocks

To strengthen the pattern tissue for repeated use, it's best either to stabilize the blocks or to make working copies from a tougher material. In production rooms, blocks are kept on a heavy paper known as tagboard, oaktag, or manila. If oaktag isn't available and you want a sturdy pattern, consider using posterboard, natural brown kraft paper, rope paper, freezer paper, or interfacing.

Stabilizing

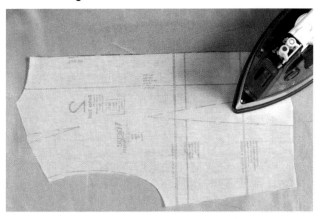

Fuse freezer paper or a stiff, nonwoven interfacing to the back of each tissue pattern piece. Place the fusible right side up on your ironing surface, set the pattern faceup on the fusible, and press the pattern only with a warm iron, taking care not to press too long or too hard. Trim off the excess interfacing.

SHOP TALK

Color Code Your Sloper

From time to time, as you make adjustments on your blocks, use a different colored pencil to record the exact adjustment and the date on the block. This information will guide you later when you compare the blocks with fashion pattern pieces.

Barbara Kelly

Copying a Block to Tagboard

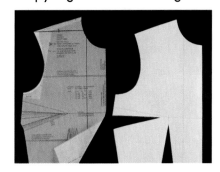

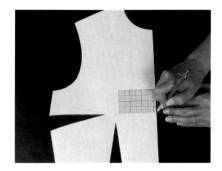

1 If you want a sturdy pattern, use tagboard, posterboard, natural brown kraft paper, or rope paper. Place your tissue blocks on the tagboard and secure them with weights, pins, or staples.

2 Accurately trace around the stitching lines with a needle-point tracing wheel. Also mark notches, circles, grainlines, and the following body lines: bicep, elbow, bust, hip, and crotch.

3 Remove the tissue pattern, and use a pencil to true the perforated lines. Label the pieces and cut them out. Also cut out the darts.

Alterations for Patterns and Blocks

Because blocks are used with working patterns, it's essential that you accurately adjust your pattern pieces and fine-tune the fit of your sloper. Measurements alone cannot guarantee a good fit. The starting point is altering the blocks and developing a customized sloper. The equipment you'll need includes a hip curve, paper, clear tape, see-through rule, tracing wheel, pen, and pencil. The following instructions are intended to help you achieve a well-fit sloper.

In this chapter, you will notice that pattern adjustments are made with a pen rather than with a pencil. This is done only for emphasis. In the industry, most pattern pieces are drawn in black ink. For quick identification, alterations, and corrections, blue, red, and green ink is used. In this chapter, such coding isn't used. When you are finished, each piece of your adjusted fitting pattern will be referred to as a block.

- To develop precise master blocks from your fitting pattern, you need to make certain the pieces are flat and wrinkle-free before adjusting them. Press the tissue pieces with a warm, dry iron. For accuracy, use a sharp pencil and appropriate ruler to draw new lines.

- Complete the lengthening or shortening adjustments first because the alignment at the side seams will be distorted.

- Always keep the grainline within the pattern continuous, and run it from the top of the pattern to the bottom.

- If the cutting line for your pattern adjustment crosses the legs at the bottom of the dart, you need to shape the cutting line. Before cutting out the block, fold the dart and tape or pin it along the stitching lines. If the dart is vertical,

also fold it toward the closest centerline. If the dart is horizontal, fold it toward the hem. Cut along the cutting line, then open the dart.

- Don't make width adjustments on the center front or center back seams. They are made by adding to the side seam or slashing within the pattern and spreading it. Mark any new width adjustments along the side seam at the bust-, waist-, and hip-lines respectively, then redraw or true the side seams using a ruler or hip curve.

- After adjusting one seam, check that the adjacent seams match.

- Date and record your adjustments on the pattern pieces.

- Use clear, removable tape so that further adjustments will not tear your pattern. Don't iron over any tape.

Pattern Adjustments for Trouble Spots

Standardized ready-to-wear clothes that you try on often give a clue to your trouble spots. Fabric strains or wrinkles form, pointing to areas that need attention. Adjustments illustrated here are for some of the most common trouble spots. Note that as in the industry, all of the seam allowances and hems are removed from the blocks.

The Long and Short of It

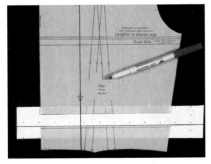

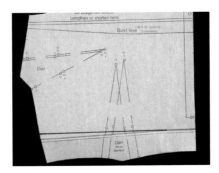

To lengthen a block, cut along the adjustment line. Tape on an extension. Measure the amount to be lengthened and draw a parallel line. Adjoining blocks must also be lengthened, and distorted darts and side seams must be trued.

To shorten any block, measure and draw a line parallel to the adjustment line printed on the block. Fold and tape a tuck joining the adjustment line and the placement line. The tuck should be half the depth that needs to be eliminated.

Long or Short Back Waistline

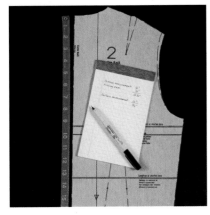

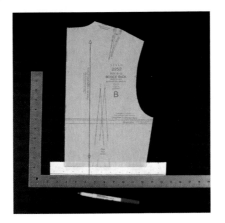

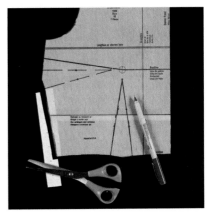

1 Add ¼ inch of fitting ease to your *waist to the floor at the center back* measurement from page 18. Compare your back waistline length measurement with ease to the back bodice block's length.

2 If the block does not equal your measurement plus the ¼-inch fitting ease, you must adjust the block. Fold the pattern if your length measurement is smaller, and slash it and insert paper if your measurement is greater.

3 For a longer back waist, tape additional paper to the side seam, close the dart, and draw a new seamline from the armhole to the waistline. True the dart legs, and lengthen the front bodice block. For a short back waist, fold the pattern, as shown.

Large or Small Bust

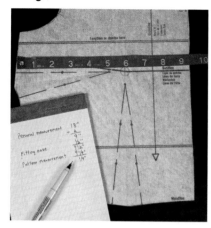

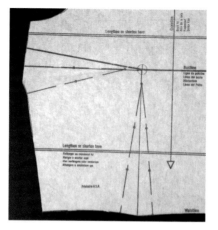

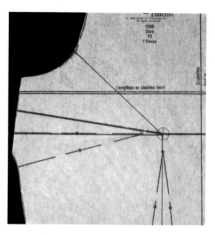

1 Measure across your bust from side seam to side seam. Divide this number in half and add ½ inch for fitting ease. Measure the front bodice block from the armhole edge to the center front. Close the side seam dart if the tape measure crosses through the dart's interior. Record the difference between the personal and pattern measurements.

2 If the block is smaller than your measurement, you must add paper. If the block is larger, you must cut and fold out the excess. Draw a line through the center of the waist dart and another through the side seam dart. The lines will intersect at the bust point, which is marked on some patterns.

3 Draw another line from the lower armscye notch to the bust point. Cut one short thread. Tape it to the seamline at the lower armscye notch.

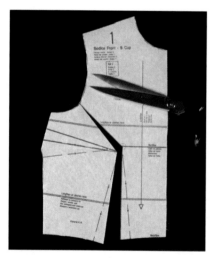

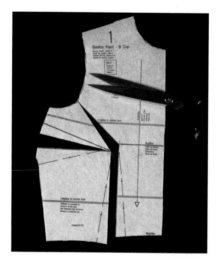

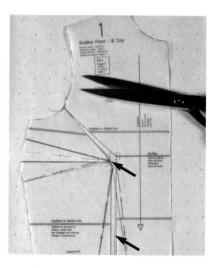

4 Cut your block along the vertical line that starts in the center of the waist dart and ends at the bust point. Cut along the line from the bust point to the armscye notch, slashing to, but not through, the thread.

5 Cut another short thread and tape it to the bust point of the lower side portion of the block. Slash through the center of the side seam dart and along the line that ends at the bust point. Cut to, but not through, the thread.

6 Place a sheet of paper under the block and tape it to the block along the center front. For a large bust, spread the bust point by the difference recorded in Step 1. (For a small bust, overlap the block.) Spread the same amount along the slash from the bust point to the waist dart. Let the other slashes spread so that the block remains flat.

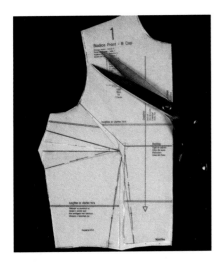

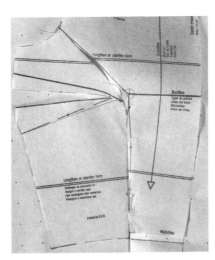

7 Tape the block to the paper. Redraw both darts, using the same starting positions at the beginning of the dart legs and making the darts their original length. You may need to adjust the dart points when you fit the muslin. The darts should stop 1 to 1½ inches from the bust tip.

8 After spreading the block, add length to the front by drawing a new waistline from the waist dart to the center front. If you overlapped the block, draw a new waistline from the waist dart to the side seam. Fold and pin your darts and cut away the excess paper. Open the dart.

SHOP TALK

Seam Allowances Excluded on Blocks

INSTRUCTIONS WITH MOST OF THE fitting patterns recommend ⅝-inch seam allowances outside the stitching lines because you will compare these lines to multi-size fashion patterns, which only have cutting lines. Seam allowances and hems are excluded from the blocks in this book, so you can use your sloper as a design tool and follow the industrial-sewing methods that do not include fittings during garment production.

Barbara Kelly

SPINNING YARNS

A Change in Plans

BESIDES HAVING DIFFERENT MEA-surements, patterns sometimes need to be adjusted so they allow for fabric shrinkage or stretching. Also, some small custom and semicustom designers will accept a special order and do pattern modifications to produce the request. These adjustments might include length and width variations. If the request is not likely to be duplicated, then the pattern is laid on the fabric, and the increased amount is drawn on the fabric to produce a new cutting line. If additional orders with this specification are anticipated, a piece of paper is stapled to the original pattern and the adjustment is drawn on the extension.

Barbara Kelly

Wide or Narrow Hips

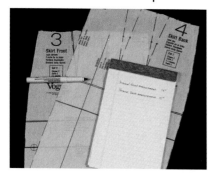

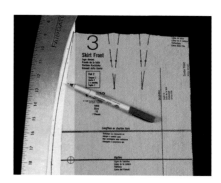

1 Treat your front and back blocks individually. Add 1 inch of fitting ease to your *hips at the fullest part from side to side through the center front* measurement. (See page 19.) Also add 1 inch of fitting ease to your *hips at the fullest part from side to side through the center back* measurement. (See page 19.)

2 Divide each of your hip measurements with ease in half to give you a measurement for each quarter of your body with ease, then compare these to the skirt blocks' measurements. If the blocks don't equal your measurements with fitting ease, adjust the side seams as instructed in Steps 3 and 4.

3 If your measurement is larger, tape additional paper to the skirt block along the side seam of the front skirt block. Measure out and mark an adjustment point away from the hipline. Using the edge of your hip curve, draw a new side seamline between the waistline and the adjustment point.

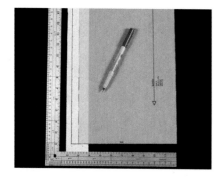

4 Continue the extended seamline to the bottom edge of the block. Increase the back skirt blocks in the same manner. If your measurement is smaller, decrease the hip and true the line between the hipline and the waistline.

Wide or Narrow Shoulders

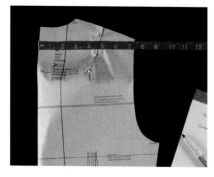

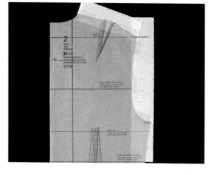

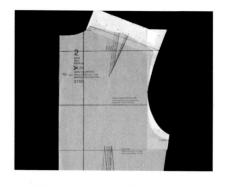

1 Obtain your *upper back from shoulder tip to shoulder tip* measurement from page 20. Divide this number in half. Compare your measurement to the measurement of the back bodice block from the armhole edge to the center back, with the dart closed.

2 Open the dart. If the block measurement is smaller, tape paper to the back bodice block at the shoulder and armhole. Draw a control line perpendicular to the grainline through the shoulder seam at the outside edge, extending it the amount you need adjusted. If your measurement is smaller, measure in from the outside edge.

3 Draw a new shoulder line with a straight ruler and pencil. Using a French curve, draw a new upper armhole. To restore the armhole depth, move the lower portion of the armhole the same distance in or out that you moved the shoulderline. Adjust the front bodice block in the same manner.

Large Arms

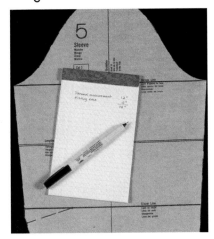

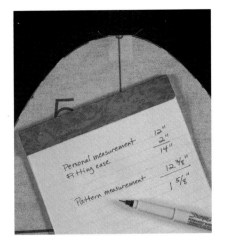

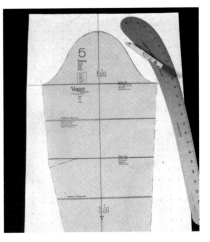

1 Add 2 inches of fitting ease to the *fullest part of your right upper arm* measurement from page 21. Obtain your left bicep measurement in the same manner. If the measurements are different, use the larger measurement to adjust your sleeve block.

2 Compare your bicep measurement with ease to the sleeve block measurement. If the measurements aren't the same, adjust the bicep by lengthening or shortening it. Cut four short threads. At each end of the bicep line and the vertical grainline, tape a thread tracing the seamline of the sleeve.

3 On a piece of paper larger than the sleeve block, draw a vertical line and a horizontal line down the center. Pin the sleeve block to the paper, matching the grainline to the vertical line and the bicep line to the horizontal line. Trace and remove the sleeve block.

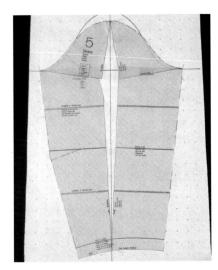

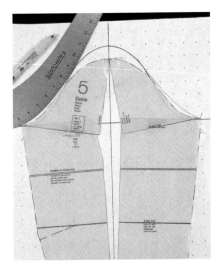

4 Cut the sleeve block along the bicep line and the center grainline, but not through the threads. Reposition the sleeve on the paper. Add width by spreading evenly on each side of the vertical line, keeping the outer points of the bicep line along the horizontal line. Narrow the spread by pushing in the outer points of the bicep line.

5 The sleeve cap has changed shape, and the cut edges of the bicep and the grainline have been distorted. Tape the sleeve cap and the cut areas in the sleeve block to your paper. True the sleeve cap by blending the underarm lines of the block with the cap you drew on the paper.

Thick or Slim Waist

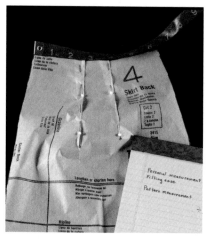

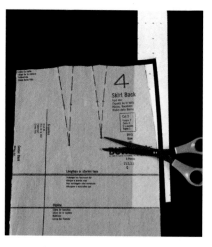

1 Treat your front and back blocks individually. Add ½ inch of fitting ease to your *waist from side to side through the center back* measurement from page 18. Also add ½ inch of fitting ease to your *waist from side to side through the center front* measurement from page 18.

2 Close the darts on your skirt blocks and measure the waist. Compare this measurement to your personal measurement with ease. If the blocks don't equal your measurement with fitting ease, adjust the side seams as instructed in Step 3 or 4.

3 If your back waist measurement is larger, tape paper to the back skirt block along the side seam between the waistline and hipline. Measure out and mark an adjustment point away from the waistline. Draw a new side seamline.

SHOP TALK

Try Changing a Dart

IN SOME INSTANCES, WAIST ADJUSTMENTS CAN ALSO be made by changing the width of the darts. For a slightly larger waist, diminish the width of the darts. For a slightly smaller waist, increase the width of the darts. Remember to adjust the bodice or waistband as well. Also see "Contouring" on page 116.

Barbara Kelly

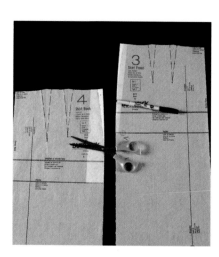

4 Increase the front skirt block in the same manner. Adjust the waist of the bodice back and front blocks also. Or narrow the waist by measuring in along each block in the same manner as in Steps 1 and 2, then adjust the side seams by folding the block along the side seams.

Protruding Abdomen

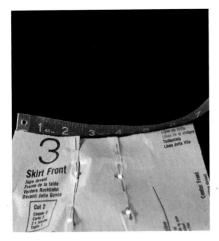

1 Add ½ inch of fitting ease to your *waist from side to side through the center front* measurement from page 18. Divide the measurement by 2. Close the darts on the front skirt block and measure the front waistline on the block. Subtract this measurement from your front waist measurement with ease.

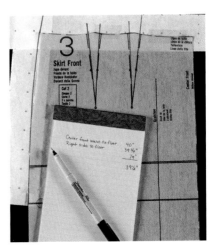

2 Tape paper to the front skirt block above the waist and along the side seam between the waistline and hipline. Proportionally reduce the width of each dart and add to the side seam until the measurement of the block equals half of your front waistline measurement with ease. Draw a new side seamline.

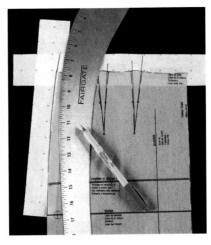

3 Compare your *waist to floor at the center front* measurement from page 18 to your *waist to floor over your right hip* and your *waist to floor over your left hip* measurements from page 18. The center front waist to floor measurement should be ¼ inch less than the side measurements.

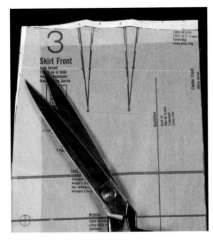

4 When the measurement is in excess, add the amount to the waist above the center front. Close the darts. With a hip curve, draw a new waist from the adjusted point above the waistline at the center front to the original waistline at the side seam.

SPINNING YARNS

Designer Saves Pattern Adjustments

APRIL EBERHARDT PRODUCES A SEMICUSTOM LINE OF WOMEN'S SUITS and dresses under the name Avril Mars. After her trunk show presentations, customers try on the samples and place orders for garments in specific colors and sizes. Customers can request a different sleeve or hem length. The staff records any adjustments that would make a garment fit better on that customer.

Then when the order arrives in the production room, Tina Smith, Avril's on-staff patternmaker, prepares a pattern for a cutter. She takes out a pattern in the appropriate style number and size. If the pattern requires customization, she changes it by taping on paper. She draws the amount needed for the adjustment and writes the customer's name, date, style number, size, and specifications on the extension in red pencil. After the pattern is cut for the customer, the extension is removed and placed in a manila folder with the customer's name on it. This allows that customer to call and order similar custom garments without a fitting.

Barbara Kelly

Short or Long Crotch Depth

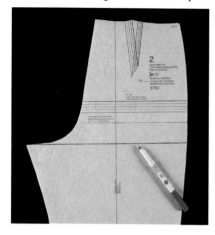

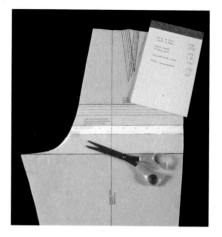

1 Before adjusting your front and back blocks, draw a crotch line perpendicular to the grainline from the crotch point to the side seam. To adjust the block to your measurements, establish the correct pattern lengths and widths and true the seams as instructed in Steps 2 and 3.

2 Subtract your *crotch to the floor at your inner leg* measurement from page 18 from the *waist to the floor over your right hip* measurement from page 18. Add fitting ease of ½ inch to both measurements if you are size 10 or smaller; ¾ inch if you are size 12, 14, or 16; or 1 inch if you are larger than size 16.

3 Compare your crotch depth measurement with ease to the back block along the side seam between the waist and crotch line. Lengthen or shorten the block along its adjustment lines to match the block's crotch depth measurement to yours. Adjust the front pants block in the same manner.

Short or Long Crotch Length

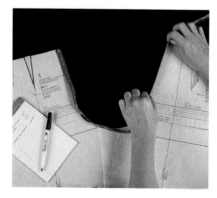

1 Add fitting ease to your *crotch to the floor at your inner leg* measurement from page 18. Add 1 inch if you are using a size 10 or smaller; 1½ inches if you are using size 12, 14, or 16; or 2 inches if you are using any size larger than 16.

2 Match the seamlines of the crotch points of your front and back pants blocks. Compare your crotch length measurement with ease with the dimension along the crotch seamline running from the waist front to the waist back. The four ways to bring the crotch length measurement in line with yours are outlined on the opposite page by body shape.

SPINNING YARNS

Fit and Flatter for All

....

P ATTERN COMPANIES DON'T expect all of their pants patterns to fit the shape of every customer, but they do check that a muslin from each pattern is suitable for their fit model. Both pattern companies and apparel manufacturers find they can "fit" or flatter more bodies when they design loose-fitting pants that accommodate figure variations.

Barbara Kelly

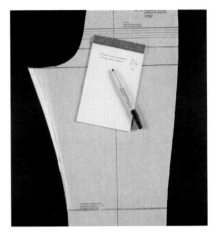

Swaybacks need a decreased block measurement. Lower the waist at the center back and taper to the side seams. See also "Custom Fitting with Contoured Darts" on page 116.

Protruding abdomens need an increased block measurement. Raise the waist at the center front and taper to the side seams. See also "Protruding Abdomen" on page 35.

Full buttocks need an increased block measurement. Extend the inseam at the crotch curve and taper to nothing before reaching the knee area.

Long or Short Legs

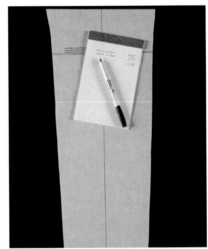

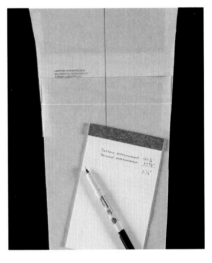

Flat buttocks need a decreased block measurement. Remove some of the inseam at the crotch curve and blend the seamline before reaching the knee area.

1 Your block should cover your ankle. Later you can adjust other pants patterns to complement your shoe height. Determine your pants length by subtracting the measurement for the *bottom of your ankle to the floor* measurement from page 18 from your *waist to the floor over your right hip* measurement from page 18.

2 Compare your pants length measurement with the back pants block along the side seam between the waistline and hemline. Lengthen or shorten the block along its leg adjustment lines to match the block's side length measurement with yours. Adjust the front pants block in the same manner.

Wide Thighs

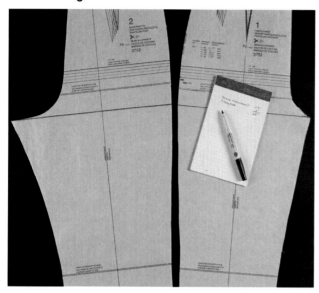

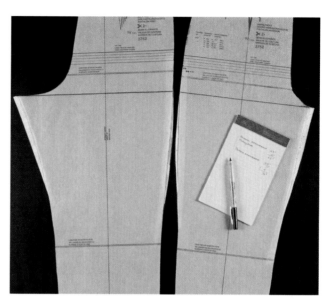

1 Add 2 inches of fitting ease to your thigh circumference *at the fullest part above your knees* measurement from page 19. Bring together the side seams of your front and back blocks. Don't tape them together.

2 Compare your thigh measurement with ease with the block dimension from inseam to inseam at the same place that you took your thigh circumference measurement. Add or subtract equally on the front and back inseams and side seams to match the block's thigh measurement with yours. Blend the adjustments along the seamlines, tapering them at the knee lines.

Thick Waist and Hips on Pants

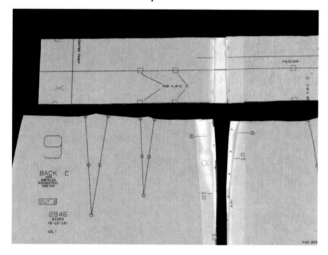

See "Wide or Narrow Hips" on page 32 and "Thick or Slim Waist" on page 34 for information about altering your blocks at the waistline and hipline. Wherever you make an adjustment on the pants block at the waistline, you need to make a corresponding adjustment on the waistband.

SPINNING YARNS

What Size Is It?

THOUGH TALLER, A RUNWAY OR PHOTOGRAPHY model has bust, waist, and hip measurements similar to a size 10 on the standardized chart used by most pattern companies. Garments she models are often ready-to-wear (RTW) size 6 prototypes from a designer or manufacturer. The same design house may establish two sets of in-house body measurements—one set from the model for the prototype garment and another set from the statistics of the target customer for the production garments. Knowing this difference, you can assume you might be two sizes larger in a pattern than you are in RTW.

Barbara Kelly

The Sloper Shortcut to Fast Pattern Alterations

Using the sloper to check fit and determine adjustments on fashion pattern pieces will cut your alteration time in half. By comparing your blocks to all future garments you plan to sew, you will achieve a better fit. And, at a glance, you can judge whether there is more or less ease than you desire. In effect, you can redesign the fashion pattern for a customized fit.

1 Separate, cut out, and press all of the tissue pieces of your fashion pattern. Draw all seamlines and hemlines if they aren't printed on the pattern.

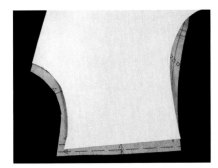

2 If your block adjustments were minor or if your fashion pattern is very loose fitting or oversize, fold under and pin the tucks, pleats, and hems in the pieces. Lay the blocks over the pattern pieces to compare the difference between the fitting and the design ease and to determine if adjustments are necessary.

3 If adjustments are necessary, flatten the pattern pieces and refer back to your blocks for adjustment information. Alter the fashion pattern pieces for length, width, proportion, contour, dart size, and placement. Many of these adjustments can be made by following the same instructions used to make changes to the fitting patterns on pages 28–38.

Making a Muslin

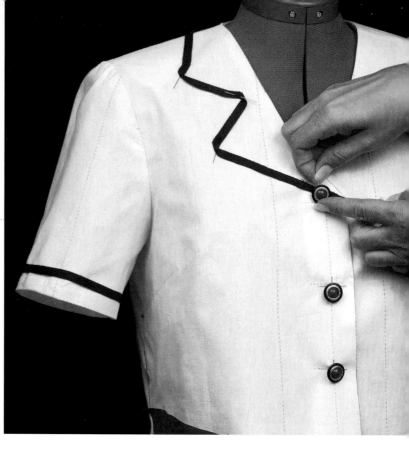

Obtaining a perfect fit is easier when you "test drive" a new pattern with a muslin. A muslin allows you to resolve fit and construction problems before cutting out more expensive fabric and to eliminate altering while assembling the fashion garment.

Fashion design studios make a test garment in unbleached muslin, which is where the term muslin originated. Some designers prefer to make muslins in fabric inventory that has a weight and hand similar to the intended garment. Others prefer to make one in the same fabric that will be used for the final garment. This latter method is always used for knits.

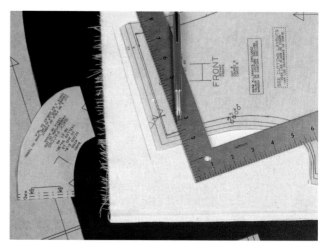

1 Prepare and alter your fashion pattern pieces. See "The Sloper Shortcut to Fast Pattern Alterations" on page 39. Choose muslin, gingham, or another fabric with a weight and hand closely related to your fashion fabric. Steam press the fabric to preshrink, smooth wrinkles, and square the grainlines. Reinforce the pattern pieces if desired. See "Reinforcing Your Blocks" on page 27.

2 Lay out your fashion pattern pieces except for the facings, upper collar, and hidden pocket. Use 1-inch seam allowances for shoulder and side seams; use ½-inch seam allowances around the neckline, armholes, and waistline. Use the pattern's hem allowances. For all other areas, follow the recommendations in "Seam Allowances" on pages 42–49.

3 Mark all of the stitching lines on one side of the muslin pattern pieces with a dressmaker's tracing paper and wheel. On the other side of the muslin pattern pieces, mark the center front, center back, waistline, bust point, grainlines, and detail lines, such as button and buttonhole placement.

4 Staystitch edges to which a facing would be sewn if this was a fashion garment rather than a muslin. Machine baste all of the darts and seams. Press the seam allowances open, the darts to the center or hemline, and the hems up. Fold and press under the unattached seam allowances.

5 Try on the muslin, right side out, over the appropriate undergarments. Insert shoulder pads if applicable. Move around to see if the muslin fits comfortably. Carefully examine the fit, ease, and silhouette, along with the scale and placement of the details. Analyze how loose or close the garment fits, then analyze the length.

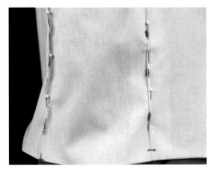

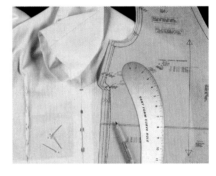

6 Pinch and pin the muslin for a better shape. If necessary, open the seams and adjust the fit, then pin the seams closed. Mark the changes and folded edges with a pen. Cross mark where seam changes begin. Rub a pen over the pins to indicate the new or adjusted stitching line.

7 When you're satisfied with your fitting changes, consider the size, shape, and placement of the details. Classically, style changes are made by pinning ¼-inch black twill tape along the new lines. The tape is easily moved until the "right" proportion, placement, or dimension is achieved.

8 Tape on buttons to assess size and style. Designers and manufacturers spend a great deal of time on their muslins, making several before they are convinced the design is ready for production. Measure the distance between the adjustment markings and the original lines, then draw new lines on the pattern reflecting the differences. When the design and fitting adjustments are complete, adjust the seam allowances as recommended and check that necessary construction symbols are included on the pattern.

SPINNING YARNS

When Is a Muslin not a Muslin?

A MUSLIN CAN BE MADE FROM GINGHAM. HOME-SEWING PATTERN companies follow procedures similar to the fashion industry. At Vogue, the sample garment, called a full muslin, is constructed from two fabrics. The right side is a solid fabric that is comparable in weight and drape to the garment's recommended fabrics; the left side is a plaid or gingham. Because woven plaid and gingham patterns follow the fabric's grainlines, these help designers evaluate the grain's response to the garment's style.

Barbara Kelly

Seam Allowances

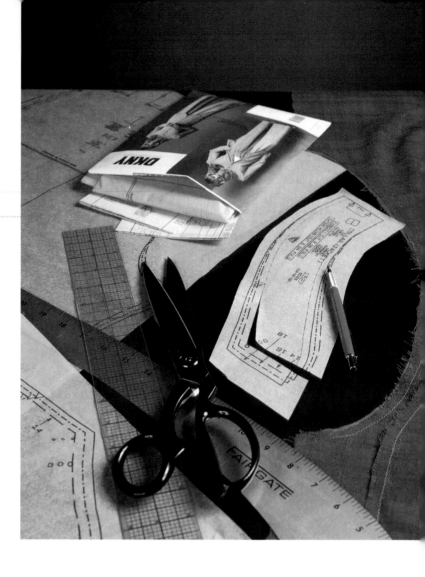

Until the mid-1990s, most pattern companies offered home sewers a single width, ⅝ inch, for seam allowances. The garment industry, on the other hand, varies seam allowance widths, based on the location and function of the seam, the fashion fabric, pressing procedure, machinery, and seam finish. These seam allowances can be as scant as ¼ inch.

Professionals say they can easily spot a home-sewn garment because the ⅝-inch seam allowances affect the way the seams—and the entire garment—hang.

You will be well on your way to achieving the look of ready-to-wear, by adjusting seam allowances before cutting out the pattern pieces for your garment. For example, the instructions for patterns with ⅝-inch seam allowances in curved areas, like the crotch of pants, advise you to either notch into the seam allowance along the curve or trim the seam allowance—or both—after the seam is sewn.

But notching weakens the seam. And trimming a seam allowance after the pattern pieces are joined can be difficult, particularly if the fashion fabric is silky. Both of these problems can be avoided by using pattern pieces with smaller seam allowances, say ⅜ inch. With this change, it won't be necessary to clip into the seam allowances, and fittings prior to assembly will be more accurate than with a large seam allowance.

Admittedly, the process of adjusting the seam allowances on tissue patterns is time-consuming. Yet investing this time up front will save a surprising amount of yardage and

eliminate the time you already spend trimming seam allowances after the seam is sewn. In addition, curved seams are easier to sew without the bulk of a ⅝-inch seam allowance.

If you look at the suggested industrial seam allowances on pages 46–49, you will note that the curved seams and the seams that lay on the finished edges of the garment have smaller seam allowances than straight seams within the garment.

At the finished edges, the straight seams' allowances are usually ¼ inch to eliminate bulk. However, within the body of a garment, like at the side seams, the pattern pieces may be cut with ½-inch seam allowances, although in couture garments, these may be ¾ inch. These straight seams have wider seam allowances so that they can be pressed flat into the garment or let out for alterations.

As a general rule, curved seams without stress, like at the neck, in a collar, or at a sleeveless armhole, have ¼-inch seam allowances. Where the stress is minimal, the seam allowance is ⅜ inch.

Seam allowances are also determined by the intended seam finish. A zipper seam at the side or back of a garment made in a woven fabric lies better with a ¾-inch seam allowance; but a fly zipper needs a ½-inch seam allowance, while zippers in a knit fashion fabric take a ⅜-inch seam allowance. And for added stability, ⅛ inch is added to the allowance for seams that will be topstitched.

Seam Allowance Guidelines

The width of seam allowances will vary depending on the assembly procedure and a sample maker's preference. Even geographic location makes a difference. Elissa Meyrich, in New York, for example, uses ½-inch seam allowances at the waist. But Laurel Hoffman, in Philadelphia, uses ⅜-inch seam allowances at the waist.

¼ inch

Used for curved seams that will not be subjected to stress:

> Center front opening
> Collar
> Cuff
> Facings
> Hip at side seams on pants and fitted skirts
> Interfacings
> Lapel
> Neck edge
> Patch pocket
> Sleeveless armhole
> Welt

⅜ inch

Used for curved areas where there will be stress, or where the seam will be serged or overlocked:

> Armscye with sleeves
> Cuff at the sleeve edge if crack stitched
> Front vest hem when there is a sew-in lining
> Interior pockets
> Lowest portion of the crotch, from the notch at center back to the point where the zipper tab rests at center front
> Side seam in knits and silky fabrics
> Zipper inserted in knit fabrics

½ inch

Employed where seam allowances must be pressed flat or additional fabric is necessary for design and structural details:

> Fly zipper
> Shoulder and side seams
> Sleeve seam
> Upper portion of the crotch, both front and back
> Waist

¾ inch

This width of seam allowance is not common. Specific design or structural details may require it so review your pattern just in case these are present before reducing your seam allowances.

> Centered and offset zippers
> Side seams on a garment that may be altered
> Zipper seam in knit fabrics

There's More!

REDUCED SEAM ALlowances on all of the standard pattern pieces for a blouse, vest, skirt, and pants are given in "At-a-Glance Seam Allowance Guide," on pages 46–49.

$\mathcal{R}$educing Seam Allowances

$\mathcal{F}$or this procedure, you will need a fine-point permanent marker, a see-through ruler, a curved edge, and paper scissors. If you intend to reuse your pattern pieces, consider backing them with a lightweight fusible interfacing for added stability.

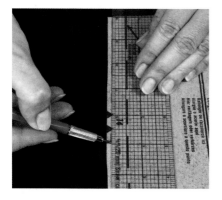

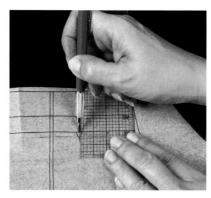

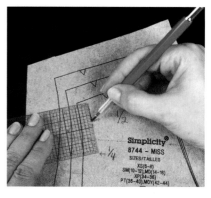

1 Place the see-through ruler on top of the pattern piece, so the ruler's edge is the desired distance from the seamline. Measure from the interior side of the line printed on the pattern piece.

2 Always move in the notches and make the mark, as well as the notch in the fabric, about ⅛ inch deep.

3 You can also draw the new seam allowance by measuring in from the existing cutting line. On a ¼-inch seam allowance, for example, the see-through ruler should be placed on the interior side of the cutting line with its edge ⅜ inch from the cutting line.

SHOP TALK

Reduction Deduction

$\mathcal{D}$ETERMINING YOUR NEW SEAM ALlowance width is easiest if you measure out from the seamline. However, seamlines aren't printed on some pattern pieces. If you find yourself in this situation, then measure in from your cutting line. For example, if you want a ½-inch seam allowance at the waist of a skirt front pattern piece, then measure in ⅛ inch from the cutting line. Cut along the marks that you made.

DESIRED SEAM ALLOWANCE WIDTH	AMOUNT TO TAKE OFF FROM THE CUTTING LINE
½ inch	⅛ inch
⅜ inch	¼ inch
¼ inch	⅜ inch

Laurel Hoffman

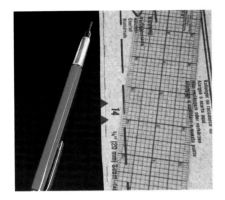

4 Place small pencil dots on the pattern piece along the ruler edge to mark the new seam allowance, shifting the ruler along the length of the seamline. When you have finished, return to the start and draw the new cutting line with the help of the ruler.

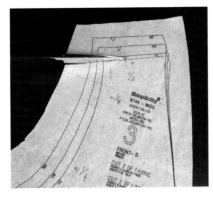

5 Write the new seam allowance on the pattern piece for reference during sewing. As you reduce each seam allowance, check the corresponding pattern pieces to ensure that you are making them all the same width.

Combination Seam Allowances

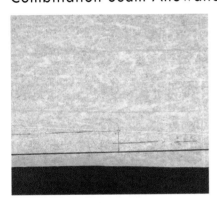

The width of a seam allowance can change along the seam. The side seam allowance on pants, for example, is ½ inch until it reaches the hip, where it is reduced to ¼ inch.

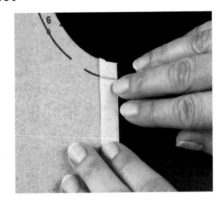

The edge of the seam allowance is shaped by folding it back on the seamline, tracing the top of the seam allowance, and then trimming it.

Extensions

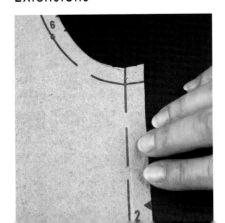

The end of a seam allowance, particularly for a curved seam, should not be square. The triangular point must be maintained if the garment is to fit properly, especially if the seam allowance will be pressed open.

At-a-Glance Seam Allowance Guide

By referring to the following photographs, you can quickly identify the recommended seam allowance widths for a vest, skirt, blouse, or pants. The pattern pieces shown here are the more common ones. The design of your garment may change the shape and, consequently, the necessary seam allowances of your pattern pieces. Use the "Seam Allowance Guidelines" on page 43 to determine any remaining seam allowance widths.

Seam Allowance Guidelines for a Vest

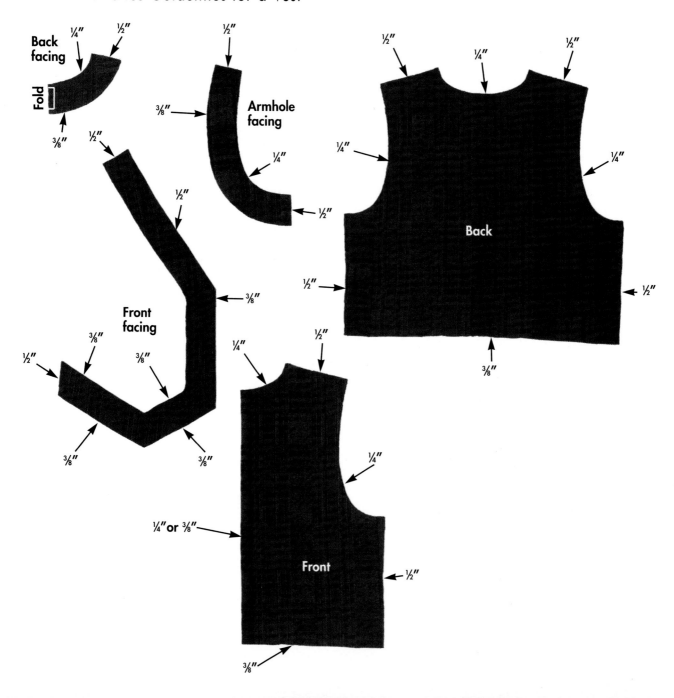

Seam Allowance Guidelines for a Skirt

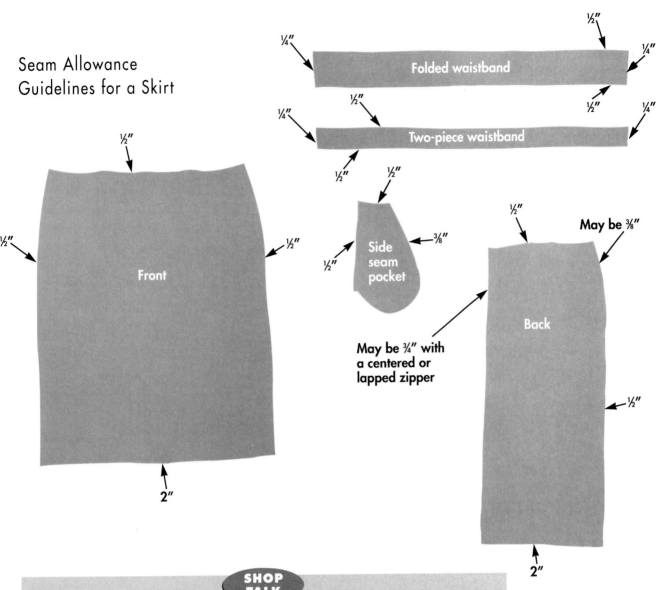

Folded waistband — ¼″, ½″, ¼″, ½″

Two-piece waistband — ¼″, ½″, ½″, ¼″, ½″

Front — ½″ (top), ½″ (left), ½″ (right), 2″ (bottom)

Side seam pocket — ½″, ½″, ½″, ³⁄₈″

Back — ½″, May be ³⁄₈″, ½″, 2″

May be ¾″ with a centered or lapped zipper

SHOP TALK

A "Fuse"ion of Ideas

I'VE NEVER UNDERSTOOD WHY SOME people go to the trouble of cutting fusible interfacing away from a seam allowance. It must remain to reinforce seams and eliminate stretch during sewing. In fact, a fusible is vital in the seam allowances of the V-neck on jackets, dresses, and blouses.

The first interfacings were made from canvas, so it was helpful to cut away extra bulk in the seam allowances. But this is no longer necessary. The garment industry's demands for time-efficient products has led to the development of fusibles that are compatible with many types of fabrics and that enhance the look of the finished garment.

Tricot fusible, for example, is one of the most popular interfacings in the garment industry. It does not create excess bulk in the seams if you trim the seam allowances on your pattern pieces properly.

Elissa Meyrich

Seam Allowance Guidelines for a Blouse

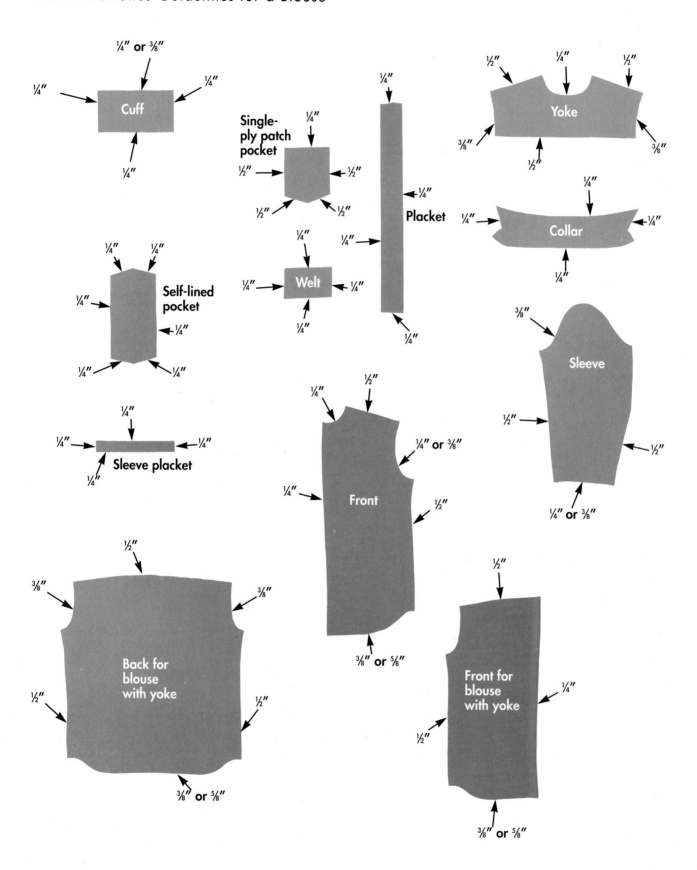

Seam Allowance Guidelines for Pants

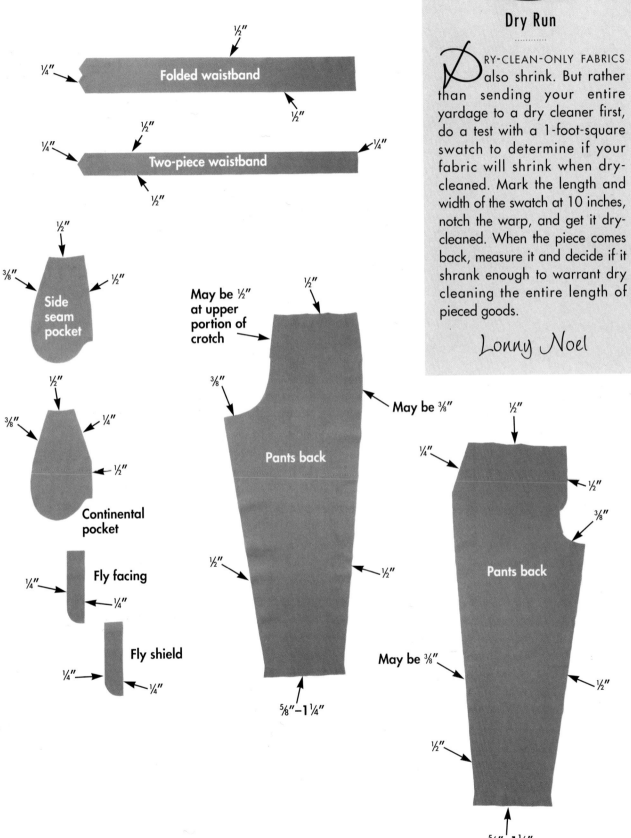

½″ — Folded waistband — ½″

¼″

½″ — Two-piece waistband — ¼″

¼″

½″

½″
⅜″ — Side seam pocket — ½″

½″
⅜″ — Continental pocket — ¼″
½″

¼″ — Fly facing — ¼″

¼″ — Fly shield — ¼″

May be ½″ at upper portion of crotch

½″

⅜″

Pants back

May be ⅜″

½″ — ½″

⅝″–1¼″

½″

¼″

½″

⅜″

Pants back

May be ⅜″

½″

⅝″–1¼″

Fabric

Prewashing fabric is not always a good idea. For example, chintz, which makes a lovely vest, is often treated with a shiny finish that may wash away. Before tossing pieced goods into the washing machine, try conducting a few simple tests. If shrinkage is minimal, there is little reason to scrub off the "new" look and feel of the fabric.

From the very first day that you entered a fabric store you were probably instructed to pretreat yardage before sewing a garment. But fabric is rarely washed in the industry.

Washing or dry cleaning literally miles of fabric is both time consuming and expensive. In addition, pretreating can wash away sizing or another finish that is sometimes added to enhance a fabric's appearance or "hand," a term used to describe stiffness or drapability. Instead, in the factory, a swatch is taken from the bolt, and a quality control supervisor subjects the material to several tests. Based on the results, the company decides if the fabric needs to be steamed and whether the dyes are colorfast. Often, testing shows that a fabric does not shrink significantly, so even this concern is eliminated.

The home sewer can easily conduct many of the same tests, thereby saving time that would be spent washing and ironing (or dry cleaning) yardage.

Throughout the instructions for these tests, advice is given to "condition" a swatch or length of fabric after it has been washed, steamed, or pressed. This industry term means that the fabric is allowed to rest and cool off. Many fabrics and processes require conditioning of little more than 15 minutes. If at all possible, however, samples should be allowed to condition overnight.

Shrinkage Tests

The primary concern of most sewers is whether their yardage will shrink after it has been made into a garment, which results in puckered seams. A simple test on a swatch will determine if the yardage needs to be dry-cleaned, washed, or merely steamed before it is cut and sewn. In many cases, sewers will discover that no pretreatment is necessary.

1 Cut two on-grain, 1-foot squares. Notch the warp, which is the set of yarns that run lengthwise and parallel to the selvage. On the wrong side of the fabric, place short lines, 10 inches apart, on all four sides of both swatches with a permanent, nonsoluble marking pen.

2 Place an iron set on high and full steam on one swatch for 20 seconds. Wait one minute. Repeat two more times. Let the swatch condition (rest undisturbed) for one hour. Gabardine, thick wool, or any other fabric that holds moisture must condition for four hours.

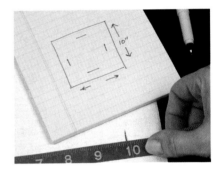

3 Compare the swatch's warp and fill measurements before and after steaming. (Shrinkage can be greater in one direction.) If the difference is significant, you should wash your fabric before cutting out the pattern pieces. If the shrinkage is minimal, you may still want to test wash a swatch.

4 Launder the second swatch. Let it condition for one hour, then measure the length and width. As shown above, the tested fabric needs to be laundered. Even though steaming didn't reveal significant shrinkage, the swatch that was machine washed and dried shrank more.

Crocking Test

A lack of colorfastness, or crocking, is the result of poor dye penetration, the use of improper dyes or dyeing methods, or insufficient washing and treatment after the dyeing operation. If your shrinkage tests determine that a fabric doesn't need to be prewashed, you need to also conduct the following crocking tests because your fabric may still need to be laundered if the dye bleeds. Fabric that is colorfast doesn't need to be washed before you assemble your garment.

It's wise to do both the wet and dry crocking tests because the dry results can sometimes be more severe than the wet results.

1 Ensure that your hands are clean, dry, and free of any perfumes and hand lotions. Cut a 4 × 6-inch swatch of fabric, on the bias, from the yardage that you want to test. Also cut a 2-inch square of white 100 percent cotton fabric.

2 Put a few drops of water on the cotton square and blot between some dry cotton fabric for the wet test. Don't apply water for the dry test.

3 Anchor the 4 × 6-inch swatch, right side up, with your thumb and index finger. Place the cotton square on top. Place your middle finger in the center of the cotton square, and anchor the square with your thumb and index finger.

4 Apply slight to medium pressure while sliding the cotton square from the lower left to the upper right corner of the fabric swatch. Repeat the back-and-forth sliding motion ten times.

5 Turn over the cotton swatch to see if the fabric's color has bled. If the results are unacceptable, laundering or dry cleaning will reduce the severity of color transfer. Some fabric shops will accept yardage returns if the fabric bleeds significantly.

There's More!

A 30-SECOND SEAM SLIPPAGE test is conducted by quality control supervisors when they need to quickly assess whether a loosely woven fabric will pull away from a seam. You can conduct the same test right in a fabric store. See "Fusible Tape" on page 62 for an explanation, as well as a solution.

Mystery Fabric

Sometimes fabric, particularly yardage that is on sale, is sold with the label "Contents Unknown." Sewers may bypass a good deal because they are nervous about selecting a fabric for which they do not know the care requirements.

Businesses in the garment industry conduct a simple "burn test" to identify fabric. Then, with the help of the "Fabric Identification" table on pages 54–55, the fabric's fiber content is determined by the personality of the flame, odor, and ash.

Conducting a Fiber Identification Test

1 A burn test is conducted on a small bundle of yarns. Cut a 4-inch swatch and pull at least five or six yarns from one side of the fabric square.

2 Blends like poly/cotton use one fiber in the warp and another in the fill. Since the yarns in the warp direction are different than the fill yarns, pull out strands from each side of the swatch and burn them separately.

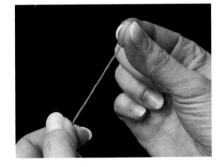

3 Twist the yarns, from one side only, into a grouping with a diameter of ⅛ inch. If necessary, add to the twisted length by pulling more yarns from either the warp or fill side of the swatch.

4 Place a large square of aluminum foil on your worktable. If a small sample burns out of control, it can be dropped onto the foil without damaging the table. Place the bundle of twisted yarns in tweezers and hold it over the aluminum foil.

5 Light the free end of the bundle and note the reaction to the flame—how it burns, its odor, and the appearance. Compare the results with those on pages 54–55. Some fabrics are made from several fibers, in which case the characteristics will be mixed.

FIBER	DESCRIPTION OF BURN	SHRINKS OR CURLS FROM FLAME	ODOR	RESIDUE
Acetate, triacetate	Burns quickly, sputters, drips melted fiber, emits black smoke	Yes	Vinegar	Dark, hard bead
Acrylic	Burns slowly, self-extinguishing, drips melted fiber	Yes	Acrid	Hard, irregular bead
Cotton, flax, ramie	Burns	No	Burning paper	Light, feathery, gray ash
Linen	Burns slowly, self-extinguishing	No	Burning paper	Light, feathery, gray ash
Nylon	Melts and shrinks from flame	Yes	Celery	Hard, tan or beige bead; will be dark if overheated

FIBER	DESCRIPTION OF BURN	SHRINKS OR CURLS FROM FLAME	ODOR	RESIDUE
Polyester	Burns quickly, has afterglow, emits black smoke, drips melted fiber	Yes	Chemical	Hard, tan bead; will be dark if overheated
Rayon	Burns, melts	No	Burning paper	Fluffy; small amount
Silk	Fuses, melts, ignites quickly	Yes	Burning hair; not as strong as wool	Black, irregular bead that crushes easily
Spandex	Shrinks or curls from flame	Yes	Chemical	Sticky, black
Wool, mohair, cashmere, alpaca	Burns, sputters, self-extinguishing	Yes	Burning hair; very strong	Black, irregular bead that crushes easily

Microfibers

Microdenier yarns, the technical name for microfibers, are very versatile and can be used in warp knits, weft knits, and wovens. They are the warmest, coolest, lightest, strongest, silkiest, toughest, softest luxury fabrics for the '90s. Yet in the mid-1990s, even the garment industry was struggling with methods to handle this unique new product. In consultation with other experts, Lonny Noel developed these guidelines for home sewers.

Fuse side seams on tailored garments with a lightweight nonwoven tape to minimize seam puckering.

Use pressure and very little, or no, steam. Press at a low heat setting because high heat may result in shine or damage, and the fabric will not recover.

A low-profile resin coating interfacing is best because large dots may show on the fabric's face. A shiny surface, like the back fusible shown here, does not always mean the resin coating is heavier.

Use fine sewing thread.

Set the sewing machine's tension as low as possible, about 10 to 12 stitches per inch (spi).

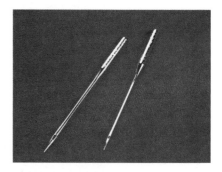

A sewing machine needle with a slim shank, like the 60/80 on the right, is more suitable for microfibers than the 100/16 on the left.

Interfacings

Essential ingredients in professionally finished apparel, interfacings add shape, support, and stability. Selecting one may be confusing at times, but if you follow the guidelines in this chapter, the correct choice will be easy.

Interfacing is the inside material that supports and reinforces the outer, or fashion, fabric. Interfacings can be woven or non-woven, sew-in, or fusible. Interfacings that are too light will not provide the required support; interfacings that are too heavy will distort the shape of the garment. Interfacings are applied in a facing, collar, cuff, placket, pocket, flap, lapel, and waistband.

Making the Right Choice

Although the choice between a sew-in and a fusible interfacing is usually a matter of personal preference, the fashion fabric may be the determining factor. Certain fabrics, including rayon and acetate velvet, fake fur, synthetic leather, open-work lace and mesh, vinyl, rainwear, textured brocades, and heat-set plissés, may not be suitable for fusing. Some fabrics with water-repellent or stain-resistant finishes may also reject the fusing process.

Sew-in interfacings are basted in place, then permanently stitched into the garment during the construction process. Fusibles have a shiny resin on one side that causes them to bond to the fashion fabric when you apply the manufacturer's recommended combination of heat, steam, time, and pressure. While most interfacings bond when ironed at the "wool" setting, several new ones, designed for sensitive and super-fine fabrics, will bond at the lower "silk" setting. Fusibles are not necessarily faster than sew-ins because time at the sewing machine is exchanged for time at the ironing board.

With a sew-in, drape the interfacing and the fashion fabric over your hand and observe how they interact. Performing a fuse test is the only true way to determine the interaction between a fusible interfacing and your fashion fabric. If you are considering a fusible and a sew-in that appear to be the same weight, note that the fusible on the right will create a slightly crisper effect than the sew-in on the left.

Conduct a fuse test by bonding a small piece of the interfacing to your fabric. Let it condition (dry undisturbed) for about an hour, then drape the fabric over your hand. It's helpful to keep several yards of a variety of weights and types of interfacing on hand. In the long run, this is more economical than the wasted yardage that occurs when you buy interfacing on a project-by-project basis.

Shopping the Market

Interfacings can be stable, which means lacking stretch; have crosswise stretch, so there is "give" across the width but not the length; or be all bias, with stretch in any direction.

Crosswise-give, nonwoven interfacings, including those engineered for knit fabrics, give a softer effect than stable interfacings. Fusi-Form Suitweight by HTC-Handler Textile Corporation is shown here.

Knit interfacings have crosswise stretch. These provide a softer effect and greater flexibility than stable interfacings. So-Sheer by HTC-Handler Textile Corporation is shown here.

Weft-insertion knit interfacings have an extra crosswise thread that offers stability. Because of the knit construction, they are more drapable than woven or stable nonwoven interfacings. Armo Weft by HTC-Handler Textile Corporation is shown here.

Warp-insertion knit interfacings stretch in all directions. They combine soft shaping with exceptional drapability. SofBrush by HTC-Handler Textile Corporation is shown here.

All-bias nonwoven interfacings stretch in every direction so that pattern pieces can be pinned to them in any direction. These interfacings provide a finished effect that is as soft as, or softer than, the crosswise-stretch interfacings. SofTouch by HTC-Handler Textile Corporation is shown here.

Stabilized tricot interfacings offer both crosswise and lengthwise stability for soft, supple shaping. The only interfacing currently in this category is Sewin Sheer, designed for sheer and lightweight fabrics. Sewin Sheer by HTC-Handler Textile Corporation is shown here.

There's More!

Heat, steam, time, and pressure—in the right combination—are absolutely necessary for bonding a fusible to fabric. Instructions for applying fusibles, as well as for a fuse test, are featured in "Fusibles Application Method" on page 61.

Interface Like the Pros

• Ensure that the interfacing requires the same care as the fabric. For example, a permanent press interfacing doesn't belong in a silk blouse, and dry clean–only hair canvas is a poor choice for a jacket that will be washed.

• Select a dark interfacing for dark fabrics and a white or beige product for light-color fabrics. This avoids interfacing show-through, as shown, prevents any chance of contrast along the cut edges of a buttonhole, and gives the inside of the garment a more pleasing appearance.

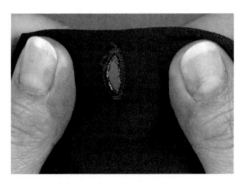

• Save an interfaced square of fabric from each garment, and label it with the name of the product. These squares will provide a quick reference for future interfacing decisions.

• Sandwich aluminum foil between your ironing board and its cover to serve as a heat conductor.

• Anchor tricky areas where fabric and fusible may shift by positioning the materials with straight pins, as shown.

SHOP TALK

Bond with Your Dry Cleaner

IF YOU WANT TO FUSE A LARGE AMOUNT OF yardage, ask your local dry cleaner to fuse your fabric on a clam shell press. If he agrees, do a test sample prior to fusing the actual garment pattern pieces.

Lonny Noel

There's More!

SLIPPERY FABRICS CAN BE DIFFIcult to cut precisely—even for experts at a factory. So once in a while, a company will block fuse pieced goods before cutting out pattern pieces. See page 76 for details on this problem-solving technique, which, as the name suggests, uses fusibles to stabilize the fabric.

If you are going to invest time, money, and energy in a sewing project, you certainly want the areas where fusibles are applied to be clean. The worst thing that can happen is to create the perfect garment and then discover that the fusible is peeling away from the fabric (delamination), bubbling (orange peel), or in some other way destroying the look of the fabric. This chart describes the common problems that occur with fusibles and explains how to solve them.

TERM	APPEARANCE	SOLUTION
 **Bubbling**	The fusible doesn't adhere uniformly to the garment fabric. Spots may be over- or under-fused.	Check your iron for uniform temperature distribution. Repeat the fusing on a new test sample, ensuring that pressure is applied when the iron is placed on the fabric. Try another fusible with a different bonding agent pattern.
 **Delamination**	The fabric may be blistered due to a breakdown of the bond between the fusible and the fabric. The fusible separates from the fabric during or after steaming, washing, or dry cleaning.	This may be caused by a finish on the fabric. Check your iron for uniform temperature distribution. Repeat the fusing on a new test sample, ensuring that pressure is evenly applied to the entire surface. Try another type of fusible.
 **Differential handle**	There is a dramatic change in the fabric's hand after the fusible is applied.	This may be due to heat sensitivity in the fabric. Check for overfusing. Try another type of fusible.
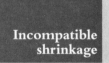 **Incompatible shrinkage**	The fabric or fusible shrinks in different amounts. The fabric or fusible bubbles, ripples, or curls. The fabric and interlining react differently to the heat or moisture of the fusing procedure.	Lower the iron's temperature and/or the fusing time. Avoid steam when fusing and pressing.
 **Orange peel**	The right side of the fabric is bubbled and coarse. The fusible is easily pulled away from the fabric.	Fuse at a lower temperature. Switch to a fusible with less bonding agent. Increase the fusing pressure. Switch to a fusible with compatible shrinkage.
 **Strike back**	The fusible has over-liquefied and seeped into the surface of the interlining, which may be shiny. In a completed garment, the fused portion sticks to unfused fabric, such as the lining.	Lower the temperature of the iron. Choose a fusible with less bonding agent or one that is intended to adhere at lower temperatures.
 **Strike-through**	The bonding agent has liquefied and seeped through. The bond between the fabric and the fusible may be weak, and the right side of the fabric may be tacky, boardy, or change color. Dots show through the fabric.	Lower the fusing time, temperature, and/or pressure. Change to a fusible with less bonding agent or one that requires a lower temperature to bond to the fabric.

Fusibles Application Method

If you are using a fusible, you must follow the manufacturer's recommendations for heat, steam, time, and pressure because all four are important components for achieving a secure bond. And always conduct a fuse test before applying the fusible to the wrong side of the fabric.

1 Some manufacturers preshrink their products, and others don't. The interleafing, or the information on the end of the bolt, that is wrapped with the interfacing will indicate if the product was treated.

2 Cut a swatch of fashion fabric at least 4 inches square. Also cut a piece of fusible to fit half of the swatch. Set the iron temperature according to the fusible manufacturer's specification.

3 Only half of the test swatch will be fused. Place the fusible with the resin side facing the wrong side of the fabric. Don't stretch the fusible.

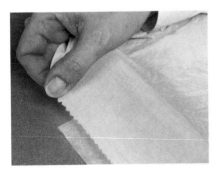

4 Cover the fusible with a damp press cloth.

5 Place the iron on top of the damp press cloth, and press firmly for the time specified by the manufacturer. This will be between 10 and 20 seconds. If the iron does not cover the entire swatch, leave the iron in one position for the specified time, then pick it up and move it to an unfused area. Don't slide the iron.

6 Turn the swatch over and steam press it. Let the fabric condition for at least an hour or overnight if possible. After conditioning, the surface of the fabric should be smooth and unchanged. The "Fusibles Troubleshooter" on the opposite page offers suggestions to improve the quality and appearance of the bond.

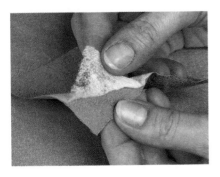

7 Check the bond by trying to peel the fusible away from the fabric. The fusible should be secure. If it isn't, more heat, time, steam, or pressure may be needed, or the fabric may require a sew-in interfacing.

8 Fold the unfused fabric back against the fused portion. If the fused fabric seems too crisp or heavy, change to a lighter weight or a sew-in interfacing. If the fabric is too limp, consider a crisper interfacing or add a second layer. For example, a collar will be crisper if both the upper collar and undercollar are interfaced.

Fusible Tape

As the term suggests, fusible tape is a strip of fusible interfacing that you can bond to fabric. The product is difficult to find, so "Buyer's Guide" on page 240 includes a supplier. However, you can make your own by cutting strips of the desired width from the taut, stable, vertical (shorter) side of fusible available by the yard. The fill on fusibles has more spring; therefore, use it as the crosswise portion of the fusible tape.

Manufactured fusible tape is used in fine tailored garments, but that shouldn't prevent you from using it to reinforce the crotch in a pair of pants.

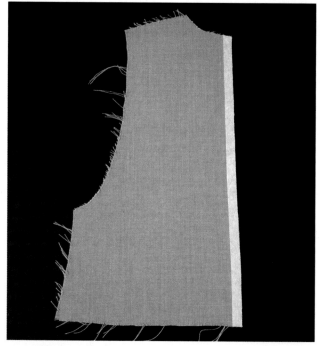

Reinforcing a loosely woven fabric that frays very easily in the handling process is possible with fusible tape. Apply the tape to all of the edges of the cut components. One edge of the tape should be flush to, or no more than ⅛ inch back from, the raw edge of the seam allowance.

Seam Slippage

This defect occurs after a seam is sewn. When stress is placed on a seam, the yarns on either side separate, pulling away from the stitching. Seam slippage is more prone to occur in smooth-yarn fabrics like microfibers and polyester, which are produced from man-made filament yarns.

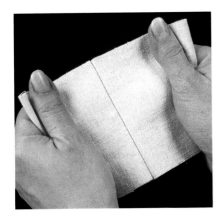

1 Cut two 4 × 6-inch swatches from your fashion fabric. The long side of both swatches must run parallel to the fabric's fill, which is the set of yarns perpendicular to the selvage. Place the swatches with right side together and sew along one lengthwise edge. Press the seam allowances open.

2 Grasp the edges of the sewn swatches in both hands, with the seam running vertically in the center. Pull out simultaneously with both hands. Release. This simulates the stress to which the center back seam of a garment will be subjected.

3 If the yarns in the fabric swatches have separated on either side of the seam, you must reinforce seams on the garment pattern pieces that will be under stress. Reinforce these seams with fusible tape that is double the width of the seam allowance. For example, apply a 1-inch fusible to a ½-inch seam allowance.

SHOP TALK

The 30-Second Test for Seam Slippage

If you are in a fabric store and want to test for possible seam slippage, ask the clerk for a small piece of the fabric. Hold it with the selvage running vertically. Place your thumb and middle finger of the same hand together on both sides of the fabric and pull. If the yarns don't recover, then you must use fusible tape.

Lonny Noel

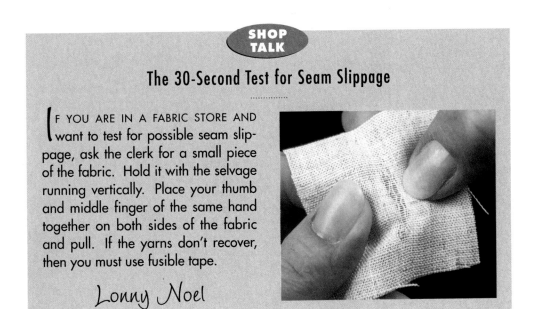

Key Application Points for Interfacing Garments

These are areas that you will probably need to interface in order to support the drape and desired hand of your garment.

Waistband

Hem

Vent or pleat (the entire pleat if it is deep or fusible strips on the fold closest to the outer side)

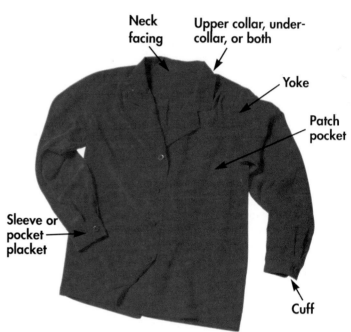

Neck facing

Upper collar, under-collar, or both

Yoke

Patch pocket

Sleeve or pocket placket

Cuff

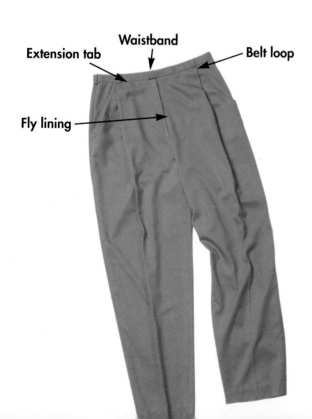

Extension tab

Waistband

Belt loop

Fly lining

Neck facing

Welt

Closed or open facing

ON BACK (not shown): Belt, Vent

Laying Up and Cutting Out Fabric

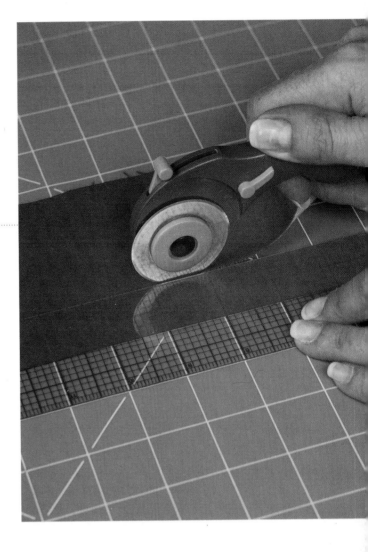

Precision layouts and cutting are essential because errors as small as ⅛ inch on each pattern piece will drastically alter fit. In the industry, highly trained operators plan layouts, then direct computerized equipment to cut the fabric, which is laid up on tables that draw air down through the fabric plies to keep them in position. Small versions of this equipment are not available for home sewers, but the principles of industrial layouts and cutting are universal.

*C*utting Edge Advice

Lonny Noel offers these suggestions for laying up and cutting out pattern pieces based on her years of factory work, plus the advice of cutters at The Greif Companies.

• Make sure your cutting table is clean and smooth. Apply a silicone spray or furniture polish to the surface, so that cut fabric will easily slide away from the pattern pieces as they are cut out.

• Examine your fabric for imperfections like holes, spots, and areas that are worn. Mark problems by taking one stitch through the fabric with doubled contrasting thread. Cut the thread tails so they are about 2 inches long. This identification method, which is similar to the industrial procedure, will allow you to quickly place pattern pieces around a problem area.

• If your pattern pieces will be cut with the fabric folded in half lengthwise, you can mark a flaw by drawing the threads through both layers of fabric or cutting the pattern pieces from a single ply.

• Make certain the selvages lay flat. If they are too tight, snip through the selvage along the entire length of the fabric. Depending on the fabric, you may be able to tear off the selvage. However, this may distort the yarns and the pattern nearest the selvage. If distorting occurs, place the pattern pieces in about 1 inch from the torn edge.

The distance required between each snip will depend on the tightness of the selvage. Start with snips every 3 to 5 inches. Lay the fabric on the cutting surface. If the selvage is rippled or stretched, try pressing it. If cutting and ironing don't work, then cut off the selvage.

• If you are tracing a pattern piece onto your fabric from a hard pattern (like cardboard), chalk the outline with very sharp chalk. If the chalk has a flat edge and you apply too much pressure, you could add another ⅛ inch to each pattern piece. On a pair of pants, this would equal an additional inch in the overall fit.

Apply slight pressure and outline the pattern with a constant, uniform stroke. Begin outlining the component at the top, working your way around the shape with a downward stroke. Hold your chalk at a slight angle, and rest your thumb along the edge of the pattern as you outline it.

• The roll of a fold will interfere with the precise cutting of a pattern piece. So if a pattern piece is positioned close to the fabric's lengthwise fold but isn't cut on the fold, you need to flatten the fabric. Cut along the fold for the length of the pattern piece.

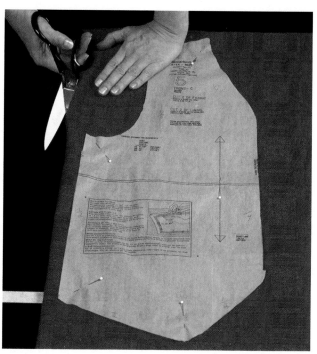

• Whether you are using shears or a rotary cutter to cut out your pattern piece, make sure the order and direction that you travel is constant.

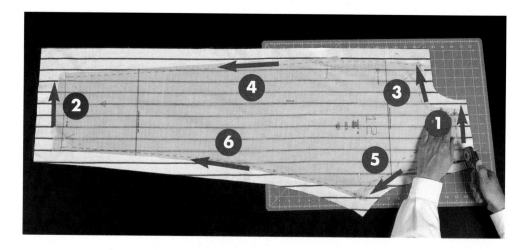

• Cut pattern pieces so that they always fall away from the path of the blade. And don't worry about getting all of the parts in one cut. It's better to cut components apart than to do the precision cutting on each pattern piece.

• Cut out the smaller pattern pieces first so they are out of the way. Then you can concentrate on the larger ones.

• Make notches after the entire pattern piece is cut out.

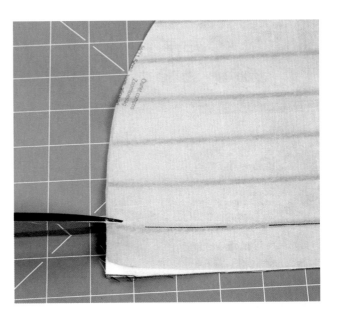

Multi"ply" Productivity

Cutting out more than a single garment in one session can be a real time-saver. In fact, some sewers who plan to make two or more garments from a single pattern take this procedure a step further. They layer single plies of fabric for each garment on the cutting surface, lay up the patterns, then cut through all of the fabric at once.

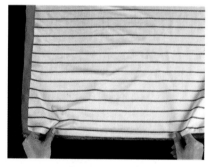

If your table is wide enough for unfolded fabric, spread one ply faceup, the second ply on top facedown, and so on. You may need help if you're dealing with wide fabric because you shouldn't disturb the bottom ply as you lay one ply on top of the next.

Folded fabric plies can be stacked before they are cut. If the fabrics vary in width, align the folds rather than the selvages when pattern pieces are cut on the fold. Depending on the thickness of the layers, you can secure the patterns with weights, staples, T-pins, or straight pins prior to cutting them out.

A problem arises if light and dark fabrics are cut simultaneously. Cut fibers have a tendency to cling; therefore, pattern pieces cut from light fabric will be contaminated with dark fibers and vice versa. To avoid this, place a lightweight paper, like waxed paper or tissue paper, between the plies.

SHOP TALK

Relax, This Won't Hurt a Bit

*C*UTTING PATTERN PIECES FROM FABRIC IS LIKE CUTting hair: If you pull a few strands taut and cut them, when you release them, they'll bounce back, and your cut edge will be uneven. Likewise, fabric should be spread in the most relaxed state possible so that there is no tension to distort the yarns.

Lonny Noel

Tilting Patterns

The industry strives for maximum efficiency when positioning pattern pieces. To prevent wasted yardage, place pattern pieces as close to one another as possible without them being off-grain. Sometimes inconsequential pattern pieces are "tilted," or shifted off-grain, for a tighter fit. If you find yourself slightly short on yardage, you may want to try tilting a few items. But don't tilt pattern pieces on plaid or striped fabric.

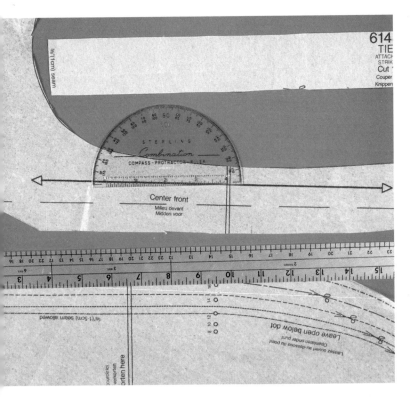

To tilt a pattern piece, pivot it up or down from its center until it fits the layout. Place a protractor on the pattern piece's grainline, and align the horizontal line with the fabric's grain. Match the pattern piece's grainline with the number closest to it on the protractor. Compare the degree on the protractor with the maximum degree of tilt allowed for the pattern piece given in "Patterns That Can Be Tilted" below. If the number is higher, then reduce the "tilt" of the pattern piece until it is the same as or smaller than indicated in the table.

PATTERNS THAT CAN BE TILTED

PATTERN	MAXIMUM TILT
Pants front	1°
Pants back	2°
Pants and skirt fly	1°
Pants and skirt belt loops	1°
Pocket facing	2°
Pants and skirt front lining	1°
Pants and skirt back lining	2°
Vest front lining	3°
Vest front facing	2°

Rotary Cutting Techniques

Some sewers perceive the rotary cutter as a small-scale version of an industrial tool. Yet others shun it, saying a rotary blade cannot be used to cut accurate corners, notches, and slash lines. Nevertheless, the position of your hands and the tool, refined through constant use, can overcome these drawbacks. Relax, but be alert and allow the blade to do the work for you.

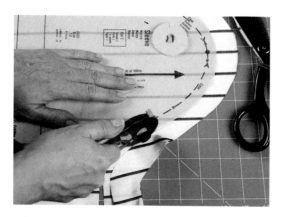

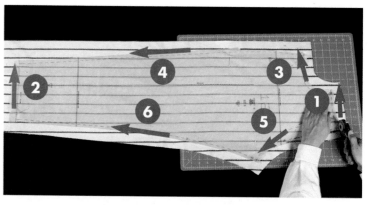

Place a hand flat on the pattern piece and the fabric. Don't push or apply pressure on either the pattern piece or the fabric. If you are directing a rotary cutter along the edge of a ruler, you may want to experiment with the grip on your ruler to prevent it from sliding.

Begin cutting at the top of the pattern piece, then cut the bottom end and any steps in the pattern piece. Next cut the pattern piece lengthwise, along the side seams for example, starting at the top and working down. This procedure will prevent the pattern piece from shifting. Use shears to cut steps and notches.

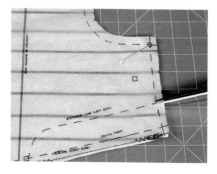

On armholes, the balls of sleeves, and any curves, try to continually move the blade on the cutting line for a smooth cut. When cutting out a pattern piece, leftover fabric should always fall away from the path of the blade.

After laying out your pattern pieces, cut out the smaller components, like collars and facings, first. Cut the general shape of your pattern pieces, then do the precision cutting for each one. Then you can concentrate on the larger ones. Make notches—with scissors—last.

If you're planning to cut out more than one fabric at a time, test the rotary cutter's ability to slice through multiple plies. Stack a swatch of each fabric on a self-healing mat, and try cutting through the fabric pile with the rotary cutter.

Notches

The manner and method that notches are used in the garment industry are slightly different than in home sewing. The notches are positioned to indicate pattern piece placement in layouts, key match points for seams, and variations from the standard seam allowances. Rather than cutting out a V, sample makers and cutters snip into the seam allowance.

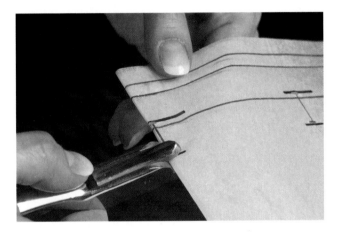

Patternmakers use a "notcher" to put holes in a tissue pattern piece when they want to transfer marks to cut components. This hand-held implement, which looks like a paper hole punch, makes a *U* in the tissue. Here, a seamstress is notching the position and width of her buttonholes.

Add notches after the pattern pieces are cut. Snip into the seam allowance ¼ inch. Circles on commercial patterns can be treated like notches. The circle marking the position of the bottom of a zipper, for example, can be replaced with a snip into the seam allowance directly beside it.

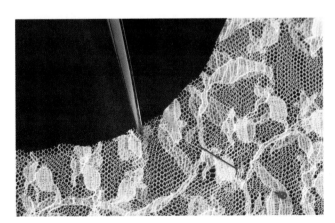

Knit fabrics and lace can be difficult to mark with a snip in the seam allowance. The fabric is often too loosely woven, or the snip is difficult to see. In these situations, blue, yellow, or white chalk is a good substitute. The mark should be in the same position as a notch.

SPINNING YARNS

The Height of Efficiency

*T*HE IDEAL HEIGHT FOR A CUTting table is 34 inches. The Greif Companies garment factory in Pennsylvania, where I worked for many years, prefers this height because it allows spreaders and cutters access to the laid out fabric, yet the table is not so low that the employees become tired.

Lonny Noel

Notches the Pattern Companies Don't Tell You About

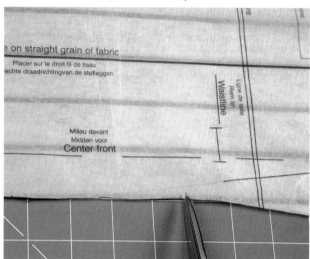

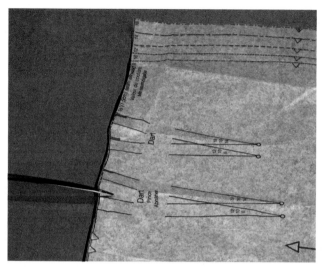

Blouses need a notch at the center front of the neck-line and hem, plus at the roll line for a self-facing and at the neckline where the collar ends. When there is a yoke, notch the shoulder line so it matches a notch at the center of the sleeve cap.

Darts and tucks are good places for notches, thereby eliminating the need for tailor's tacks. Mark the dart legs (wide ends) with notches. On tucks, place a notch in the seam allowance at the end of both the solid and broken lines, as well as at the fold.

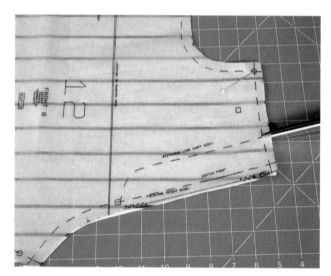

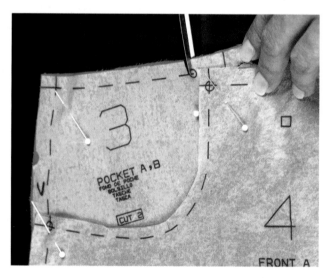

Pants need a notch at the center front or side closure. Also, at the waist, notch the stitching line for the fly. You can also notch the fly front in the seam allowance parallel to the dot that marks the bottom of the zipper.

On pants with a continental pocket, notch the side front and pocket pattern pieces at the waistline and hipline where the pants front overlaps it.

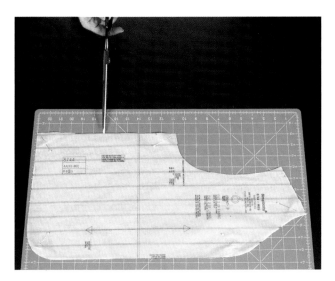

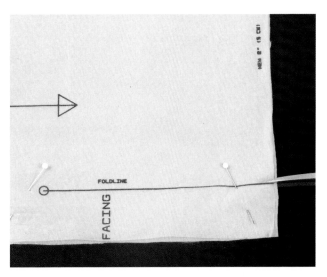

Lined vests need notches to ensure that the fashion fabric and lining pattern pieces match. Place a notch at the center back of the neck and hem, at the lower third of the armscye, at the front neckline halfway between the shoulder seam and the center front, and at the midpoint on the side seams and fronts.

Skirts always need a notch at the center front, and the dart legs need a notch at the waistline. If the skirt has a slit back, vent, or kick pleat, notch the release point and the foldline.

The foldline on any pattern piece is easier to locate when the top and bottom of the fold are notched in the seam allowance.

SHOP TALK

A "Hole" New Marking System

IN THE INDUSTRY, IMMEDIATELY AFTER CUTTING PATTERN pieces, a hole is drilled ½ inch away from the dart point. If the dart is a double fisheye, holes are also drilled ⅛ inch in from the widest area. This forces operators to stitch accurately. Sample makers and workers in small-production rooms mark darts by puncturing holes in the fabric with an awl. But I recommend that you don't make holes in your pattern pieces because these weaken the fabric and prevent later fitting adjustments. On oak tag patterns, notches are cut at the dart legs. Holes are punched ¼ or ½ inch from dart points and ⅛ inch from the widest part. The notches provide an opening so that a worker can snip the fabric underneath. The holes are used to mark one layer of fabric with chalk, two layers with a tailor's tack, or multiple layers with an awl.

Barbara Kelly

Bundling

An identification system is a must when working on more than one project at a time. On the factory floor, pattern pieces are identified and grouped according to the parts that will be joined. The cut components are "bundled" and sent to areas where machine operators trained in particular techniques will sew, press, or perform some other procedure with them. You can apply this same concept to your work in progress.

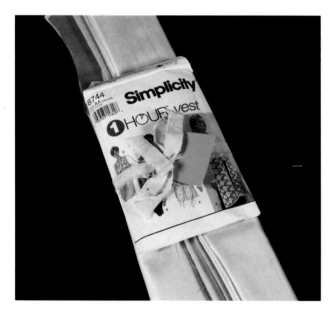

After the components are cut and design details like darts are marked, you may want to identify the items. For example, a Simplicity 8744 size small vest front pattern piece could be (S) 8744 SVF, while a Simplicity 8744 size medium vest back could be (S) 8744 MVB.

Consider placing identifying adhesive tags on the wrong side of the pattern pieces. Wherever the tag is placed, be consistent. But don't place the ticket on the very edge because fibers may cling to the ticket. When the ticket is removed, the yarns may fray, reducing the width of the seam allowance.

Pig Latin, Maybe?

SYSTEMS FOR IDENTIFYING CUT COMponents vary greatly from one factory to the next, so you should also consider options. Other identification methods are to pin an information ticket to the cut components or mark them with tailor's chalk. Be very consistent in the placement. You could also label a ticket with pertinent information, punch a hole into the ticket, thread it with string, and tie it around the pattern pieces. You may want to consider storing the pattern with your bundle.

Lonny Noel

Handling Special Fabrics

Napped, plaid, striped, and silky fabrics all require special layout and cutting techniques to ensure the best possible results. If you pay attention to match points, directional cutting, and fabric stability, you'll find that the pattern pieces sew together easier and the resulting garment hangs better.

Silks, Microfibers, and Other Slippery Fabrics

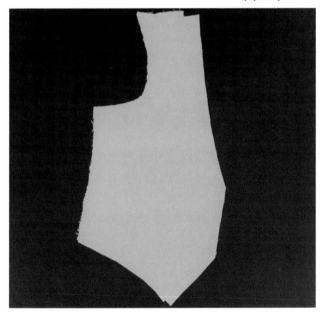

Microfibers, knits, and loosely woven fabrics demand special attention because it's very easy to cut out a poorly shaped pattern piece. In the photo above, the vest front on the bottom was block-fused, so its shape is accurate. The vest front layered on top, cut only from the fabric, is off-grain and distorted.

Difficult fabric can ruin a garment before it is sewn. If you pull it taut, it will shift when cut, and the shapes will be distorted, as shown by the vest front on the right. The block-fused vest front on the left was stabilized, so the shape is correct, and the edges don't fray or curl.

Lay paper on the table before spreading the fabric to prevent the material from shifting as you cut it. Waxed paper and tissue paper are effective, and newspaper can be used if you are not concerned about ink bleeding onto the fabric.

Block-Fusing Procedure for Slippery Fabrics

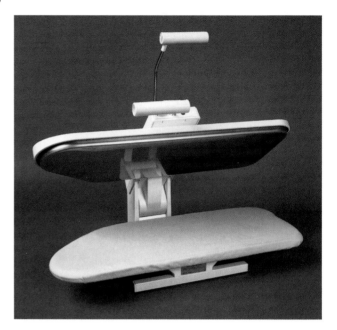

1 Choose the pattern pieces to be blocked based on the desired finish appearance and feel of your garment. Plan the layout so that pattern pieces that will be cut from block-fused fabric are positioned together. Calculate the yardage these pattern pieces will cover and cut off this length.

2 The easiest way to block fuse a large area is on a clam shell press at a dry cleaner. If the shop agrees, do a test prior to fusing the entire yardage. Sewing schools and home-based professionals who fuse frequently often have a smaller home version, like the Elnapress shown here.

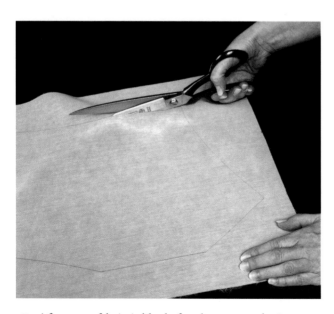

3 After your fabric is block-fused, you must let it condition. Lay up the pattern pieces and cut the fabric as usual. See the "Fusibles Application Method" on page 61 for directions on bonding fusible interfacing to yardage at home.

SHOP TALK

Going around the Block

BLOCK-FUSING CANNOT BE USED FOR ALL PATtern pieces. Consider it for a vest front and back or a pocket facing on a skirt. Pants components generally are not block-fused, except for the cuffs, waistband, pocket facing, and belt loops.

Lonny Noel

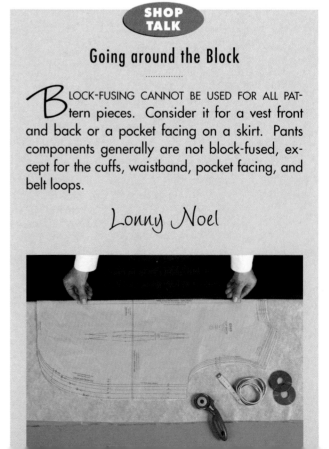

SHOP TALK

Designer Drapes

AWARD WINNING DESIGNER MARIAN Clayden prefers to develop patterns by draping because the velvets and chiffons she often chooses have a life of their own. She sculpts and arranges these elegant fabrics on her own body to achieve a precise artistic expression. The draping may take anywhere from one hour to an entire day. When Marian is satisfied with the creation, Sarah Brown, her design assistant, marks the fabric, trues all of the lines, adds seam allowances, and cuts away excess material. Then Sarah repins the fabric and places it on Marian again to check for fit, accuracy, and hang. Any necessary adjustments are made. When Marian is pleased with this "pin fitting," the fabric is re-marked and disassembled. Sarah flattens the pattern pieces and transfers them to paper, which becomes the patterns.

Barbara Kelly

SPINNING YARNS

Cheating Isn't Always Wrong

IF YOU ARE RUNNING SHORT OF fabric but need bias binding, you can cheat a bit. Rather than cutting strips on the true bias, cut them on slightly less than the true bias. I do this all the time because I never have enough fabric. I break every rule and cheat as much as I can. It's important to know all the rules so that you know which ones you can break.

Julia Linger

Velvet

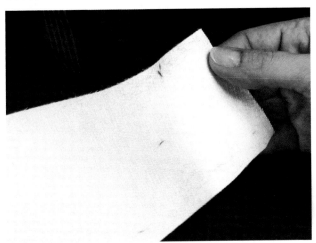

Velvet should not be cut with any other fabric because the short, dense pile causes excessive fiber contamination. Other fabrics will be covered with fibers from the velvet.

Laying Out Napped, One-Way Fabric

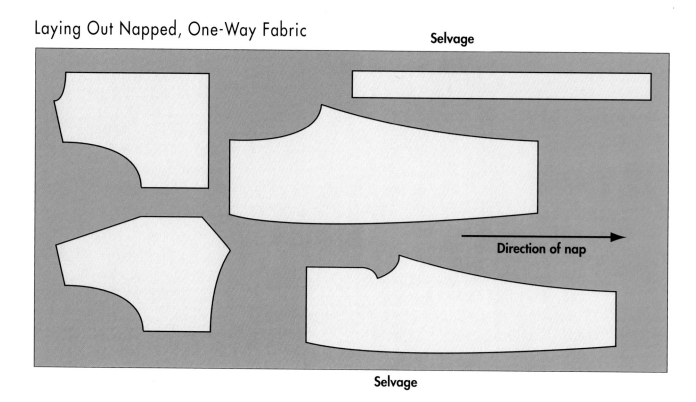

Selvage

Direction of nap

Selvage

Laying Out Velvet

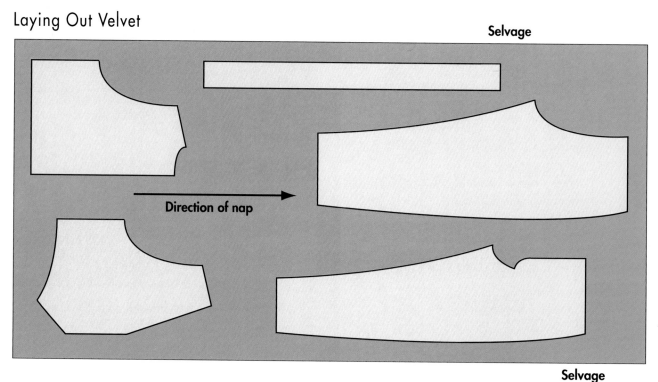

Selvage

Direction of nap

Selvage

Run your hand down a piece of velvet. Unlike other napped one-way fabrics that lie down when smoothed, velvet fibers stand up. So velvets are laid out as "napped one way" with the nap running "up." When laying out patterns, make sure the top of all of the patterns point in the same direction as the nap.

Laying Out Plaids, Stripes, and Patterns

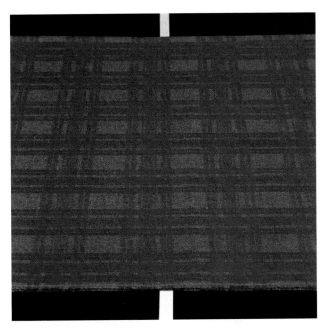

1 This technique for matching plaids also applies to stripes and repeating patterns. Place one side of a T-square on the lower edge of your cutting table. Press masking tape vertically across the entire width of the table, using the T-square as a guide. Keep the tape straight and perpendicular to the edge.

2 If your fabric is slippery, place a sheet of paper on top of the table. Fold the plaid fabric in half lengthwise, with the selvages matching. Line up one of the vertical lines of a plaid repeat with the masking tape extending beyond the fabric's fold and selvages.

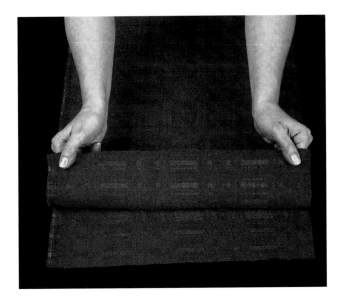

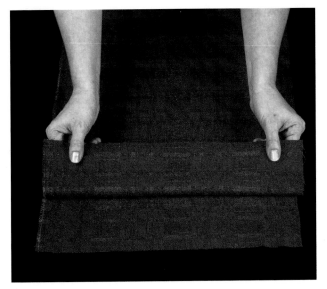

3 Make sure the repeats in the bottom ply line up with the top layer. If none of your pattern pieces need to be cut on the fold, cut the length of fabric in half lengthwise along the fold. This makes it easier to check the repeats since you can roll back the top layer.

4 Grasp the corners of the top layer at the short end and roll back the fabric as far as you can. As the fabric is rolling back, check that the lines, or repeats, of the plaid on the top fabric mirror the repeats on the bottom layer. If the repeats don't match, shift one of the two layers until they do.

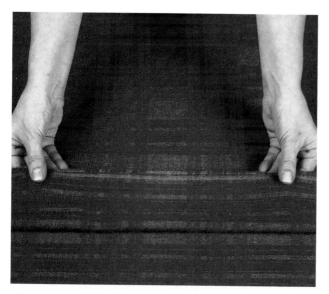

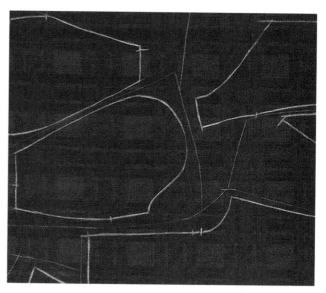

5 Repeat this procedure to check the alignment of the horizontal repeats. Grasp the top layer at the selvage and roll back the fabric as far as you can. Now roll it forward while continuously checking and adjusting the alignment. When you are satisfied, begin placing your patterns. Lay out the pattern pieces according to the instructions in "Key Match Points" on the opposite page.

6 "Hard" pattern pieces (made from cardboard) are optional. If you are using hard pattern pieces, trace their outlines with chalk and remove them. If you are using tissue pattern pieces, cut them out outside the cutting lines.

Chalk an outline about ½ inch outside the cutting line for the hard or tissue pattern pieces. This outline is called the blocking line. Cut out each pattern piece along its blocking line.

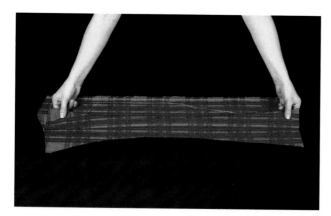

7 Place one pattern piece on the cutting table and roll the top layer back, then forward, both horizontally and vertically, to check the repeat alignment. Adjust if necessary, then cut out the pattern piece along the inner chalk outline or the cutting lines on the tissue pattern. Repeat with the remaining pattern pieces.

SHOP TALK

Don't Tilt

....

I STRONGLY RECOMMEND THAT YOU don't deviate from the grainline when working with a fabric that has a pattern, plaid, or stripe.

Lonny Noel

Key Match Points

The industry has identified key match points on garments. These are places along seams where plaids, stripes, and patterns must line up. Some, but not all, match points are identified with notches. The notches are used as guides to line up and roll cut components in order to match dominant lines in a fabric's pattern.

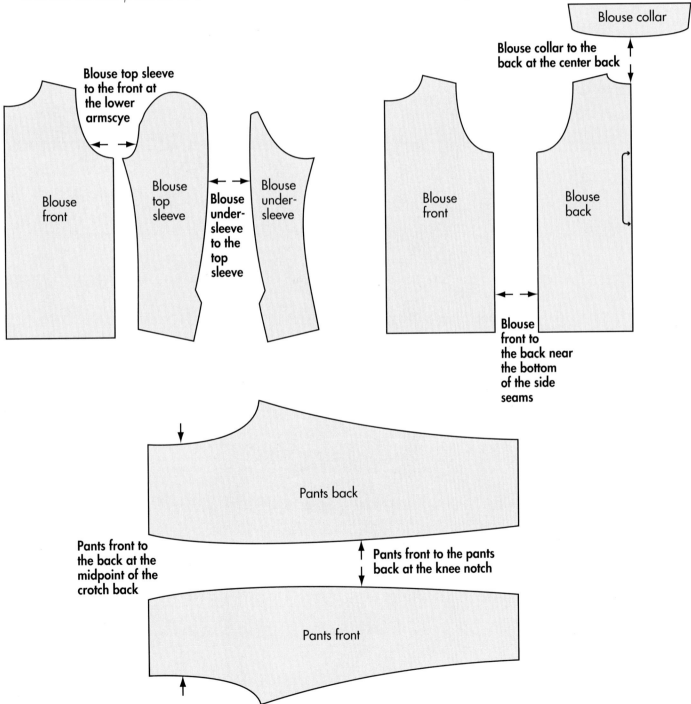

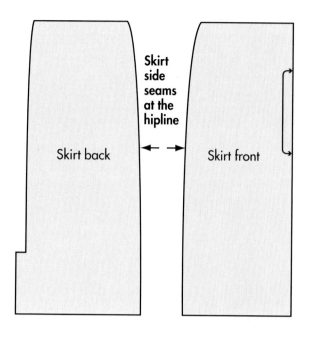

Skirt side seams at the hipline

Skirt back

Skirt front

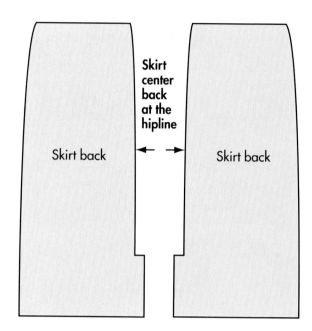

Skirt center back at the hipline

Skirt back

Skirt back

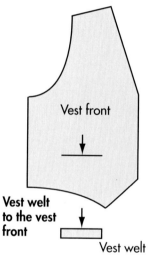

Vest front

Vest welt to the vest front

Vest welt

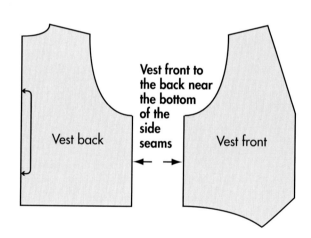

Vest front to the back near the bottom of the side seams

Vest back

Vest front

SHOP TALK

Split Personality

IF YOU PLAN TO MAKE A GARMENT FROM plaid fabric, split the collar or body back at the center back. Cut the pattern in half along the entire length of the center back and lay out the two sections as separate pattern pieces. Place the center back on an area of the repeat that isn't too busy. This will give the illusion of a single pattern piece when the seam is sewn.

Lonny Noel

Tips and Techniques

wl

Best known by people who work with wood or leather, an awl is a pointed tool that is commonly used to punch holes. But in the fashion industry, this piece of equipment is an indispensable sewing aid. In fact, every sample maker always has an awl next to the sewing machine, ready to be used when needed.

An awl functions like an extra finger. It provides additional control when manipulating fabric, and its strong, narrow point can access areas that fingers cannot reach. In addition, an awl comes in handy when adding ease to a sleeve cap, sewing gathers, and attaching bias piping at a neckline.

Awls are available in a variety of shapes and sizes, with both sharp and rounded points. The Clover brand, above (top, right) is made for sewers. By way of comparison, the larger Stanley awl, above (left), is a woodworking tool. (Some sewing machine operators believe the brands found in hardware stores last longer.)

A seam ripper or trolley needle, above (center), can be substituted for an awl. The trolley needle slips over the index finger of the left hand, with the needle on the pad of the finger. Be careful when using this tool. It is so light that it is easily forgotten, and a simple motion, like brushing hair away from your eyes, can have tragic consequences.

SHOP TALK

Awl Brands Are Not the Same

I PREFER THE AWL MADE BY DRITZ because its rounded point won't snag fabric.

Elissa Meyrich

Thick fabric is eased under the presser foot with a blunt-tipped awl by pressing the awl across the fabric just in front of the presser foot. When the fabric is flattened, it moves smoothly under the feed dogs, and an even stitch is maintained.

Easing a sleeve cap into the armscye is easier when you use an awl to position the excess fabric. Place the garment body on the bed, with the sleeve on top. While sewing, use the awl to push more ease, or gathers, under the presser foot.

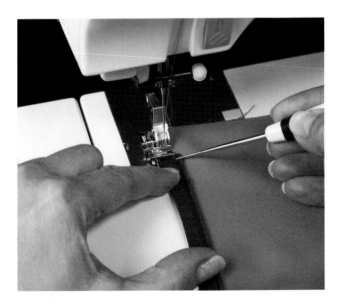

Zipper insertion is jump-started with an awl. Some feed systems are too weak to pull both the zipper tape and fabric under the presser foot. Push the start of the zipper tape under the presser foot with the awl to prevent the machine from jamming.

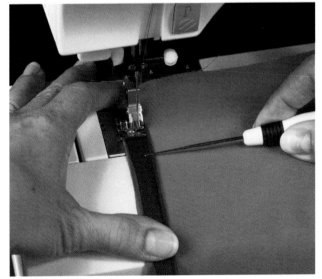

Flattened teeth on an invisible zipper flow smoothly under a presser foot. The conventional approach is to iron the teeth down. But with an awl, you can go directly to the sewing machine and use this handy tool to fold down the teeth as you sew.

Backstitching

Backstitching is used to secure the beginning and end of a row of stitching without tying the thread ends. The most common method used by sample makers operating a lock-stitch machine with a reverse feature is to slowly sew three stitches forward, reverse three, then proceed with the seam. At the very end of the seam, the operator will reverse three stitches, then go forward three to the end again.

For efficiency, this same industrial machine can have a needle positioner attached to the motor so it will always backstitch when the operator starts and stops. Industrial machines with memory banks allow the operator to program the backstitch (or reverse three) into an electronic control panel. Cutters can be programmed to clip the threads when the sewing is complete.

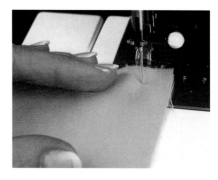

1 Position the garment under the presser foot. Lower the machine needle into the fabric about ⅜ inch from the beginning of the desired stitching line. Leave the presser foot on the machine for this step—it was removed in the photograph above only to show the position of the needle.

2 Hold the thread tails and lower the presser foot into the fabric. Reverse stitch three or four stitches, then proceed forward with straight stitches.

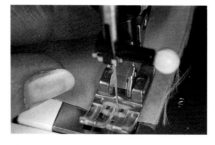

3 When you reach the end of the stitching line, reverse stitch three or four stitches again. Raise the needle and the presser foot.

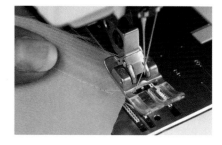

4 Pull the garment to the back and cut the threads close to the stitches.

SHOP TALK

Backstitching without Going in Reverse

IN SAMPLE MAKING AND SMALL PRODUCTION ROOMS, two common backstitching techniques prevail among operators of lockstitch industrial-sewing machines without a reverse feature. The first method involves sewing a few stitches, lifting the presser foot with the knee lever, then shifting the garment back to repeat the beginning stitches.

In the second method, the operator sews a few stitches, lifts the presser foot with the knee lever, and holds the garment in place to prevent the feed dogs from carrying the garment along. After a few stitches are accumulated in the same spot, she lowers the presser foot and resumes normal sewing. Both techniques are done so automatically and quickly that you would hardly even notice that something besides seaming occurred.

Barbara Kelly

$\mathcal{B}$ias Binding

Ready-to-wear garments use bias-cut fabric for both structural and design elements. Bias binding is found at armholes and necklines; piping accents seams and waistbands; and spaghetti tubing replaces buttonholes. In the industry, a "jobber" cuts and folds fabric, by machine, into bias strips. Since you probably don't have access to an industrial machine, this chapter explains how to make bias strips and replace facings. See also "Spaghetti Tubing" on pages 181–183.

Making Bias Strips

Bias is more elastic than the warp and fill of a fabric; therefore, bias-cut strips are your best choice for making binding and piping for curved areas on a garment. Bias piping and binding stretches around necklines and armholes and easily forms spaghetti tubing for straps and button loops. Sample makers will cut pattern pieces on the bias when they want a skirt to have draped, sensuous curves.

Generally speaking, bias is difficult to cut, especially if you are working with slippery fabrics like silk crepe, rayon, georgette, and chiffon. Because bias stretches, it's important to prevent the fabric from slipping off-grain.

1 Place a length of paper on a table and spread your fabric, one ply thick, on top. In the industry, Alphanumeric Marking Paper is used, but you can substitute an inexpensive tissue paper or examination table paper that is sold in rolls at medical-supply stores.

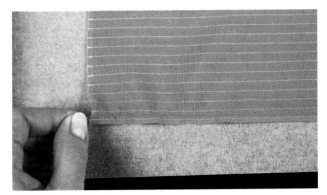

2 Identify both the warp and fill. The warp is parallel to the selvage, while yarns in the fill run from selvage to selvage. If you find it difficult to identify the warp and fill visually, pull two or three threads until the fabric puckers. Cut the fabric along the pulled strands to make straight edges along the warp and fill.

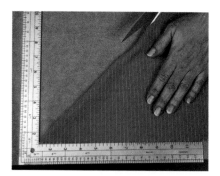

3 Place one edge of an L-square ruler along the selvage, with the other edge of the ruler parallel to the fill. Fold the fabric diagonally so that the fill meets the warp. The diagonal fold created is the true bias. Cut the fabric along the foldline to make two pieces.

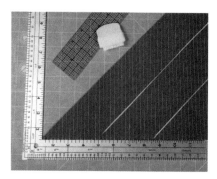

4 On one piece of fabric, chalk lines parallel to the true bias. These are the cutting lines for your strips, so each should be placed for the desired width of your strips.

5 With right sides facing, sew the bias strips together on the warp, using a ¼-inch seam allowance. Press the seams open. Always sew the strips together so they are at right angles to each other.

Replacing Facings with Bias Binding

Most ready-to-wear blouses and some dresses replace facings with bias binding made from self-fabric or even a complementary piece of fabric to finish the neckline and armhole edges. Facings are normally only used when additional support and body is desired around a neck opening. The bias strips are usually 1 inch wide and are cut along the true bias.

Applying Self-Fabric Bias Binding

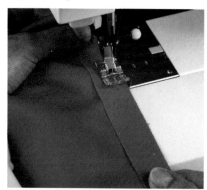

1 This set of instructions tells you how to apply bias binding to an armhole. However, the same procedure can be applied to a neckline. Fold under ¼ inch at the beginning of a 1-inch-wide length of bias binding. With right sides together, sew the bias binding to the raw edge of the armhole.

2 Continue sewing the bias around the armhole until you reach the starting point. Overlap the end of the bias binding on top of the beginning of the bias binding (the portion that has been turned under). Diagonally cut the end of the bias binding past the start of the seamline.

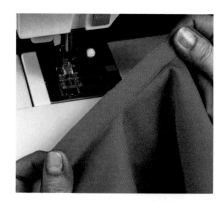

3 Open out the bias binding and finger press the seam allowances toward the binding. Understitch the bias binding to the seam allowances by stitching ⅛ inch from the seamline.

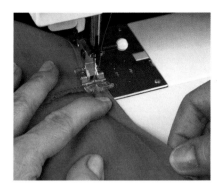

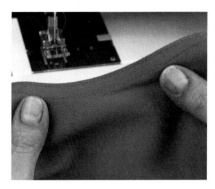

4 With the wrong side of the underarm facing up, fold a few
inches of the bias binding in half
lengthwise so that the raw edge is
adjacent to the seamline. Now fold
the bias binding to the wrong side
of the armhole, making sure the
seamline and understitching aren't
visible from the right side. Secure
the folds by stitching ⅛ inch from
the folded edge.

5 Continue to sew the bias
binding in position around the
armhole, folding under the raw edge
as you sew. When you finish sewing
the bias binding to the wrong side of
the armhole, a single line of topstitching will be visible from the
right side of the garment.

6 With the right side of the garment facing up, apply another
row of topstitching close to the edge
of the armhole.

Applying Purchased Bias Tape

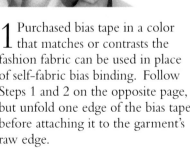

1 Purchased bias tape in a color
that matches or contrasts the
fashion fabric can be used in place
of self-fabric bias binding. Follow
Steps 1 and 2 on the opposite page,
but unfold one edge of the bias tape
before attaching it to the garment's
raw edge.

2 Open out the bias binding and
finger press the seam allowances
toward the binding. Understitch
the bias binding to the seam allowances by stitching ⅛ inch from
the seamline.

3 Fold the bias tape to the wrong
side of the armhole, making sure
the seamline and understitching
aren't visible from the right side.
Sew ⅛ inch from the folded edge.
Turn the garment over and topstitch
as close as possible to the fold.

Buttons, Buttonholes, and Lappage

It's very important to pay special attention to the focal points on a blouse. The two main areas are usually the front placket, which contains the button and buttonholes, and the collar. You should also pay special attention to cuffs, sleeve plackets, decorative trims, and any special style lines that provide decorative shaping for the blouse.

This chapter explains the need to adjust fronts to accommodate variations in button size and shape, recommends positions for buttons and buttonholes, and explains how to make bound buttonholes as they're done in sample rooms.

Sample Room Guidelines

Few rules are "firm" within the garment industry because time, economics, desired quality, and design elements all infringe on standard garment construction procedures. However, here are some guidelines that will improve the appearance of both buttonholes and buttons.

• Add ⅛ inch to the diameter of a two- or four-hole flat standard button to determine the corresponding buttonhole width. This rule does not work with odd-shaped buttons.

• Cut buttonholes with a chisel so they're neat.

• To avoid blank spots, either use a heavier thread or double stitch around the buttonhole.

• Use interfacing that doesn't contrast with your fabric at the buttonholes.

• Place buttons in the following areas: at the bust line; between the bust line and the waistline; above the waistline but just high enough to prevent the button from interfering with a waistband or belt; below the waistline, using the same approximate spacing as that between the other buttons; and at the neckline down from the seamline half of the button's diameter plus ¼ inch, adjusting the placement of the other buttons to maintain even spacing.

Lappage

Correct placement of both buttons and buttonholes provides the fabric needed to support the closures, maintain correct fit, and prevent the front of the garment from gaping. The amount of fabric that "overlaps" at the buttons and buttonholes, called the lappage, is of utmost importance. When you choose a button size or shape that deviates from what your pattern recommends, you must also adjust the lappage.

The positions of the buttons and buttonholes are established in relation to the closure line, which is the vertical line on both fronts that runs through the center of the area where the two fronts overlap. (See the heavy line in the photo.)

The size of your button and the choice of either a vertical or horizontal buttonhole determine the width of the fabric that extends beyond the closure line toward the other front. This area is called the lappage closure extension. (See the heavy line in the photo.)

Although home-sewing pattern pieces come printed with that styles' correct size buttons and buttonholes, you may need to modify the lappage closure extensions if your button isn't the same size as the one recommended on the pattern envelope, if you use a vertical buttonhole even though the pattern calls for a horizontal orientation, or if the buttonhole must accommodate a ball, semiball, square, or other odd-shaped button.

A horizontal buttonhole is placed almost entirely on the body side of the closure line.

About $\frac{1}{8}$ inch of the buttonhole extends past the closure line into the lappage closure extension. For a button with a large shank, $\frac{3}{16}$ inch of the horizontal buttonhole's opening is in the lappage closure extension.

Vertical buttonholes hang on a button shank on ready-to-wear garments from high-end manufacturers. The top of the buttonhole is sewn $\frac{1}{8}$ inch above the location of the center of a standard button on the opposite front. The finished lappage closure extensions on both fronts are the same width as the button.

SHOP TALK

The No-Sew, 30-Second Buttonhole Test

$\int$EST YOUR BUTTONHOLE WIDTH WHEN USING A semiball, ball, square, or other odd-shaped button. First measure the button's diameter. To this measurement add $\frac{1}{8}$ inch if your button is flat and $\frac{1}{4}$ inch if your button is a ball, semiball, square, or another odd shape. Mark this length on a piece of paper. Tape each end of the mark and cut along the line. Slide your button through the slit to determine if that length is appropriate.

Laurel Hoffman

Bound Buttonholes

A *distinctive feature that often sets apart high-end garments is bound buttonholes. In quantity production, these are typically formed on a machine that makes bound buttonholes. But in a sample studio and small-production rooms, a sewer will carefully make each one individually. A popular method that creates an effect similar to the results of the bound buttonhole machine is to construct bound buttonholes using a folded patch. It is efficient and ensures precision, provided that you mark and sew accurately.*

Preparing the Garment Pattern Piece

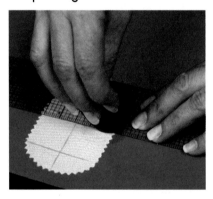

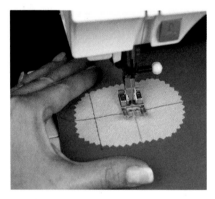

1 Cut a piece of lightweight fusible interfacing 2 inches longer and wider than your buttonhole. Reinforce the back of the buttonhole with the interfacing. With a sharp fabric marking pencil, draw one horizontal and two vertical lines for the buttonhole on the interfacing. The vertical lines should extend 1 inch beyond each side of the intended opening.

2 With a contrasting thread in the bobbin and the tension slightly loosened, machine baste over the buttonhole markings to create one long horizontal and two short vertical thread tracings on the right side of the garment.

Making the Welts

1 Cut a buttonhole patch 1 inch wide and 1 inch longer than the desired buttonhole. Using a grid ruler and rotary cutter is efficient and ensures accurate results. If your fabric ravels, reinforce a piece of it with a lightweight fusible interfacing before cutting out the patch.

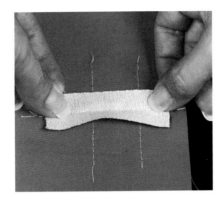

2 With wrong sides together, fold and press the patch in half lengthwise, identifying the center with a crease. Open out the patch. With right sides together, place the crease of the patch over the horizontal thread-traced buttonhole marking, leaving ½ inch extending beyond each of the two vertical markings.

3 Machine baste through all thicknesses exactly along the patch crease and over the horizontal marking. Fold and press the long raw edges of the patch, so they touch the center basting line and one another. The folded patch should now measure ½ inch wide.

4 Using a grid ruler and chalk, mark a thin line through the center of each folded section, accurately dividing each in half.

5 Turn your grid ruler and place it alongside one vertical thread tracing. Then draw a line over the folded patch to mark the edge of the buttonhole on it. Repeat to make a similar line on the other side of the patch, using the other vertical thread marking. You now know precisely where to begin and end your stitching.

SHOP TALK

Machine-Stitched Buttons

WHY NOT TRY ATTACHING YOUR two-hole buttons by machine? Change to the presser foot recommended by your sewing machine's owner manual, or attach a satin stitch foot. Dab the button with glue, position it on the garment, and insert it under the presser foot. Adjust your stitch width so the needle moves from one hole to the other and back again. Also adjust your stitch length to 0.

Laurel Hoffman

Securing the Welts

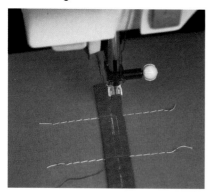

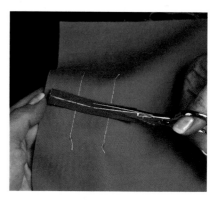

1 Sew through the center of each folded section, using a fine stitch length (15 to 20 stitches per inch) and starting and stopping at the lines. Cut the thread tails 3 to 4 inches long. The presser foot was removed here for better visibility. Don't remove your presser foot.

2 If you are making several buttonholes, check now to make sure they are all the same length and width. Remove the horizontal basting threads. Pull the thread tails to the inside of the garment. Tie and cut the threads close to the knots. Press.

3 Cut through the center of the strip. Don't cut through the garment fabric underneath the strip yet.

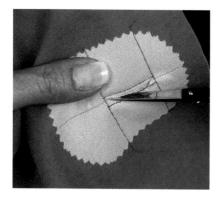

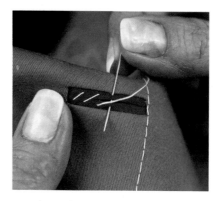

4 Turn to the inside of the garment. Using small, sharp scissors, cut evenly between the two rows of stitching, stopping about ¼ inch from each end of the stitching. Carefully snip into the corners to create a small triangle at each end.

5 Push the strips through to the inside of the garment and adjust them to form a rectangle. Press. Remove the vertical basting threads and hand baste (or carefully zigzag) the welts together. Press.

6 Position the buttonhole under the presser foot with the fabric right side up and folded back to expose one triangular tip and the welt ends. Starting in the center of the line, sew across the triangle. Sew again to secure, flatten, and strengthen. Repeat at the other end. The presser foot was removed here for better visibility. Don't remove your presser foot.

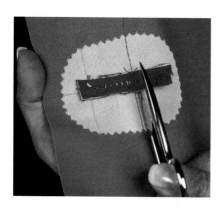

7 Trim the welt ends to ¼ inch and press them with the tip of your iron. Finish the garment's facing, and secure it to the wrong side of each buttonhole. See "Completing the Facing with a Slash, or Eye Slit, Finish" on the opposite page or "Completing the Facing with a Windowpane Finish" on page 96.

Completing the Facing with a Slash, or Eye Slit, Finish

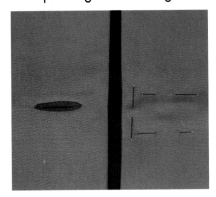

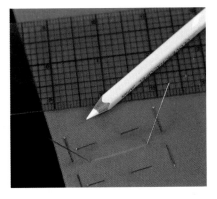

1 Sew the facing to the garment. Align the facing behind the garment, and position pins around the buttonhole to prevent the fabric layers from slipping. If you have multiple buttonholes in your garment, start pinning at the center buttonhole and work up, then down, until the facing is secure.

2 Insert a pin at each end of the buttonhole opening from the right side of the garment through to the wrong side.

3 Carefully turn over the garment so the facing is up. The cross-grain lines of the facing should run between pairs of the pins. Adjust if necessary. Mark a line between the pins with a fabric pencil.

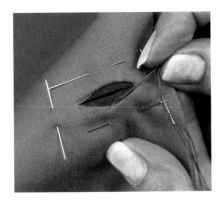

4 Remove the pins. Again, using small, sharp scissors, slash along the line you just drew. You can further prevent your cut edges from fraying by applying a thin strand of liquid seam sealant along the slash. Allow it to dry before proceeding with the next step.

5 Turn under the cut edges of the slashed opening. Using a fine needle and matching thread, slip stitch the edges while exposing the welts. Remove the basting from the welts and press.

SPINNING YARNS

No Backstitching Necessary

·············

A N INDUSTRIAL MACHINE CAN be programmed to make smaller stitches at the beginning and the end of a line of stitching.

Barbara Kelly

Completing the Facing with a Windowpane Finish

1 The windowpane method for attaching a facing behind a bound buttonhole always looks neat and can be used on all types of fabrics. This photograph shows the back of a buttonhole finished in this way. First attach the facing along the edge adjacent to the buttonholes. Press and trim. Work in stages with multiple buttonholes.

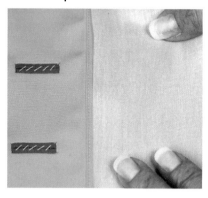

2 Cut a strip of lightweight, crisp fabric 2 inches wider and longer than your buttonhole. Use a continuous strip if you are working on a row of buttonholes. Place your garment right side up on a flat surface, with the right side of the facing adjacent. Place the strip of fabric on the facing over the buttonhole opening.

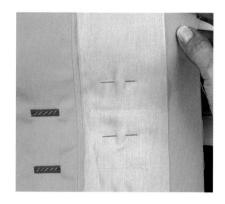

3 Anchor the fabric strip with pins. Draw a horizontal line on the fabric strip directly across from each buttonhole. Machine baste along each line through the fabric strip and the facing.

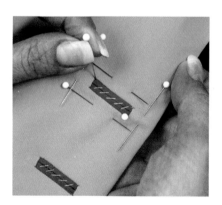

4 With wrong sides together, fold the facing behind the garment. Working on the right side of the garment, pin around the buttonhole to prevent the facing from slipping. Then insert a pin at each corner of the buttonhole through to the other side. If you have multiple buttonholes, start with the center one.

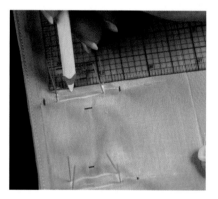

5 Turn to the facing side. Ideally, your horizontal lines will be centered between the pairs of pins. Carefully mark the rectangular outline from pin point to pin point. Check that all of the windowpanes are the same length and width. These rectangles should correspond with the seams that secure the welts to the garment.

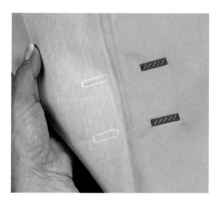

6 Remove the pins and open the facing away from the garment.

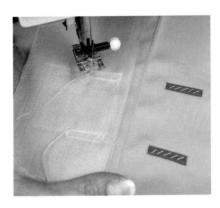

7 Position the facing under the presser foot with the strip side up. Starting at the middle of one long "window" marking and with your sewing machine set for a very fine stitch (20 stitches per inch), sew around the rectangular outline, pivoting at each corner and continuing over a few beginning stitches. Don't backstitch.

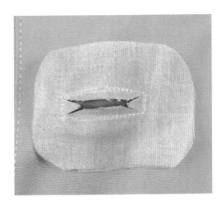

8 Remove the basting from Step 3. Cut away the fabric strip around the window, leaving a ½-inch margin of fabric outside the stitching lines and around the corners. Using small, sharp scissors, cut through the center of the window, stopping ¼ inch from each end. Carefully snip into the corners to create small triangles. Press.

9 Push the patch through the window to the wrong side of the facing. From the wrong side, press around the folded edges of the window, making certain that the patch doesn't show on the right side of the facing.

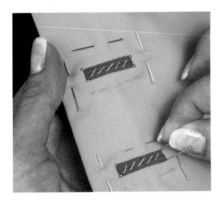

10 Complete the facing. Trim, turn, and press. The windowpane buttonhole should be aligned under the bound buttonhole. Pin it in position.

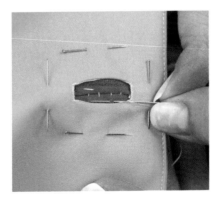

11 Slip stitch the folded edges of the windowpane to cover the stitches that secure the welts. Press.

There's More!

W HAT COUNTS ARE LITTLE DE-tails, including the method you use to close your garment. So rather than making buttonholes yet again, replace them with loops of spaghetti tubing that extend from the closure line.

*C*hain Stitching

This timesaving technique is suitable for most garments. Basically you feed several components through your sewing machine one after another, leaving 1 inch of stitching between each. For example, when assembling a blouse, most sewers complete a single cuff, attach this to the sleeve, then turn their attention to the second cuff and sleeve. But with this technique, both cuffs are completed at the same time.

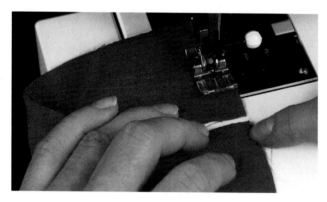

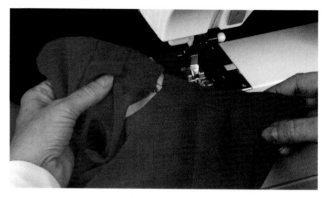

Sew both cuff ends at once. Fold one cuff with right sides together so that both of its short ends are on the sewing machine bed. Continue sewing, letting the needle run off the first cuff and making several stitches without fabric. Sew the seam on the second cuff, break your threads, and cut the threads between the two seams.

Baste pleats on both blouse fronts one after the other. Prior to attaching a yoke, baste the tucks on the right front and then sew off the pattern piece. Make a few stitches without fabric, then mount and baste the left front. Cut the threads between the two pattern pieces after basting the left front.

SHOP TALK

"Chain" Your Continuous-Lap Sleeve Plackets

*T*O CHAIN STITCH SLEEVE PLACKETS, double the length of a single placket pattern piece and add 1 inch. Cut this out and press under ¼ inch on one lengthwise edge. Spread the bottom of the sleeve along the slash, and sew the right side of the placket to the wrong side of the sleeve. At the uppermost point of the slash, reduce the seam allowance. At the end of the first sleeve, break your threads but don't cut the placket. Leave a 1-inch gap on the placket, then attach the second sleeve. Fold the placket to the right side, crack stitch, and then cut the placket between the sleeves.

Laurel Hoffman

Collars

Whether you are creating a mandarin, two-piece, or flat collar or a collar with a stand, there are sample room techniques that will improve the quality of your workmanship. These ideas, gleaned from many hours in several sample and production rooms, are presented here. Usually collar pieces aren't cut on a fold. If the fabric for a collar has some density, the patternmaker will prepare the upper collar slightly larger than the undercollar. A ⅛-inch increase is standard. Shown on the right is a pointed collar with a partial facing.

Flat Collar

A patternmaker reduces the inner curve of a flat collar to create a slight roll and to prevent a neckline seam from showing. Since the undercollar and upper collar are marginally different, they're cut out separately.

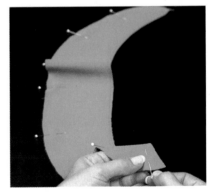

1 Cut the outer edges, but not the neckline edge, of the upper collar ⅛ inch larger than the undercollar. Notch the neckline seam allowance at the centers and shoulder seams to match the corresponding locations on the garment.

2 To prevent the impression of the seam allowances from showing when pressed, apply interfacing to the wrong side of the upper collar. If you're using a sew-in interfacing, baste it in the seam allowance next to the seamline to prevent slippage. It's not necessary to baste it along the neckline edge.

3 With right sides together, match and pin the undercollar to the upper collar along the outer edges.

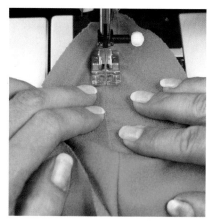

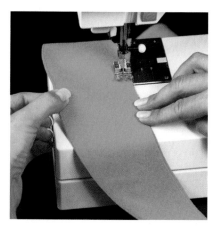

4 Position the outer seam under the presser foot at the center back with the undercollar up and to the left. Sew the seamline to the center front. Don't sew the neckline. Turn the collar around, but not over. Overlap ½ inch of the stitching at the center back. Sew to the center front on the other side.

5 Press the stitches flat, then press the seam allowances open. If your fabric is heavier than shirt weight, grade the undercollar seam allowances to ⅛ inch. Understitch the seam along the undercollar to prevent it from rolling.

6 Press the collar flat. Turn it right side out and press again. Pin the raw edges of the inner neckline together. Removing the pins as you sew, baste the layers in place. The collar should now form a slight roll and can be attached to the garment.

Convertible Collar

Many call this a rolled, or basic shirt, collar. It's constructed with front facings, so it can be worn open or closed. A stand and a roll line are created within the convertible collar when it's curved around a neck. This occurs because the neckline edge of the convertible collar is shaped in the opposite direction to the garment's neckline edge. To make a basic shirt collar, you must first construct a collar with points.

Constructing a Collar with Points

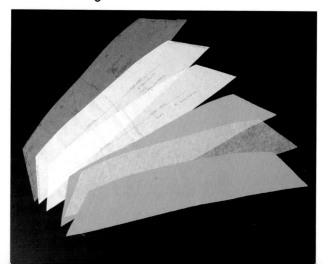

1 Cut the upper collar ⅛ inch larger than the undercollar on the outer edge and 1/16 inch larger along both short front edges. Cut the interfacing the same size as the upper collar. Diagonally trim the interfacing's corners so that they don't catch in the stitching at the points.

2 To prevent the seam allowances from showing when pressed, apply the interfacing to the wrong side of the upper collar. Notch the neckline seam allowance at the center back and the shoulder seams. Staystitch the neck edge of the upper collar in the seam allowance a thread's distance away from the seamline.

3 Sew the outer edge of the collar pieces together with the right sides facing and the under-collar on top. Backstitch. Sew along the seamline while pulling the layers taut. Backstitch at the end of the seam.

4 If your collar won't be top-stitched, understitch it now. Finger press the seam allowances toward the undercollar. To keep your sewing consistent, switch to a presser foot that will guide your sewing, such as an edge stitching foot. Understitch. In this photo, the presser foot was intentionally installed backwards because the right toe is an excellent guide.

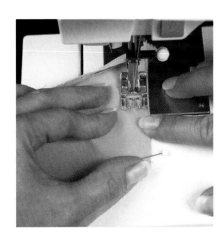

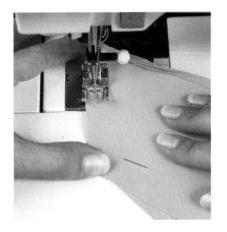

5 Fold the collar with the right sides together and the front seams matching. Position a front seam under the presser foot with the undercollar faceup. Insert your needle into the fabric at the point. Lower the presser foot, backstitch, and sew the remainder of the seam at the regulation stitch length. Backstitch at the end of the seam.

6 Move the collar to sew the other side. Don't turn the collar over. Position the collar to the right of the presser foot and the seam allowance to the left. Sew this front collar seam in the same manner as the other one. By using this directional sewing, both points are favored in the same way.

7 Trim the seam allowances at the point, so they're slightly smaller than the collar point. Repeat on the other side. Press the stitches flat, then press the seam allowances open.

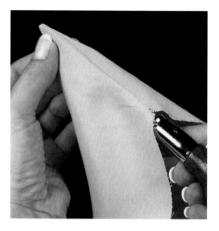

8 To turn the collar, insert your thumb inside a point. With your index finger as close to the point as possible, pinch the seam allowance and turn the collar right side out, pushing your fingernail into the point. Repeat on the other side.

9 If some of the fabric has not turned to form the perfect point, use a point turner to push it out. If more turning is still necessary, insert an awl into the point of the undercollar and coax the seam allowance flat and into the point.

10 Press the collar flat from the wrong side. Turn in the seam allowance and press a crease along the staystitching between the notches on the upper collar. Place one front seam on top of the other to check that the distance between the neck edges and the points are identical.

Attaching a Collar with a Partial Facing

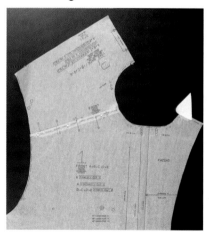

1 Adjust and trim the seam allowances on your pattern pieces. Mark your neck seamline along the front, self-facing, and back pattern pieces. Tape a 2-inch paper triangle to the neck/shoulder edge of the self-facing. Pin the front pattern piece to the back at the shoulder seamline.

2 Fold the self-facing along the vertical foldline to match the neckline edge. Draw a smooth line along the straight part of the facing to 1 inch beyond the shoulder seam on the neckline. Add a ¼-inch hem to blend with the unadjusted facing. Mark the neck point on the pattern pieces. Add a ¼-inch seam allowance at the top of the facing and along the neckline edge.

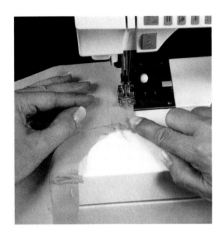

3 Notch the neckline seam allowance at the center front, the foldlines, and the center back. Narrow hem the long edge of the self-facings. With right sides together, sew the front and back at the shoulder. With raw edges even, baste a 1½-inch loop of spaghetti tubing to the right neckline facing beside the foldline.

4 Make your collar. See "Constructing a Collar with Points" on page 100. Pin the collar to the right side of the neckline edge, matching the notches at the center front, the center back, and the shoulder seams. Keep the upper collar free between the notches.

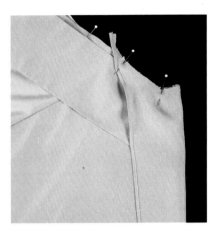

5 Turn back the facings along their foldlines, and place them on top of the collar with the neckline seams matched. At the shoulder seam of the facings, notch to the seamline. Don't pin the facings past the shoulder notches.

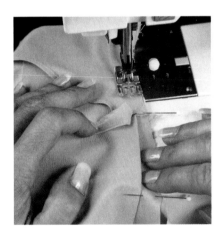

6 With the facing side up, sew the neckline seam. Keep the last, notched inch of the facing out of the seamline, and make sure the upper collar doesn't get caught in the stitching between the notches.

7 Snip along the neckline seam allowance to release the curve. Clip the seam allowances at the shoulder, and trim the seam allowances under the facings to ⅛ inch. Turn the facings right side out. Use a point turner to push the corners out.

There's More!

POORLY STITCHED OR TURNED collars can ruin an otherwise beautiful garment. To make your work outstanding, borrow the tricks in "Corners" on pages 108–109.

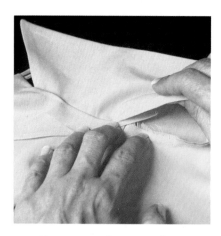

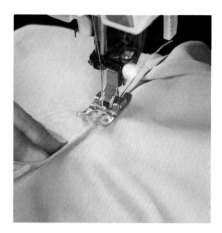

8 Finger press the seam allowances toward the collar. Fold the seam allowance of the upper collar into the neck opening. Push the seam allowance of the small unattached facing section under the upper collar and into the neck opening.

9 Place the fold of the upper collar over the neckline seam. Pin if desired. Production sewers don't pin. They "feel" their way along the seam as they sew. Position the neck opening under the presser foot. Insert the needle into the edge of the upper collar next to the shoulder seam.

10 Lower the presser foot, backstitch, and then sew along the edge of the unattached, folded upper collar. Keep the fold aligned with the stitching of the neckline seam. Backstitch when you reach the other shoulder seam.

SPINNING YARNS

Use Your Hemmer

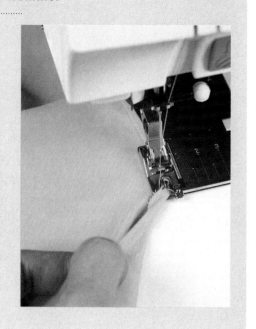

*D*URING THE PRODUCTION OF shirts at Think Tank in San Francisco, some sewers use a straight stitch hemmer attachment to finish the facing edge, while others prefer turning the edge with their fingers as they proceed with the stitches. If you have a hemmer, this is an ideal time to use it because the facing edge is mostly on the straight of grain and will give consistent results. Keep your edge taut while sewing the "baby hem" with fine stitches, so it won't pucker when you are finished.

Barbara Kelly

Standing Collars

Mandarin collars and collars with a stand can be constructed from the lengthwise or crosswise grain of the garment fabric. Two methods are presented here. After you are comfortable creating an edge stitched standing collar, you may want to try the interesting "pull-through" procedure in "The Ten-Minute Collar with Stand" on page 107. Hand sewing is kept to a minimum, and the procedure produces a clean corner at the top of the placket.

Popular Edge Stitched Standing Collar

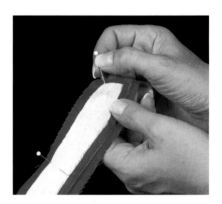

1 Attach the interfacing to the wrong side of the outside collar. If you want a stiffer collar, attach another layer of interfacing to the inside collar. Don't include interfacing in the seam allowances so that it can act as a template to guide your stitches.

2 To prevent stretching, staystitch ¹⁄₁₆ inch inside the neckline seam allowance of the inside collar. Turn in the seam allowance along the neckline, and press so the stitches are visible only in the seam allowance.

3 With right sides together, match and pin the inside and outside collars along the front and top edges.

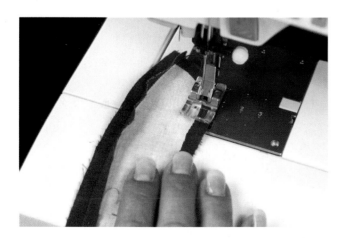

4 With the inside collar facing up, position the front edge of the seam allowance under the presser foot. Open the pressed neckline seam allowance. Start sewing at the intersection of the neckline seam and the collar seam. Don't let any stitches stray into the neckline seam allowance. Stitch around the collar seam.

5 Press the stitches flat to set them, then press the seam allowances open with the tip of your iron. Press over a point presser or tailor board for greater ease. If the fabric has density, the seam allowance of the inside collar may need to be trimmed to ⅛ inch. Trim the curved areas to ⅛ inch.

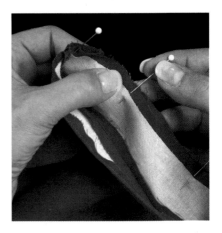

6 Turn the collar right side out and press it flat, taking care to maintain the pressed edge of the inside collar. With right sides together, pin the outside collar to the garment along the neck edge, matching all of the notches.

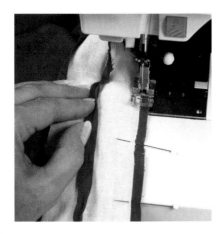

7 With the wrong side of the outside collar facing up, place the neckline seam under the presser foot. Keep the neckline seam allowance of the undercollar free. Insert the needle at the front edge of the neckline seam. Sew the seam, backstitching at the beginning and the end.

8 Wrap the right side of the inside collar around to the wrong side of the garment. Align the neckline seams. You will have a little "sandwich" of collar-garment-collar. Starting at the front intersection, sew, backstitch, and stitch along the neckline seam for 1 or 2 inches. Trim the corners.

9 Pull the garment out from the collar "sandwich." Finger press the remainder of the neckline seam toward the collar. From the right side, pin the inside collar to the neckline seam. Edge stitch around the collar.

The Ten-Minute Collar with Stand

1 Make a collar with points. See page 100. Place the finished collar between the two right sides of the neckband, and sew them together along the raw upper edge, using a ¼-inch seam allowance. Turn the neckband right side out, and press the edge where the collar and neckband are joined.

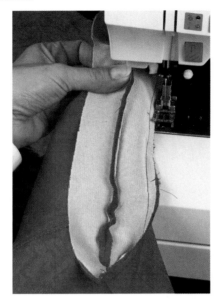

2 Place the right side of the neckband to the wrong side of the neckline with raw edges even. Sew along the neck edge, using the center back and shoulder notches as placement guides.

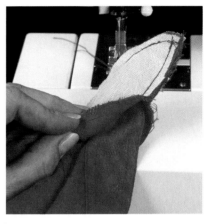

3 With right sides together, fold the neckband, encasing the collar and the neck edge above the placket. Stitch together the raw edges along the width of the placket.

4 Carefully trim back the seam allowance at the center front corner of the neckband to reduce the bulk. Turn the collar right side out.

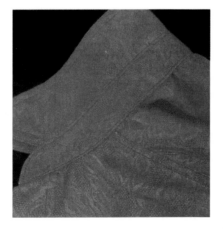

5 Starting where the neckband is seamed together above the placket, topstitch along the outer edges of the neckband. Leave the needle down in the fabric when turning the corners so that you have one continuous line of stitching. When stitching along the side with the raw edge, turn it under and place it along the neck edge seamline.

*C*orners

A *corner is such a simple detail, yet it's one of the more noticeable signs of a poorly constructed garment. Collars and cuffs, the obvious location of corners, are focal points; therefore, any error—however small—is glaring. So it's important to use an effective method for handling these areas on your garments. In a factory setting, stitching and turning corners is not a complicated procedure. It is frequently done by hand with the aid of tools that are similar to the point turners you can purchase. There are, however, a few simple tricks to make your corners smoother and straighter.*

Making a Point

A *crisp, precise point doesn't necessarily require a sharp turn in the stitching line. In fact, making two diagonal stitches across the point will give your work an attractive shape.*

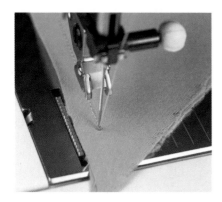

1 Sew along the seamline until you are about ½ inch from the point. At this location, stop stitching and shorten the stitch length. It should be set at 18 stitches per inch (spi). Continue stitching until you are one stitch shy of the point.

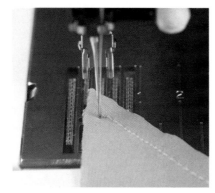

2 With the needle through the layers, raise the presser foot and pivot the collar. Take two diagonal stitches across the point, then raise the presser foot again and pivot with the needle through the layers.

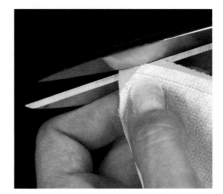

3 Continue with the shortened stitch length for about ½ inch, then resume regulation stitching. Trim the seam allowances diagonally at the point.

4 Now you should take the time to leave your sewing machine and use your iron. Press the stitches flat to set them. Then press the seams open. This is easier to do if you use a point presser.

5 Turn the garment right side out. Use a point turner or awl to coax the corner out, as shown. If necessary, insert a substantial needle into the tip of the undercollar from the right side to further coax the seam allowance flat and into the point. This is a puncture-and-pull action. Press.

Turning a Corner

Finger pressing is a quick technique for turning the corners of waistbands and collars. After sewing the corner, you use your fingers to fold the seam allowances and turn the work right side out. With this technique, it's unlikely that you will need to push out the point after you turn the corner.

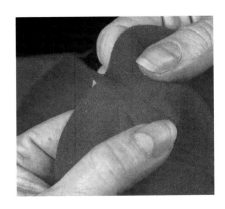

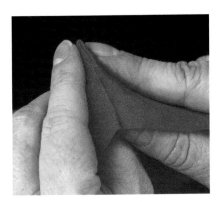

1 If necessary, diagonally trim only the corner seam allowances. Place the forefinger of your left hand into the corner's point. Fold the seam allowance to one side with the thumb of your left hand on the other side of the fabric.

2 Grasp the fabric with your right-hand forefinger and thumb, and slide your right forefinger into the corner beside your left forefinger. With a twist of both wrists, turn the corner right side out. Don't shift the position of your fingers.

Crack Stitching

Also called stitch in the ditch, this eliminates hand sewing. Rather than slip stitching a folded seam allowance to the seamline in the garment's interior, the un-attached seam allowance is secured with a line of stitching in the "crack" of the previous seamline. The fabric underneath will catch in the stitching.

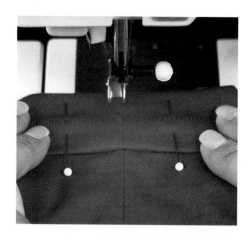

1 Fold under the seam allowance on the pattern piece that will be secured in later steps with the crack stitching. Sew your combined pattern pieces to the garment. Press the seam allowances toward the portion of the garment that will be encased when the crack stitching is complete.

2 Fold the loose edge of the garment to the interior, and pin it in place so that the folded edge extends just past the seamline. Instead of pinning, you can place the folded edge as you sew, using your fingertips to feel its location just before it goes under the presser foot.

3 Insert the garment right side up (or wrong side up, if desired) under the presser foot. Set your machine to a regulation stitch length, between 10 and 15 stitches per inch (spi). Holding your fabric taut, sew in the seamline to secure the folded edge.

Tips and Applications

In some instances, you will find it easier to make the line of stitching with the garment wrong side up.

You can reverse the procedure so that the unattached pattern piece is folded forward, to the right side, and crack stitched with the folded seam allowance over the seamline.

An overlocked edge on a waistband doesn't need to be pressed under and neither does a waistband cut on the selvage. Place the seam allowances just past the seamline and crack stitch from the right side.

The width of the folded edge that extends past the seamline varies. On a cuff, the fold is close to the seamline because it isn't visible when the garment is worn. On the waistband, the fold is ⅜ inch past the seamline.

Crowding

This technique puckers an edge of fabric to make it smaller. It doesn't cause gathers, but it reduces the length of an area that needs to fit into a shorter or smaller area. An industrial machine with differential feed can be set to ease in the given amount to a specific dimension. Crowding can be considered the manual version of differential feed.

On a fabric scrap, test the degree of pressure you need to exert and the length at which your stitch should be regulated to determine what combination will work best for your project.

1 Position the beginning of the section to be eased under the presser foot. Insert the needle to the right of the seamline just slightly inside the seam allowance.

3 If you find you have crowded too much, you can snip a few threads along your work.

2 Lower the presser foot, then place and hold a finger behind it. Slowly begin machine stitching, crowding the fabric as you sew. After a few inches have bunched, release your finger and proceed again. Continue with this technique until you have reached the end of the section to be eased.

SHOP TALK

"Ease"y to Fit

OFTEN CROWDING IS NECESsary for rounding a curve such as a princess seam at the bust line. It is also useful when easing in a turned hem on a flared skirt, an elbow in a sleeve seam, the back at the shoulder seam, a waist into a waistband, or an area that has accidentally stretched.

Barbara Kelly

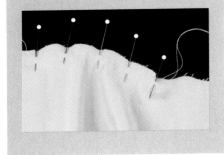

*C*uffs

A *pinless, painless method to attach cuffs is to work from the wrong side. Rather than sewing the cuff and sleeve with the right sides together, you will attach the right side of the cuff to the wrong side of the sleeve. Seeing the edge that you are finishing eliminates the need for pins and enables you to achieve perfect topstitching on both the inside and outside of the cuff.*

1 Sew the sleeve side seam and finish the raw edges. Attach the placket at the slash. See Step 8 on page 217. Sew the right side of the notched edge of the cuff (or cuff facing if you have a two-piece cuff) to the wrong side of the lower sleeve edge with the placket edges ⅜ inch from the raw edges of the cuff.

2 If you have a two-piece cuff, attach the second portion now. Place the right sides of the cuff pieces together, and sew the components around the outer edges of the cuff, using a ⅜-inch seam allowance.

SHOP TALK

Don't Baste Your Time

IF YOUR SLEEVE HAS TUCKS, POSItion these by folding along the notches as you sew the cuff to the sleeve. Following the notches will eliminate the need to baste the tucks prior to joining the garment pieces.

Julia Linger

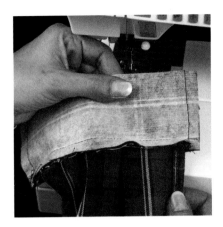

3 If you have a one-piece cuff, fold the seam allowance made in Step 1 toward the sleeve. Don't press. Fold the cuff in half lengthwise, so that the raw edges match. Join with a seam, starting at the fold and ending at the seam that joins the cuff and the sleeve. Fold the seam allowances made in Step 1 toward the cuff.

4 Turn the cuff right side out. Starting at the outer edge of the cuff, topstitch around one side, the top, and the remaining side of the cuff. Leave the needle in the fabric, and pivot at the corners for a continuous stitching line.

5 Fold under the seam allowance of the remaining lengthwise raw edge. Place the fold along the seamline that joins the cuff to the bottom of the sleeve, and sew it in place by stitching as close to the fold as possible. On the inside of the sleeve, the stitching should just catch the bottom of the cuff.

6 As a finishing detail, topstitch the cuff ¼ inch from the outer edge. You can sight by your standard presser foot, which is ¼ inch wide.

There's More!

YOU CAN REDUCE THE AMOUNT of time you spend assembling sleeves and cuffs by chain stitching them. For instructions, see page 98.

SPINNING YARNS

Not "Pin"staking Work

SKILLED PRODUCTION SEWERS don't use pins because they are capable of feeling their way around the collar as they attach the inside collar and stitch around the outside edge.

Barbara Kelly

*D*arts

There are several techniques for creating a dart, and the use of each is determined by the equipment and the operator's skill. A sewing operator who produces many darts becomes skilled enough to backstitch at the dart point. An operator at a nonreverse industrial machine starts at the wide end of the dart, advances to the point, pivots the work, and sews a few stitches back into the dart. An operator of a reverse-stitch machine can start at the point and backstitch before continuing to the wide end. An "industrial" technique suitable for a home-sewing machine is explained on page 117.

Transferring Pattern Markings to Fabric

Because there are so many weights, types, and textures of fabrics, you should know a variety of marking techniques so that you can choose the one most suitable for your fashion fabric. The methods on the opposite page were done on two layers of fabric that were cut with the right sides together. As shown, you can accurately make matching marks on both layers at the same time.

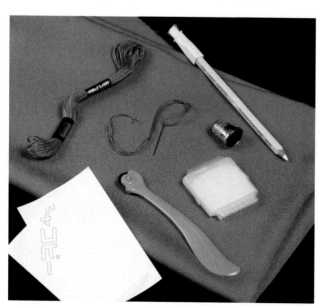

The preferred method for marking darts in delicate and lofty fabrics is with tailor's tacks. They are easy to remove and prevent permanent damage. The efficient method described on the opposite page is a simplified version used by many dressmakers.

A dressmaker's tracing paper and wheel will help you conveniently transfer a single mark or an entire stitching line onto two layers at the same time. This method is especially helpful when marking an uneven, angled dart under a notched or cowl collar. It works best on opaque fabrics.

Chalk or wax is the most efficient way of marking a dart if you formed it with pins during a fitting. These markers are used with pins to make a single mark or a series of marks.

Tailor's Tacks

 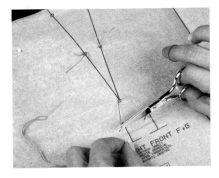 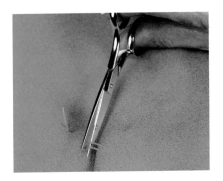

1 Cotton basting thread is the best choice for making tailor's tacks in delicate fabrics. It contains no dyes and has a loose twist to hold it in place until removed. If this product isn't available, select a fine silk thread. A great choice for other fabrics is two plies of embroidery floss.

2 At a dart point or another interior dart marking on your pattern, take a small, single stitch through both the fabric and tissue pattern pieces with a needle and thread. Leave a 2-inch unknotted thread tail on each side of your stitch.

3 Carefully lift the pattern off the fabric. Raise the top layer of fabric about an inch. Cut the threads between the two fabric layers.

Dressmaker's Tracing Paper and Wheel

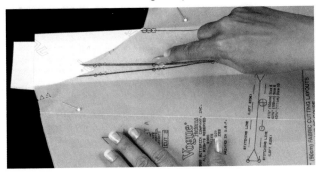 

1 Place dressmaker's tracing paper, tracing side up, under both fabric pattern pieces. Place another piece of tracing paper, tracing side down, between the tissue pattern piece and the top fabric pattern piece. The result will be (from top to bottom): tissue pattern piece, tracing paper, two cutout fabric pattern pieces, and tracing paper. On the tissue pattern, trace the dart legs with a dressmaker's wheel.

2 Top the dart point with a ½-inch line running perpendicular to the center of the dart. On the wrong side of the fabric, trace short horizontal lines at the other interior dart markings.

Chalk and Wax

 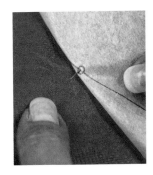

1 Insert pins through the marks on the pattern and both layers of the fabric pattern pieces. Turn the pattern and fabric pieces over. Push each pin in the direction of the dart point. Rub a chalk pencil or wax on the fabric over each pin, leaving you crisp lines.

2 Turn the fabric and pattern pieces over again. Carefully pull the pattern off while holding each pin in place from the bottom. Angle the pins in the direction of the dart legs. Again rub a chalk pencil or wax on the fabric over each pin.

Contouring

In the patternmaking process, straight lines are used to make dart legs. These lines create a point, not a body-flattering curve. When the final pattern is drafted, the dart is usually shortened and shaped. Patternmakers move from a straight dart to a contoured dart on the final draft for a B-cup figure. You can establish the specific contouring for your body during the fitting of your basic blocks.

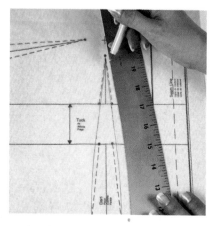

A double fisheye dart is redrawn from the point nearest the bust. Bring in the area under the bust $\frac{1}{16}$ inch on each leg. Then reverse the new lines, extending the dart legs out $\frac{1}{8}$ inch through the midriff before returning to the original location at the waist. Between the waist and the bottom point, the dart legs contour in a total of $\frac{1}{8}$ inch.

A single dart is redrawn in two steps. Bring in each leg $\frac{1}{16}$ inch between the dart point and the deepest point under the bust. The line then crosses the original dart leg and extends out $\frac{3}{16}$ inch before returning to the original location at the waist.

Custom Fitting with Contoured Darts

Constructing darts to follow your contours will give you the best fit. First angle the dart to the area where you need fabric released, then curve the legs of the darts the way you curve.

Often when wrinkles form below the waist on pants and skirts, it's because a person is swaybacked. The excess fabric is removed by widening the back darts. To avoid a bubble at the end of the dart, the line needs to be drawn in two parts. When darts are straining over a rounded part of your body, such as a high hip area, they may be taking in too much fabric. You can release some by contouring the darts.

Swayback

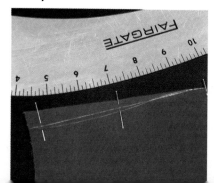

Fold the dart. Place a French curve between the notches and the dart point with the outer curve facing the garment and the hook at the waist. Chalk a sewing line from the base, stopping $\frac{3}{4}$ inch from the point. Flip the ruler so that the outer curve faces the fold. Continue the line to the point.

High Hip

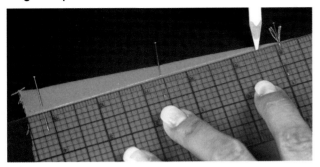

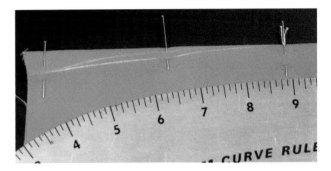

1 With right sides together, fold your dart through the center. Match the notches at the cut edge, and continue the fold past the dart point. Chalk a straight line between the notches and the point.

2 Place a French or hip curve between the notches and the point with the outer curve facing the fold and the hook (the curved end) at the waist. The position of the ruler depends on your figure. The more rounded you are, the more fabric you will release. Chalk a seamline, following the ruler's edge.

Single Tapered Dart

Some industrial production sewing machine operators don't see the subtlety of curved darts because sewing a straight line between notches and a point is faster.

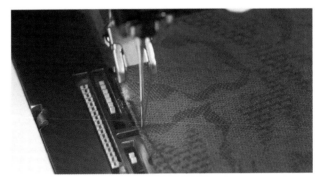

1 Transfer the dart markings to the wrong side of the fabric. At the cut edge of the seam allowance, notch about ⅛ inch into the dart legs. With right sides together, fold the dart through its center. Starting from the notched end of the dart, backstitch, then stitch toward the point. Taper the last ½ inch of stitches very close to the fold.

2 Lift the needle and presser foot, and pull the dart ¼ inch to the back of the sewing machine. Pivot the dart and sew three stitches into the fold ¼ inch from the point. The presser foot was removed here for better visibility. Don't remove your presser foot. Cut the thread tails after your last stitch. Press.

SHOP TALK

For Gentle Contouring

THE POINT OF THE BUST DART SHOULD end 1 or 1½ inches away from the bust point. Lower the top of the dart for a low bust. Narrow the dart intake for a thick waist. Darts take in fabric then release it. Prepare your dart with this in mind so that you can see what a difference contouring will make for you. For consistency, I record the numbers from the curve ruler that I started and ended with when I drew my line.

Barbara Kelly

Double Fisheye Dart

A *double fisheye dart is particularly unique because it blends contouring from the upper torso to the lower torso. This produces a continuous vertical line on the outside of the garment, which can be very flattering as well as functional. Shape your double fisheye dart to match the length and shape of the midriff dart from your bodice and the hip dart from your skirt.*

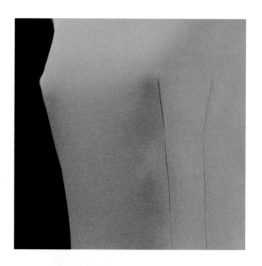

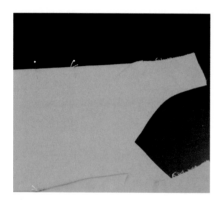

1 Transfer the dart markings from the pattern piece to the wrong side of the fabric. (See "Transferring Pattern Markings to Fabric" on page 114.) With right sides together and all markings matching, fold the dart through its center. Secure by placing pins perpendicular to the fold.

2 Begin stitching the dart in the middle, which is the widest part, and continue along the leg. Taper the last ½ inch of the stitching, eventually stitching very close to the fold.

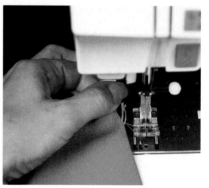

3 Raise the needle and the presser foot. Pull the dart about ¼ inch to the back of the sewing machine.

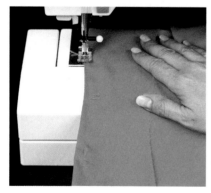

4 Pivot the dart. Sew three or four stitches into the fold about ¼ inch down from the point. Cut the thread tails after your last stitch. Press.

5 Turn the garment around to complete the remaining half of the dart in the same manner. Start by overlapping a few stitches at the widest part, then continue to sew and finish in the same manner as the other point.

Hems

A *hem should be flat, smooth, and a uniform depth. It should have enough weight to suit its style and hang well at an even distance from the floor. And unless it is topstitched for a tailored or decorative effect, it should also be invisible.*

Hems can be found in a variety of lengths and assorted depths. Designers base a hem's depth on the style of the garment, the type and drape of the fabric, and the final effect. Price points and available machinery also influence the decision. Though the finished hem will either have blind stitching or topstitching, several methods can be employed to produce each effect.

Top Ten Rules about Hems

1. Trim the seam allowances of the hem to half their original width.

2. Make straight hems deeper than shaped hems.

3. The more a hem curves, the narrower it should be.

4. Hems in sheer fabrics can be the narrowest of all or the deepest—whatever the designer prefers.

5. If you want to give a hem a little more weight, interface it.

6. Deep hems, especially curved ones, are difficult to manipulate, so don't topstitch them.

7. Add topstitching for a sporty look.

8. The smaller the needle you use to hand stitch a hem, the better the results will be because you are inclined to pick up less fabric in each stitch.

9. Keep your hand stitches loose to prevent puckering.

10. To totally avoid the hem and any stitches from showing on the garment, sew the hem to an underlining or lining.

SHOP TALK

Deep Thoughts

Hem depth isn't really determined by the type of fabric from which your garment is made. Whether your skirt is crepe de chine or wool, it will have a blind hem that is between 1 and 2 inches deep. Similarly, a coat made of melton or linen will have the same hem.

Barbara Kelly

PROFESSIONAL HEM DEPTHS AND STITCHES

The following chart contains guidelines that are used in the industry. There are variations among ready-to-wear garments, but these are based mainly on hem shapes and special effects intended by the designer.

GARMENT	HEM DEPTH	HEM TYPE
Blouse	$\frac{3}{8}$ to $\frac{5}{8}$ inch	Topstitched
Coat	$1\frac{1}{2}$ to 2 inches	Blindstitched and interfaced
Jacket	$1\frac{1}{2}$ to 2 inches	Blindstitched and interfaced
Pants/jeans	$\frac{5}{8}$ to $1\frac{1}{4}$ inches	Topstitched
Pullover	$\frac{3}{4}$ to $1\frac{1}{4}$ inches	Blindstitched or topstitched
Shirt	$\frac{3}{8}$ to $\frac{5}{8}$ inch	Topstitched
Shorts	$\frac{5}{8}$ to $1\frac{1}{4}$ inches	Topstitched
Skirt, full	$\frac{3}{8}$ to $1\frac{1}{4}$ inches	Blindstitched or topstitched
Skirt, pegged	2 inches	Faced and blindstitched
Skirt—straight, pleated, or flared	$1\frac{1}{4}$ to 2 inches	Blindstitched
Top	$\frac{3}{4}$ to $1\frac{1}{4}$ inches	Blindstitched or topstitched
Trousers	$1\frac{1}{2}$ to 2 inches	Blindstitched

SPINNING YARNS

Rules Are Meant to Be Broken

IN A SAMPLE ROOM, PRACTICALITY IS MOST IMPORtant when choosing, say, a seam finish or assembly technique. There's more than one right way to do something. The same idea applies to home sewing. You choose the technique—one that's comfortable for you.

Julia Linger

Interfacing a Garment's Hem

Whether lined or unlined, garments made of soft, pliable fabrics benefit from a bias strip of interfacing in the hem. It will add weight, reduce wrinkling, and also prevent the impression of the hem allowance from showing through.

Sew-in interfacings for hems include bias strips of organza, batiste, muslin, hair canvas, flannel, lamb's wool, and horsehair braid. It's more cost effective for designers and manufacturers to use a fusible interfacing.

The following instructions are specific to velvet, but you can apply the same procedure to other fabrics by excluding the needle board and selecting a compatible interfacing.

1 Use a 1-inch hem allowance. Cut ¼-inch-wide bias strips of fusible tricot that are long enough to circle around the bottom edge. At the seam allowances, extend the bias strips past the seamlines about 1 inch. Cut the ends on a diagonal.

2 Place the hem facedown on a needle board. Position a tricot strip on top, with the resin coating facedown and one edge even with the bottom of the hem. Tack. Cover with a press cloth and lightly fuse. A strong bond isn't essential.

3 Continue until the entire hem allowance is fused. Overlap the diagonal edges of the tricot strip where they meet. When complete, hang your garment for 15 minutes to condition (cool and set).

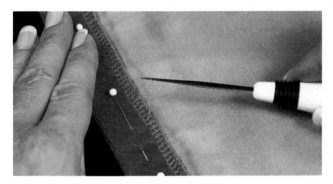

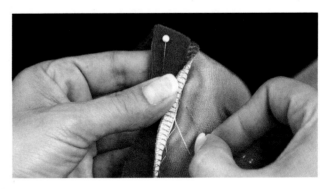

4 Apply a four-thread overlock around the edge of the hem allowance. Pin the hem. To ease in any excess hem allowance, pull the stabilizing needle thread every 8 inches to redistribute the hem allowance.

5 Hem by hand with a blindhem stitch. Very lightly steam press on the needle board with the velvet side down. Hang to dry.

Blindhem Stitch

This is the most popular invisibly stitched hem used in ready-to-wear. As the hem is fed through a blind hemming machine, a curved needle penetrates a few threads of the garment and sews the edge in place with a single-needle chain stitch. The blind stitch on your machine is a combination of several straight stitches separated by a zigzag stitch that attaches the hem to the garment.

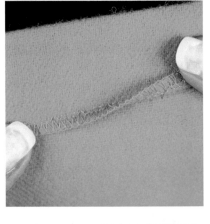

1 A blindhem stitch works best on straight edges. Adjust your machine's controls, and change the foot as recommended in your owner's manual. Sew a test row to ensure that your tension is loose. This example is a suitable tension for a lightweight wool. The finer the fabric, the looser your tension should be.

2 Clean-finish the edge of the garment's hem by overlocking, then fold and press along the hemline. Pin or thread baste the hem's bottom foldline in place to prevent slippage.

3 Place the garment on the sewing surface with the wrong side up and the hem to your right. Fold the hem under to expose ¼ inch of the wrong side of the clean-finished edge. Position the hem under the presser foot so that the right toe is anchoring the clean-finished edge and the left toe is holding the garment.

4 Start sewing. The straight stitches should be in the clean-finished edge to your right, and each zigzag stitch should "bite" into only a few threads of the folded garment to the left. Control the zigzag action by changing the width of the stitch or by repositioning the garment.

SHOP TALK

Invisible Thread Works Wonders

*B*ESIDES THE PRODUCTION ROOM, BLIND HEMMERS CAN often be found in businesses that alter and sew hems of pants, skirts, dresses, and jackets. To avoid changing and rethreading to match every fabric, some blind hemmers keep a clear or smoky monofilament thread on their machine. If you are not quite satisfied with the blindhem stitch made by your machine, try invisible 0.004 Nylon Wonder Thread. It's softer and more pliable than the monofilament thread many alteration departments use. Use it as your needle thread to eliminate the need to color match.

Barbara Kelly

Rolled Hem

Also called a baby hem, this treatment is suitable for crepe, chiffon, and other very fine fabrics. It can be sewn by hand, but it's much faster to sew by machine. There's a knack to holding and feeding the fabric into a rolled hem presser foot. By using the following instructions, you can imitate the effect that an industrial machine produces.

1 Set the length for a straight stitch at no more than 13 stitches per inch, and install your rolled hem presser foot.

2 Fold the start of the hem twice, making the folded width the same width as the sole of your presser foot. Position the fabric under the presser foot and sew a few stitches. Stop with the needle down in the fabric. Lift the presser foot, insert the fabric into the spiral, and lower the foot.

3 Carefully shift the fabric that is feeding into the presser foot spiral to the left. Start sewing, continuing to hold the fabric at an angle to your left and slightly taut so that the spiral is always filled with fabric.

SPINNING YARNS

Designers Take Chances

*C*REATIVE DESIGNERS OFTEN EXPERIMENT WITH FABrics and techniques. To produce an interesting result, they may disregard any previously recommended set of hem depths, and so should you. When designers find what they like and what works best for their line, they establish a "house" standard. At the same time, manufacturers will find consistent results when staying within certain parameters for their machinery and their sewers.

Barbara Kelly

Adding Cuffs to Pants or Sleeves

These instructions are for a shaped pants cuff, but you can apply the same procedure to sleeves. To establish the length on your pants pattern, compare the outer seam with the outer seam of a pair of pants that you like. Then adjust the pattern length so the hemline and the favored pants are equal. Before cutting your fabric, adjust the pattern pieces to include the exact garment length, cuff depth, turn back, and hem.

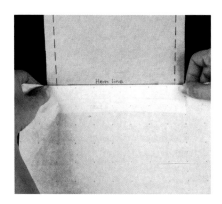

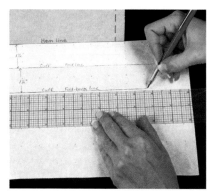

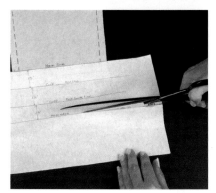

1 Highlight and label the hemline on the pattern. Tape on extra paper to complete the cuff draft. The cuff on the pants shown in the photographs in this sequence is 1½ inches deep.

2 Measure the cuff depth below the hemline. Draw and label the cuff foldline. Measure the same distance (1½ inches) again below the cuff foldline for a cuff return. Draw this second line and label it the fold-back line.

3 Add a hem below the fold-back line. The hem should be ¼ inch less than the depth of the cuff. In this case, the hem depth is 1¼ inches. Cut off the excess tissue below this last measurement, at the hem's edge.

SHOP TALK

Collapsed Cuffs Need Interfacing

YOU CAN PREVENT A CUFF FROM collapsing by interfacing it with a bias strip of a woven, lightweight sew-in interfacing. Cut the interfacing strip 1 inch wider than the depth of the cuff. The distance between the cuff foldline and the cuff fold-back line is the depth of the finished cuff. If the interfacing strip is 1 inch deeper than the finished cuff depth, then the strip will extend ½ inch above the cuff foldline and ½ inch below the fold-back line. Before sewing the front and back pants legs together, center the strip between the cuff foldline and the fold-back line with the edges extending ½ inch beyond each of these lines. Stitch the strip ⅛ inch above the cuff foldline and ⅛ inch below the fold-back line.

Barbara Kelly

4 Fold the pattern extension along the new lines to form the cuff. Cut the seam allowances for the inseam and the side seam on the cuff extension, following the lines of the pants leg. If your pants leg is tapered, the cuff now corresponds with it. Prepare your other pants pattern piece with an identical cuff extension.

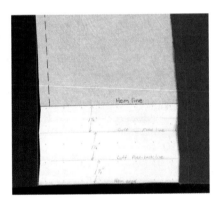

5 Open the pattern. Cut, mark, and assemble your pants as directed in the pattern guide sheet except for the final hemming. Take special care to stitch accurately along the angled seam allowances you created when you drafted the cuff. Clip and press open the angled seam allowances at the cuff area.

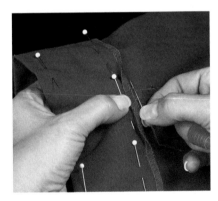

6 Turn under and press the lower edge of the pants at the cuff foldline. Pin or thread baste close to the cuff foldline to prevent slippage. Clean-finish the bottom edge. Pin the hem in place, then blind hem it.

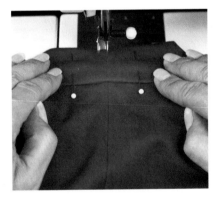

7 Turn the cuff along the fold-back line to the right side of the pants leg. Press. To secure the cuff to the pants leg, crack stitch along the cuff's side seam and inseam. The presser foot was removed here for better visibility. Don't remove your presser foot.

Kick Pleats, Slits, and Vents

A *design element often found on quality ready-to-wear skirts and dresses is a slit, vent, or kick pleat. Patterns for home sewers frequently include such a detail, yet it's possible to improve both the assembly method and the appearance of what is offered. In addition, you can easily convert a simple slit to an appealing kick pleat or vent to give your skirt a more professional and expensive look.*

A Perfect Slit

Many *patterns for basic straight skirts are designed with a simple slit at the center back. It's easy to master this design detail, but you can elevate your work above the ordinary with the addition of strips of a two-sided adhesive fusible web tape like Stitch Witchery. It will help reinforce folds and make them more crisp.*

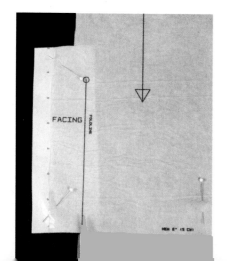

1 If your skirt pattern has a narrow hem on the slit, add a 2-inch extension to both lengthwise sides of the slit, from the hem to the release point, before cutting your fabric. When cutting your fabric pattern pieces, notch the hem at the foldline for the facing.

2 Cut out your fabric pattern pieces. Overlock all of the raw edges except the waist. You can narrow hem the facing rather than overlocking it. Sew together the back pattern pieces above the release point at the top of the slit, install the zipper, sew the side seams, and attach the waistband. Don't sew in the lining if one is planned.

3 Press open the seam allowance for the center back seam, then press the slit facing along the foldline on both the right and left skirt back pattern pieces to the wrong side.

There's More!

Kick the habit of settling for a slit just because that's what your skirt pattern is offering! It's easy to convert a slit to a kick pleat by making a minor change when cutting out your left back pattern piece. See "Kick Pleats without a Separate Facing" on page 130.

4 With the skirt still on the ironing board, measure and cut two lengths of fusible web tape, each one the same length as the slit opening.

5 Sandwich the fusible web tape between the facing and the wrong side of the skirt, with one edge of the tape butted against the foldline for the facing. If your slit has a 2-inch-wide facing, use two strips of fusible tape, placed side by side, for each facing.

6 Press in place, using a low steam setting on your iron. If desired, insert strips of paper between the seam allowance and the garment before pressing. This will prevent the facing allowance from showing through to the right side of the garment. Now sew the hem.

Crisp Vent

Many commercial skirt patterns don't include vents that are as nicely styled as those found in ready-to-wear garments. Yet with a few adjustments, a vent in any skirt pattern is easy to improve. In fact, even a slit can be converted to a vent. If you are adding a vent, it should be 5 inches long after your skirt is hemmed.

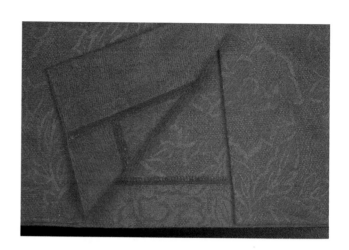

There's More!

A MITERED CORNER IS AN EXceptional finish for the hem and facing of a slit. Follow Steps 1 and 2 of "A Perfect Slit" on pages 126–127. Next, review "Mitered Corners" on pages 141–142 to finish the hem and facing, then insert the fuse tape between the facing and the skirt.

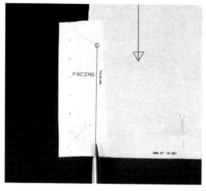

1 Make a 2½-inch-wide × 7-inch-long vent facing for both the right and left back pattern pieces. Mark a release point at the center back 6 inches above the hem. Below the release point, the center back seamline will be the facing foldline for the right back pattern piece.

2 Cut out your pattern pieces and notch them, including the center back at the hem. Overlock all raw edges except for the waist. Cut a piece of fusible tricot interfacing the same size as the facing. Fuse the interfacing to the facing of the left back pattern piece.

SPINNING YARNS

Wonder Tapes

THE GARMENT INDUSTRY USES FUSIBLE WEB tape in some slits, not in vents or kick pleats. But in today's new soft fabrics, bonding tape to kick pleats and vents will help them look crisp. As with most innovations, I came up with this solution while experimenting in my design room. The methods described here are quick-and-easy ways to bond the extension of a slit, leaving a beautiful, clean finish with no additional sewing.

You probably know fusible web tape by the brand name Stitch Witchery. This product is sold by the roll or the yard. In the garment industry, it's called fuse tape. You can certainly cut stripes from fusible web to fit your slit.

However, using the tape will make this a quick, simple, and easy process. That is precisely the point. On Seventh Avenue, we try to save time and money—getting it done without overworking and beating the garment to death.

Elissa Meyrich

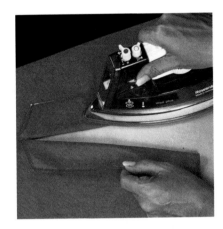

3 Sew the center back seam from the waist (or the bottom of the zipper) to the release point at the top of the vent. Install the zipper. Press open the center back seam allowances. Press the left back facing to the wrong side along the foldline.

4 Cut out and apply fusible tape to a piece of skirt fabric 2½ inches wide and the same length as your facing. With right sides together, sew the separate facing to the right back pattern piece along the lengthwise edge of the facing, using a ½-inch seam allowance.

5 Press the fabric extension on the right back pattern piece to the wrong side along the seamline. If desired, insert fusible web tape between the wrong sides of the facing and the extension. See Steps 4 and 5 on page 127.

6 Still at the ironing board, arrange the two sides of the vent so that the lengthwise edges are straight. Insert a pin at the release point to secure the left and right vent facings.

7 From the right side, sew a 2-inch-long diagonal line from the release point to the outer edge of the left facing through all thicknesses. The presser foot was removed here for better visibility. Don't remove your presser foot to sew this diagonal line.

Kick Pleat without a Separate Facing

This vent is sewn closed and doesn't require a separate facing. If you are adding a kick pleat to a skirt or are converting a slit, start by taping facings to the left and right back pattern pieces. See "Crisp Vent" on pages 128–129. After your skirt is hemmed, your kick pleat should be 5 inches long and at least 1¼ inches wide. These instructions will produce a 2-inch-wide kick pleat.

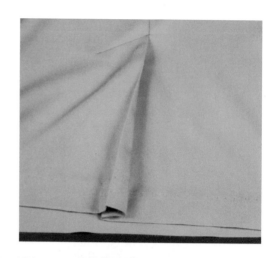

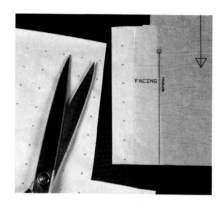

1 Make left and right back facings that extend 2½ inches beyond the center back for 7 inches above the skirt's bottom edge. Cut out and overlock the pattern pieces, apply a piece of fusible tricot interfacing, press under the right back facing, and assemble as in Steps 1 and 2 on page 128.

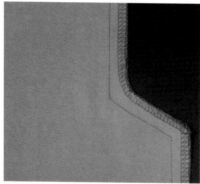

2 Open out the facing. Sew the center back seam from the waist (or bottom of the zipper) to the release point at the top of the facings. Without breaking your thread, pivot at the release point. Sew the extensions together across the top and down the lengthwise side.

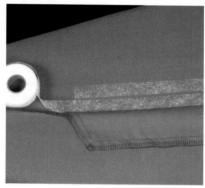

3 Install the zipper. Open the right facing. If desired, insert fusible web tape between the wrong sides of the facing and the skirt back. See Steps 3, 4, and 5 on page 127.

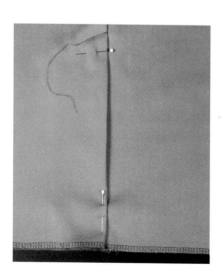

4 Arrange the kick pleat and secure it with a diagonal line of stitching at the release point. See Steps 6 and 7 on page 129.

Lapel

A *lapel on a vest or a faced notched collar on a blouse is a focal point; therefore, it requires special care. To this end, you can perfect your corners by stitching them diagonally across the point and turning them properly. See "Corners" on pages 108–109. Understitching is the final step if you don't plan to topstitch. This is a continuous stitching line on the facing below the break point that then switches to the garment side.*

1 Sew the collar to the garment and interface the facing. If you use a sew-in, you can apply the interfacing and finish the long lengthwise edge of the facing in one step. With right sides facing, sew the interfacing and facing along the long, unnotched edge that you usually narrow hem.

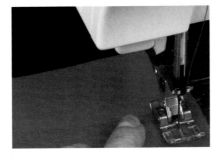

2 Press the seam allowances toward the sew-in interfacing. (In this case, the sew-in is organza.) Understitch the seam allowances to the organza. With wrong sides together, fold the organza to the lapel facing. Baste together the remaining edges. With right sides together, sew the facing to the blouse.

3 Insert a pin on the seamline at the break point, where the facing starts to roll to the outside of the garment. Clip the seam allowances to the seamline at the pin. Finger press the seam allowances above the pin toward the lapel; below the pin, press toward the facing.

4 Insert the garment under the presser foot with the lapel on the left and the facing on the right. Understitch the seam allowances to the lapel by stitching 1/16 inch to the left of the seamline. Stop sewing at the pin with your needle down in the fabric.

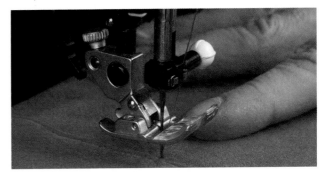

5 Lift the presser foot. Remove your needle from the fabric and shift the garment to the left. Without breaking your threads, insert the needle into the facing 1/16 inch to the right of the seamline. Continue understitching, making sure that the remaining seam allowances are toward the facing.

Lining a Skirt or Vest

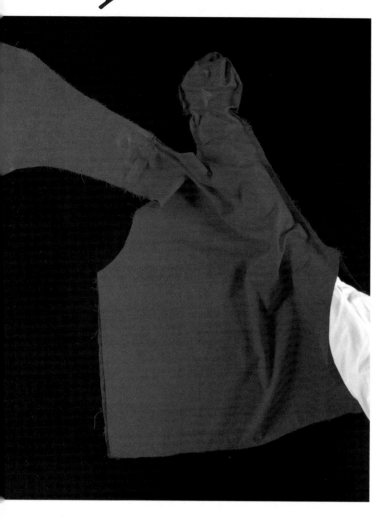

Creating a lining for a skirt, vest, or pair of trousers is a relatively simple process, in many cases involving little more than cutting and assembling the garment pattern pieces from a finer, static-free fabric.

There are, however, some interesting techniques. The bagged lining for a vest in this chapter involves no hand sewing. See pages 134–135. You can attach a lining to a skirt by sewing it to one side of the waistband, joining the skirt on the opposite side, and then topstitching the waistband in position. See "Lining and Waistband Assembly for a Skirt" on pages 136–137. And you can attach a lining to the zipper tape invisibly, by machine, or by trace stitching along the previous stitching, as explained in Step 5 on page 137. Finally, the steps for attaching a lining to a skirt at the side seams is detailed below.

Securing a Lining at a Zipper Tape

The lining on better ready-to-wear skirts is often attached to the garment at the zipper tape, although this is done less frequently today because it drives up labor costs. Home sewers hand stitch the lining, but sample makers use a sewing machine. This requires careful handling to avoid puckers. The procedure is simple enough, but you may need to practice in order to develop the control of a professional sewer.

1 Cut out the lining pattern pieces and notch the center back where the zipper tape ends. Sew the lining together at the center back below the notch and press open the seam allowances. Above the notch, press the seam allowances to the wrong side. Finish the skirt and lining, install the lining, and hem both.

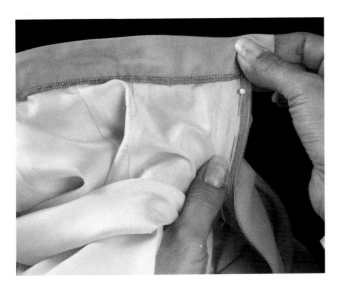

2 With wrong sides together, match one side of the zipper tape to one side of the lining above the notch. The lining seam allowance should still be turned to the wrong side. Secure the lining's folded edge to the zipper tape with one or two pins. Place the pins parallel to the zipper and as close to the fold as possible. Don't pin the skirt. Skilled sewers don't use pins for this procedure.

3 Insert your hand into the garment between the lining and the skirt. Grasp the seam allowance of the lining and the zipper tape at the pin(s).

4 Without turning the entire garment wrong side out, pull the lining seam allowance and zipper tape out through the bottom of the skirt. Be careful that the lining and zipper tape don't slip out of position, or the lining will pucker when sewn.

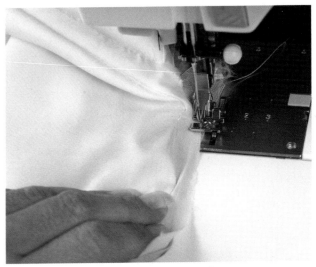

5 Still without shifting the lining and the zipper tape, place them with right sides together under the presser foot of your sewing machine. Sew them together, extending the seam as far as possible toward the waistband, using the crease line on the lining as your seamline guide. Repeat this procedure for the other side of the lining and zipper tape.

Bagged Lining for a Vest

Ready-to-wear manufacturers have basically eliminated the need for any hand sewing in the production of clothing. Even lined garments are assembled completely with machine-sewing techniques. When a lining is attached to the outside edges of a garment, a "bag" is created, hence the term "bagged" lining. The garment is turned right side out through a small opening in the bag, and the opening is then stitched closed.

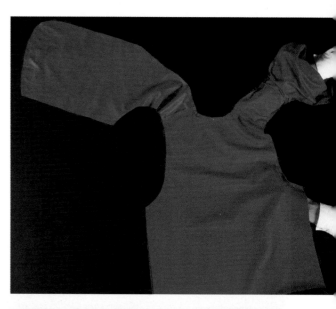

1 With right sides facing, sew together the vest fronts and vest back at the shoulder seams. Sew the vest lining pieces together in the same manner. Press the shoulder seams of both the vest and the lining open.

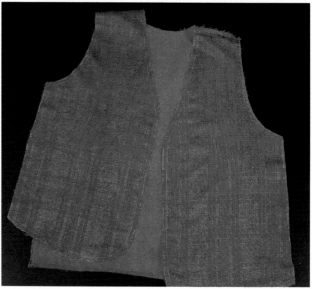

2 With right sides together, sew the lining to the vest at the armholes; at the bottom, along the front and neck edge of the vest front; and around the neck of the vest back. Leave the side seams open.

3 Reach into the vest through one of the open side seams in the vest back, so that your hand and arm go between the back vest and back vest lining and up through the shoulder. Grasp the vest back. If you find this awkward, use both hands.

SPINNING YARNS

From Bag to Box in Minutes

AT AN INDUSTRY SHOW, I WATCHED A DEMONSTRATION of team assembly for garment manufacturing. A lined baseball-style jacket with a zipper front, welt pockets, and ribbed waistband was sewn, bagged, and boxed in 15 minutes. Bagging the lining was just one of the techniques used by the team in this demonstration.

Julia Linger

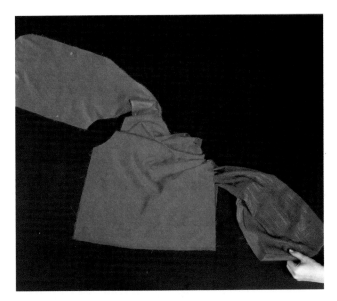

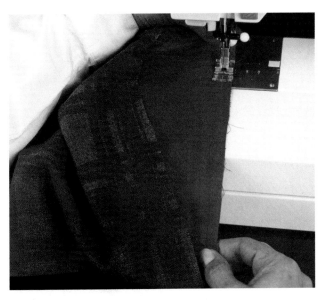

4 Pull one vest front through the shoulder. Gently pull it completely through the shoulder and out the open side seam of the vest back. Pull the second vest front through the same side seam. Now turn the back right side out. Press the front and armhole seams carefully, making sure the lining fabric is not rolling to the outside of the garment.

5 Sew together the side seams of the vest by placing the right side of the lining and the vest front to the right side of the vest back lining. Leave the raw edge of the vest back open because it will not be sewn in the seam.

6 Sew together the three layers of fabric (vest front, vest front lining, and vest back lining), starting the seam at the bottom of the vest and catching the seam allowances in the stitching.

7 Press the seam allowance toward the vest back. Turn under the raw edge of the vest back side seam. Starting at the armhole, sew the vest back to the side seam by turning under the seam allowance, placing it on the seamline, and topstitching through all of the layers.

8 Topstitch around the front, neck edge, bottom, and armholes. Start at the side seams so that the break points of the stitching line aren't noticeable.

Lining and Waistband Assembly for a Skirt

The most common method of lining a skirt is attaching the lining in a single seam with the waistband. Julia Linger describes a more finished but more costly method of joining the skirt to one edge of the waistband and joining the lining to the opposite edge.

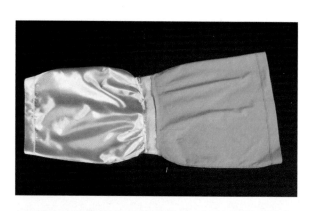

1 Sew the darts, insert the zipper, and sew the side seams of your skirt. Sew together the lining pattern pieces, but replace the darts with tucks.

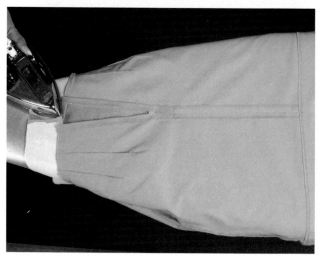

2 Fuse interfacing to the wrong side of the entire waistband. With right sides together, sew the waistband to the top of the skirt. Press the seam allowances toward the waistband.

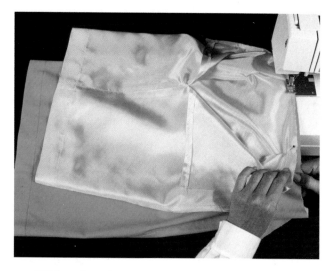

3 With right sides together, sew the opposite edge of the skirt lining to the remaining edge of the waistband. Press this seam toward the waistband.

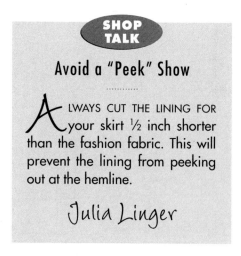

SHOP TALK

Avoid a "Peek" Show

ALWAYS CUT THE LINING FOR your skirt ½ inch shorter than the fashion fabric. This will prevent the lining from peeking out at the hemline.

Julia Linger

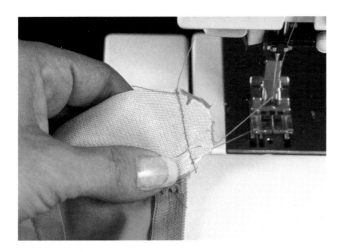

4 Fold the waistband in half with right sides together. Turn, but don't press, the seam allowances away from the waistband. Sew across the two short ends of the waistband. After stitching, fold the seam allowances back toward the waistband and turn the ends right side out.

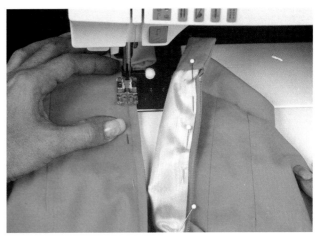

5 With the wrong side up, lay the lining just inside the zipper teeth. Pin if desired. Turn the garment right side out, and trace stitch along the previous topstitching for the zipper.

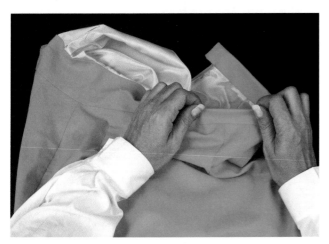

6 Fold the waistband in half, and place the skirt's seam allowance directly over the lining's seam allowance. With the right side up, place the garment under the presser foot in order to secure the waistband by topstitching along the seamline a needle width from the edge.

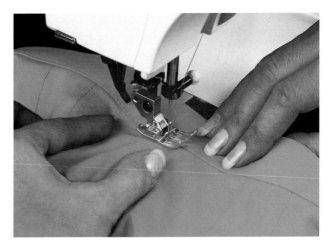

7 Topstitch, keeping the two seamlines on top of each other with your fingers. Use the index finger of your left hand to feel the thickness of the inside waistband seam allowance. Then roll the waistband so that the bulk of the skirt's seam allowance rests on top of the lining's seam allowance.

SHOP TALK

Press As You Go

It's very important to do the pressing in Steps 3 and 4 on these pages. If it's not done while the waistband is still flat, it will be next to impossible to do later. These edges must be flat in order to line them up for the final topstitching.

Julia Linger

Securing a Lining to the Side Seams of a Skirt

The next time you're in a store, flip up the side seam hem of a designer dress. You'll probably find that a serged chain is loosely holding the lining in position. This is used when the lining is not stitched into a slit and is added after hemming. You can substitute a crocheted chain if you don't own an overlocker or serger.

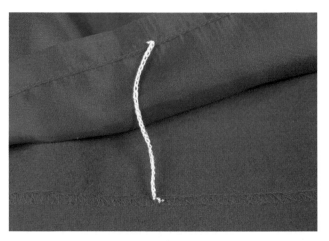

1 Thread a 4-inch tail chain through a hand-sewing needle. Draw a bit of the tail chain through the lining at the top of the hem at the side seam. Most of the tail chain should be hanging from the wrong side of the lining, facing the wrong side of the skirt.

2 Secure the tail chain to the lining with a few stitches. Secure the tail chain at the top of the hem at the side seam to the skirt's interior in the same manner. The tail chain linking the skirt and lining should be about 2 to 3 inches long when stitched in position

There's More!

AN EASY AND VERY QUICK WAY to attach the lining to a skirt at the zipper tape is by trace stitching along the zipper's top-stitching. See Step 5 of "Lining and Waistband Assembly for a Skirt" on pages 136–137.

See Step 5 of "Lining and Waistband Assembly for a Skirt" on pages 136–137.

SHOP TALK

Magic Marker

I PREFER A TRACING PAPER CALLED CHACOPY BECAUSE the marks left by any of its five available colors behave just like wax when pressed: The white disappears into the fabric, and the yellow pigment usually disappears, depending upon the type and color of the fabric. The red, blue, and green pigments are strong and should be tested if removal is imperative.

Barbara Kelly

Crochet a Chain in Four Easy Steps

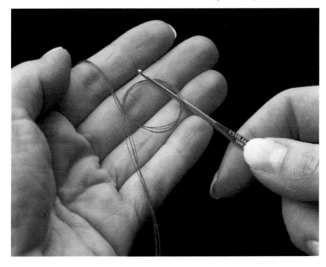

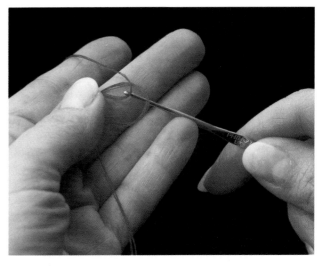

1 Cut four lengths of matching sewing thread, each 2 feet long. Treat the lengths as a single thread. Make a loop in the palm of your left hand. The thread on one side of the loop should be 4 inches long. Insert a crochet hook through the loop from back to front.

2 Wrap a bit of thread from the bottom of the loop around the crochet hook. Pull the thread through the loop. Pull on both ends of the thread until the newly created knot is almost snug around the crochet hook. You should be able to slide it up and down the shank.

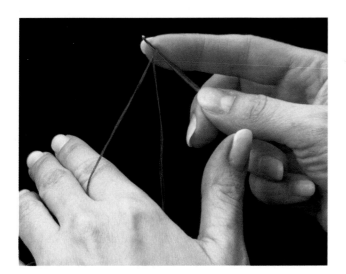

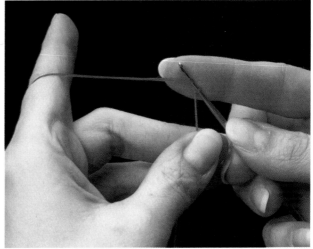

3 Feed the longer thread through the fingers of your left hand to control the tension in your thread. Wrap the thread over your left-hand index finger, under your two middle fingers, and over your baby finger. The tail should hang from the crochet hook. Left-handed people should feed the longer thread through their right-hand fingers.

4 Guide the longer thread around the back of the crochet hook and across the front with your index finger. Grasp the tail, or shorter thread, between your thumb and second finger. Slide the crochet hook down so that it catches the loop at the top of the crochet hook and pulls it through the lower loop. This completes one stitch. Continue until the chain is the desired length.

Matching Seams

In sample making and small-production sewing rooms, sewing machine operators have little more help with matching plaids than you do. Yet seldom does the professional use pins. The key points are starting out evenly, checking the work, and manipulating the fabric. To ensure that plaid seams can be sewn together so that the bars match, the pieces must first be plotted and cut properly. See "Key Match Points" on pages 81–82.

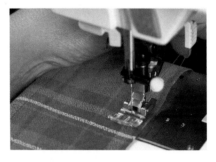

1 Match the bars (dominant lines) of the plaid exactly, and place the edge of the seam allowances under the presser foot. Lower the needle into the fabric. Fold open the seam allowance and check that the plaid bars match. Lower the presser foot.

2 Hold the thread tails, proceed with a few stitches, and then backstitch. Next, you'll use a little manual differential feed to counter-balance the pull of the feed dogs and the drag from the presser foot.

3 Separate the layers. Hold the lower layer. Keep your wrist at the same level but rotate your hand in an upward fashion. The more you turn your hand, the greater the resistance.

4 Place the fingertips of your left hand on the top layer, and push its dominant plaid bars slightly ahead of the plaid bars of the lower layer. Sew. Stop at each prominent bar to check that the sewn and ap-proaching bars match. Continue sewing, manipulating your work, and checking it.

SHOP TALK

Seams Incredible

T HERE IS A RANGE OF POSSIBILITIES IN PRODUCTION EQUIPMENT BASED ON the sophistication of each machine. With a needle-feed ma-chine, the feed dogs and needle travel together. If plaid fabric is fed with the plaids matching, there will be no shifting.

A machine with a differential feed can be calibrated to allow two layers of plaid to travel through at the same pace. A walking foot on a lockstitch machine has a presser foot to hold both layers of fabric; the other part of the machine pulls the top and lower layers.

The best machine controls the seam allowance of the two layers of plaid and also has an electronic beam that reads the bars in the plaid.

Barbara Kelly

Mitered Corners

This treatment for handling a corner has a neat appearance and eliminates bulk. Commonly, the edges that are joined on the diagonal to form a mitered corner are of equal length and are seamed at a 45 degree angle to make a square corner. However, this is not a requirement. The diagonal edges can be unequal, and the corner can be greater, or less, than a true right angle.

Seam allowances at corners are easily mitered before a piece is sewn to a garment. And trims and facing strips are typically mitered at the corners as they are applied around the edges of a garment. Tailored jackets usually have a mitered corner in the vented hem of the upper sleeve.

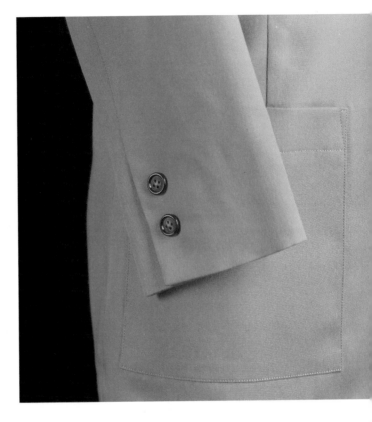

Mitered Patch Pocket

A piece, such as a patch pocket, can be mitered at the corners before it is sewn to a garment. Try using staystitching around the seamline before pressing. Although this is not done in the industry during production, Barbara Kelly finds it most helpful because it prevents stretching while pressing and gives a clean line along which to press.

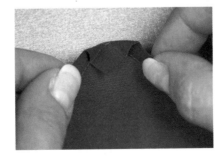

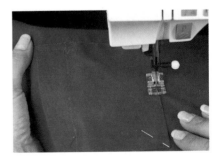

1 Hem the top of the patch pocket. Staystitch in the side and bottom seam allowances next to the seamline. Press these three seam allowances to the inside.

2 Unfold the seam allowance at one lower corner, and form a triangle by turning the corner in on the diagonal.

3 Fold the seam allowances back in. Press. Repeat on the other corner. Turn the pocket faceup, and sew it to the right side of the garment.

Mitered Hems of Unequal Lengths

Connecting hems of unequal lengths may seem like joining mismatched puzzle pieces. But when you follow these easy steps and see the perfect results, you will marvel at its simplicity.

1 Staystitch ¼ inch from each raw edge that will be hemmed. To clean-finish the raw edges, turn them in and press them along the stitching line.

2 Turn your work faceup. With right sides together, reverse the fold of the hems. Press along the hemlines. For a temporary hold, insert a pin through the two folded edges at the inside corner. Draw a line along one hem between the pin and the corner to form the miter.

3 Fold back the top hem. On the other hem, draw a line along the side of the crease.

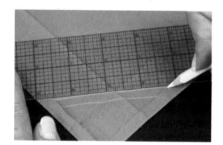

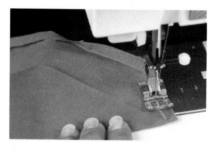

4 Remove the pin. Open the hems and finished edges and turn your piece to the wrong side. Place a ruler beside the lines. Connect and complete them as one line between the clean-finished folds. Draw another line ¼ inch away. Cut along the line closest to the outer corner.

5 With right sides together, fold half of the line exactly on top of the other to form the corner seam. Sew along the line between the staystitching and the corner. Backstitch at each end.

6 Press the stitches flat to set them, then press the seam open. Trim the corner on the diagonal for bulky fabrics. For thin fabrics, flatten the point evenly, forming a triangle at the corner.

7 Turn the corner right side out. Use a point turner to push out a clean corner. Fold in the clean-finished edges. Press again. Sew the hems in place.

SPINNING YARNS

Chanel, Miyake Use Mitered Corners

THE REVERED COCO CHANEL IS one designer who incorporated mitering techniques in many of her jackets.

The Japanese designer Issey Miyake often designs unlined garments with all edges hemmed. Where two hemmed edges meet on his clothing, you will usually find a mitered corner.

Barbara Kelly

Pintucks

Pintucking is most cost effective if a "pieced" approach is used. By pintucking the fabric before cutting out the pattern piece, you know that your pattern dimensions are accurate, and you can center your tissue or hard pattern piece on the pintucks as desired. If you make a pintucked collar, as shown, you must seam your collar at the center back. First cut your collar pattern in half at the center back and add ¼-inch seam allowances to each new edge. When laying up your pattern pieces, place the center back along the crosswise grain.

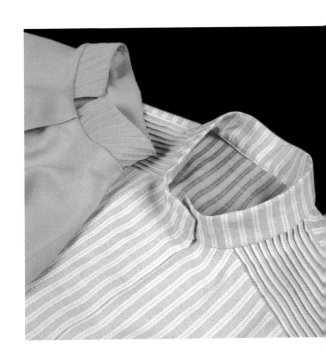

Preparation

Pintuck on the straight of grain for the best results. Use a presser foot that has a guide or toes that spread a measurable distance, so you can use the inner edge of the right toe as a guide for the fold of the pintuck and the outer edge of the left toe as a guide to distance each pintuck. An edge stitching foot works well.

Single-Needle Pintucks

The traditional way of forming a pintuck is by stitching a narrow fold in the garment.

1 Determine the amount of fabric to pintuck, as well as the number of pintucks required, by following the instructions in "How Much Fabric Do You Need?" on page 144. Here, a pintuck will be sewn in the middle of each white stripe.

2 With the tip of an iron, press a fold for each pintuck that will be sewn. The pintucks are a generous ¼ inch apart. This tiny amount of extra fabric (the "generous" portion) is lost during this pressing step.

3 Place the fabric facedown on the machine. Fold back the right edge to expose the first fold and place it under the presser foot. Lower the needle into the fabric 1⁄16 inch from the fold. Hold the thread tails to prevent any tangling.

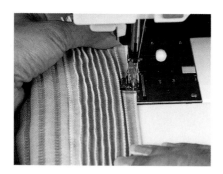

4 Begin stitching, but don't back-stitch. Fold the fabric taut in order to keep the grain straight and to prevent puckered stitches. Continue sewing evenly to the end of the fabric. Repeat this process for each fold.

5 After all of the pintucks are sewn, stretch and lightly press the back of the fabric. Turn the fabric right side up and press all of the pintucks in one direction. If the fabric doesn't lay flat, pin it to an ironing board, press it, and then use a clapper.

6 Place your pattern piece faceup over the right side of the pintucked fabric. Cut out your pattern piece and use it as planned.

SHOP TALK

How Much Fabric Do You Need?

TO CALCULATE THE AMOUNT OF FABRIC YOU will lose in the pintucking process, first determine the finished depth of the pintuck. Multiply this fraction by two to allow for both sides of the tuck. Then multiply that amount by the number of pintucks you plan to sew. It's always a good idea to allow yourself a little extra for turn of cloth or shrinkage. Add this total amount to the width of your pattern piece.

The calculation for determining the amount of fabric you need to pintuck yardage for a specific pattern piece is given below. In the example, the pattern piece is 5 inches wide, and each pintuck is $\frac{1}{16}$ inch deep. You will cut out $7\frac{1}{2}$ inches of fabric ($\frac{1}{2}$ inch is excess) and make 20 pintucks.

Barbara Kelly

FORMULA	EXAMPLE
Depth of pintuck × 2	$\frac{1}{8}$ inch deep
Number of pintucks in an inch	4
Size of pattern piece	$5 \times 7\frac{1}{4}$ inches
Number of pintucks in an inch × pattern width	4×5 inches = 20 pintucks
Total number of pintucks × depth of pintuck	$20 \times \frac{1}{8}$ inch = $2\frac{1}{2}$ inches
Pattern width + fabric used for pintucks	5 inches + $2\frac{1}{2}$ inches = $7\frac{1}{2}$ inches of fabric

Double-Needle Pintucks

Using double needles and pintuck feet is an alternative method that produces a ridge between two rows of stitching. This technique resembles the industrial process. At Bay Bias Binding and Quilting in San Francisco, pintucking goes quickly on an elaborate chain stitch machine that tucks and sews with 16 needles.

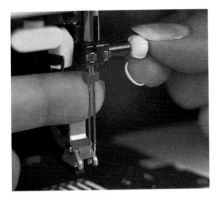

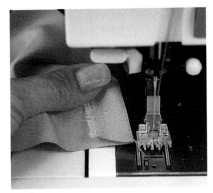

1 Choose an appropriate presser foot and double needle for the type of fabric, desired width of the pintucks, and type of sewing machine. Thread your machine with two spools of sewing thread. It's best to use two spools so that the threads' twist is in the same direction.

2 Including a selvage along one edge, cut a 4-inch square of the garment fabric. Make a pintuck sample using the procedure described in Steps 3 through 5. Measure the amount of fabric that was taken up by your pattern, and calculate the total yardage that you need for your pattern piece.

3 Place your fabric right side up under the presser foot with the selvage to the right of the presser foot. The selvage ensures that you are sewing along the lengthwise grain. Sew a row of pintucking. Don't backstitch. Raise the presser foot and pull the fabric to the back.

What Size Are Your Feet?

*P*INTUCK FEET COME IN A VA-
riety of sizes. The more grooves on the underside of the foot, the finer the pintucks will be. The double needle recommended for the finer pintucks is designed for use with fine fabrics.

Barbara Kelly

PINTUCK FOOT SIZE	DOUBLE-NEEDLE WIDTH/SIZE
3 groove	4.0 mm/90
5 groove	3.0 mm/90
7 groove	2.0 mm/80
9 groove	1.6 mm/80

4 Turn your work and lower the presser foot, fitting the ridge created by your row of tucking into one of the grooves on the foot's underside. Sew another row of tucking parallel to the first. Turn your work again and fit the second ridge into a groove. Sew successive rows evenly with the grain. Press.

5 Place your pattern piece over the pintucked fabric. Cut out your piece and use it as planned.

Plackets

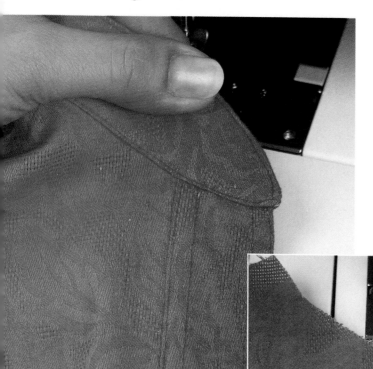

Rather than simply accepting the placket offered on your pattern pieces, you may want to explore other options. Since the placket is as much a design element as it is the functional method for closing your garment, you might consider making the placket wider or narrower. The standard width for a placket is 1¼ to 1½ inches. In the techniques that follow, the finished width is 1¼ inches.

False Placket

This gives a shirt the appearance of a placket by using a small pleat to simulate the bulk of the seamed edge of a separate pattern piece. Home-sewing patterns don't allow for the pleated method of a false placket, so you must adjust your pattern. In the following example, the placket is 1¼ inches wide.

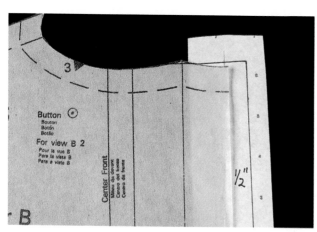

1 Tape a strip of paper to the entire lengthwise edge of the blouse front. Draw a line ½ inch from this edge. This addition will be taken up in the pleat. Draw a line along the neckline edge from the center front to the new line, squaring off any curvature in this portion of the neckline.

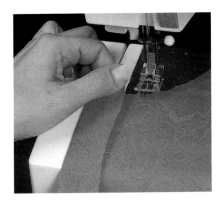

2 Fold under the front, raw edge of the blouse 1¼ inches, which is the desired finished width of the placket. Press.

3 Turn the edge of the front to the wrong side again. Fold under the same amount as in Step 2: 1¼ inches or the desired finished width of the placket. The front raw edge of the shirt is encased in fabric and should just touch the inside of the second fold. Press.

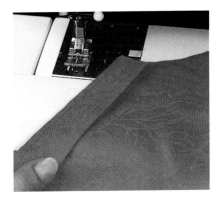

4 With the blouse front right side up, topstitch ¼ inch from the fold. This will create your placket and encase the raw edge within the folded edge. The topstitching has been completed in this photograph. The blouse front is turned wrong side up to show the placement of the folds and the stitching line.

SHOP TALK

Add More for Patterns with a Single Fold

IF YOUR PATTERN PIECE HAS ONLY A facing (a single fold under), you have to add 1¼ inches for the second fold, then ½ inch for the pleat. Draw a line along the neckline edge from the center front to the new line, squaring off any curvature in this portion of the neckline.

Julia Linger

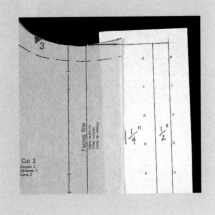

5 Flip the folded, stitched edge back out to the front and finger press the edge toward the side seam. Topstitch along the inner placket edge through all thicknesses.

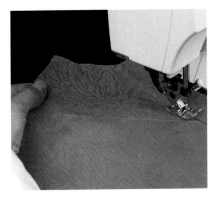

6 Sew two rows of topstitching at the placket's outer edge, with the first row about a needle width away from the fold and the second row ¼ inch from the fold.

Traditional Placket

The traditional tailored shirt has a separate placket. It was originally used as an added layer of stability for the buttonhole area, but now it often acts as a design statement for the garment. In the following instructions, the front raw edge on the front pattern pieces is called the center front. In reality, the center front of your garment is in the middle of the placket.

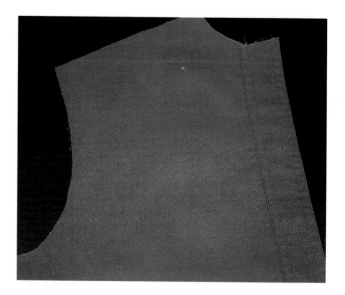

1 Overlock the lengthwise outer edge of the placket. This will be a guide for turning under the edge and will prevent it from stretching. With raw edges even, place the right sides of the unstitched long edge of the placket and the shirt together at the center front. Sew with a ¼-inch seam allowance.

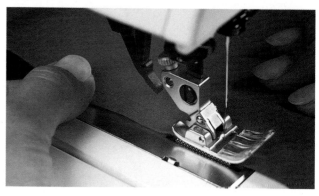

2 Fold the placket to the right side of the blouse. Finger press along the seamline and topstitch ¼ inch from the outer edge, thereby encasing the raw edges of the seam allowance from the previous seam.

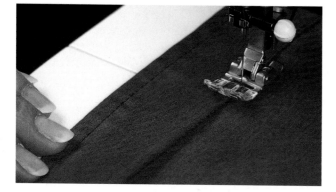

3 Turn under the inside edge of the placket, using the row of overlocked stitches as a guide. Sew the remaining edge of the placket in place by topstitching it to the blouse ¼ inch from the edge that you have just folded under.

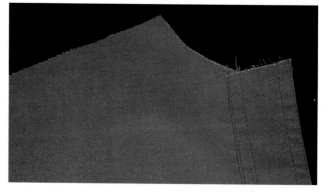

4 For a professional finish, topstitch the placket's outer edge a needle width away from the fold, then topstitch another row ¼ inch away from the inside edge of the placket. Use your presser foot as a guide. This will help you keep the topstitching along the inside edge of the placket straight.

Pockets

Design features and structural details vary greatly among pocket styles that are specialized by both function and appearance. Within the garment industry, the cost of fabric, available machinery, and time are factored into any decision about the type of pocket that will be used on a garment.

The invisible side seam pocket, for example, is suitable for snug-fitting clothes, while the faced pocket will keep costs down if your fashion fabric is expensive. A sportswear side seam pocket, shown here, is designed for rough-and-tumble action.

Welt and patch pockets are often installed by machines. As an alternative, this chapter introduces methods used by sample makers, as well as a small mechanism that produces results that are just as good as you'll find in ready-to-wear.

The industry terms for pocket and pocket facing are pocket and pocket bag.

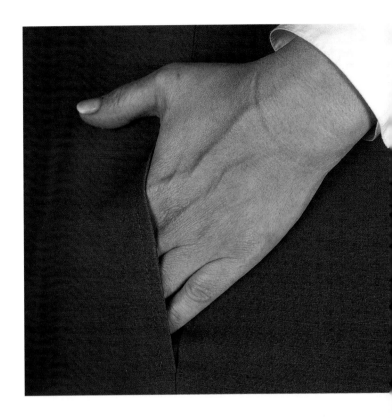

Invisible Side Seam Pocket

This is a great treatment for clothes that fit too tightly because even if the pocket pulls open slightly, the seam edge of the pocket won't show. In this particular style of pocket, all of the pieces are just called pocket. There is no pocket facing because the opening is not faced; instead, it's identical on both sides.

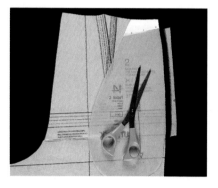

1 Redraw your pocket pattern, removing the extension and extending the long, straight edge the full length of the pocket. Don't overlock your pocket and pants side seams on your pattern pieces. The raw edges will be finished later in this procedure.

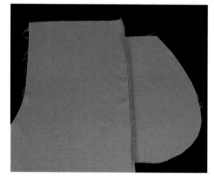

2 With right sides together, serge the long raw edge of the pocket bag to the side seam. The seam allowance should be no more than ¼ inch.

3 Fold the pocket pattern piece out across the seam allowance and edgestitch. This line of stitching will reinforce the seam and prevent the pocket from rolling out from the inside.

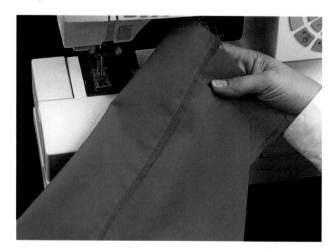

4 Place the right sides of your garment front and back together with raw edges even. Starting at the waist, sew the side seam, stopping 1 inch inside the top of the pocket. Backstitch and break your threads. Move down the side seam 6 inches for the pocket opening and resume stitching the side seam.

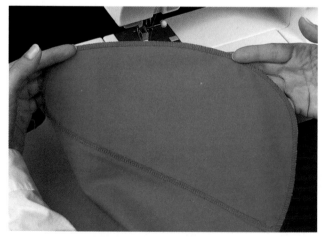

5 Sew the pocket pieces together along the outer edges. Finish the seam by overlocking along the side seam and around the pocket in one continuous operation, starting at the top of the pants. Press the seam allowances and the pocket forward.

Sportswear Side Seam Pocket

This type of pocket creates a more durable opening than the invisible side seam pocket. It's recommended for use in any garment where the pocket openings will be under a great deal of stress from constant use.

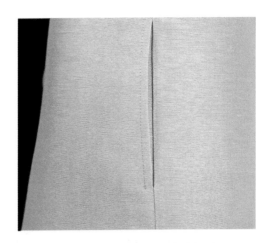

1 Place the long raw edge of the pocket facing to the side seam of the garment front, with the right sides facing and notches matching. Sew the pattern pieces together between the notches, using a seam allowance that is the same width as the garment side seam, usually ⅜ inch.

2 Turn the pocket facing to the inside of the garment and press. Topstitch ¼ inch from the finished edge of the pocket opening. The seam allowance won't be totally encased by this topstitching.

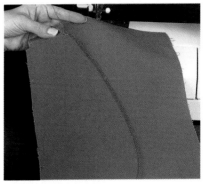

3 With the right sides of the pocket and pocket facing together, sew along the curved outer edge. Overlock the seam allowances.

4 With the right sides of the garment front and back together, sew the side seam. Use care when stitching between the notches so that you don't catch the finished edge of the pocket opening in the side seam. Overlock the seam allowance.

5 Press the pocket bag toward the front of the garment, and press the side seam toward the back. Bartack both ends of the pocket opening.

Faced Pocket

These are used when a limited amount of self-fabric is available, when pocket fabric becomes a cost factor, or when a different weight or type of fabric is more practical for the pocket.

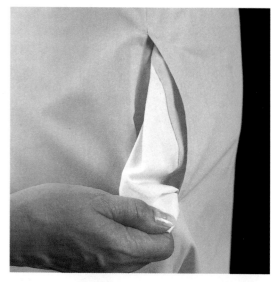

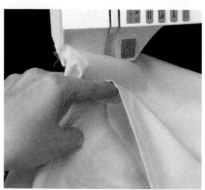

1 Cut a 2-inch-wide strip of the self-fabric to the same length as the straight edge of the pocket. Turn under ¼ inch along one long raw edge of the fabric strip.

2 Lay the wrong side of the facing piece on the right side of the pocket bag with the long raw edges together. Sew the fabric strip to the pocket along the turned-under edge.

3 Complete the pocket assembly in your garment using your desired method. As this photograph shows, only the self-fabric is visible at the side seam.

SPINNING YARNS

What's the Flap?

SIDE SEAM POCKETS IN READY-TO-WEAR GARMENTS HAVE A long, straight edge along the opening rather than the added extension and the flapping shape found on home-sewing patterns. Having the entire straight edge of the pocket attached to the garment provides added stability that is often lacking in home-sewn garments. The extension is not necessary because of the way the pocket is attached.

Julia Linger

Inside Patch Pocket

These are used when the pocket is more decorative than functional or when a fully faced pocket will create too much bulk inside the garment. The first step for making this pocket is binding the edge with a strip of self-fabric. Don't use bias binding to finish off the edge of the pocket opening because it will cause the edge to stretch out of shape.

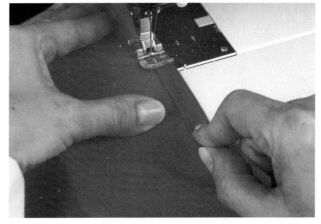

1 From the lengthwise grain of self-fabric, cut a strip 1 inch wide and the same length as the opening. This will bind the raw edge of the pocket opening. With right sides together, sew an edge of the strip to the edge of the pocket opening, using a ⅜-inch seam allowance.

2 Finger press the strip of self-fabric to the wrong side. Roll under the remaining raw edge of the binding and sew it in place. Topstitch close to the outer folded edge for added stability.

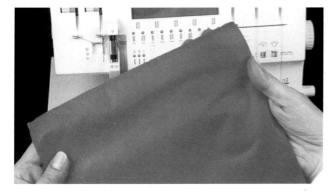

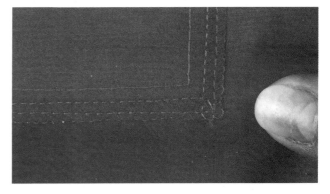

3 Clean-finish or overlock the two inside edges of the pocket. Since patch pockets are generally used as a design option or for the front of a jacket or sweatshirt when bulk is a factor, there are no standard dimensions.

4 Place the right side of the pocket against the wrong side of the skirt or pants front. Sew the pocket in place by stitching close to the two inside edges. Keep the needle down in the fabric when turning the corner of the pocket so that the stitching line is continuous. Sew another line of stitching in the same manner ¼ inch away from the previous stitching line.

The No-Fail, Perfectly Shaped Patch Pocket

With this method, you interface and line the pocket and encase the seam allowances before you apply the pocket to the garment. The pocket is formed perfectly, will not bag, and feels good when you put your hand inside of it. All types of fabrics can be used to make this pocket.

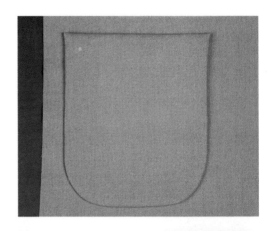

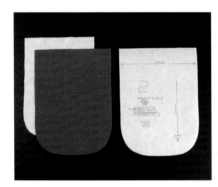

1 Cut out your fabric and interfacing using a patch pocket pattern piece that either includes a 1-inch-deep self-facing or has a 1-inch hem. Trim the interfacing piece to eliminate the seam allowances. Fuse it to the wrong side of the pocket. Notch the foldline in the seam allowance of the fabric.

2 Cut a lining using the lining pattern piece. If the pattern doesn't include a pocket lining, create one using the pocket piece. Turn the self-facing (or hem) down along the marked foldline on the tissue. Turn the top down again ¾ inch. Trace it and include a grainline.

3 Trim ¹⁄₁₆ inch off the sides and bottom of the lining pattern. Cut the lining from this pattern piece. The lining is made slightly smaller so that it won't show when the pocket is complete. You will have to stretch the lining when pinning and sewing it to the pocket seams.

4 With right sides together, sew the top of the lining to the edge of the pocket self-facing with a ⅜-inch seam allowance. Leave a 2-inch opening in the center of the seam for turning the pocket later. Press the seam allowances toward the lining.

5 Again, with right sides together, fold the pocket and the lining along the foldline and match the raw edges at the sides and bottom. The pocket will curve toward the lining since it's smaller. With the lining side up, stitch around the raw edges.

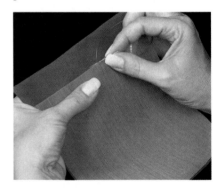

6 Notch the seam allowances around the curves and trim the corners diagonally. Press. Turn the pocket right side out and press it from the lining side. The seam should be visible only on this side. Slip stitch the opening closed. Attach the pocket to the garment.

Faced Single Welt Pocket

When using anything but self-fabric for this type of pocket, you will need to cut two strips of self-fabric to be used as the welt and the facing. Using a contrasting fabric is also an option. The pocket bag for the single welt pocket is almost the same dimensions as the pocket in "Single Welt Sportswear Pocket" on pages 156–157. The faced pocket bag is $6\frac{1}{2} \times 14\frac{3}{4}$ inches. Here, the pocket bag is $\frac{1}{2}$ inch shorter because you are adding a welt to one end instead of folding down the self-fabric pocket bag to create a welt.

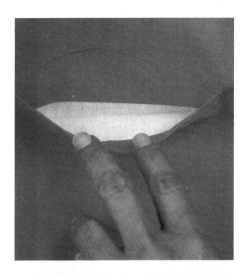

1 Cut out your pocket bag. Notch both long edges 1 and $2\frac{1}{2}$ inches from one end. Cut two self-fabric strips, each $2 \times 6\frac{1}{2}$ inches. With right sides together, sew one of the fabric strips, the welt, to the top edge of the pocket bag, using a $\frac{1}{4}$-inch seam allowance.

2 Place the right side of the second fabric strip, the facing, to the right side of the bag at the notches that are $2\frac{1}{2}$ inches from the end. Sew, using a $\frac{1}{4}$-inch seam allowance.

3 Fold 1 inch of the welt end to the wrong side. Fold the facing over the previous stitching line, so that the wrong side of the facing is now against the right side of the pocket bag. Sew the long raw edge in place.

4 Place the welt end of the pocket bag into the window frame, and assemble as described in Steps 5 through 10 of "Single Welt Sportswear Pocket" on pages 156–157.

SPINNING YARNS

"On the Double" Welts

ONE TYPE OF INDUSTRIAL POCKET MACHINE completes the entire process of putting double welts in a pocket opening. An operator places a patch of fabric over a marked area. An electronic beam reads the marking, and in less than 30 seconds, the ingenious machine completes the operation of sewing, cutting, and folding a pair of matching welts.

Barbara Kelly

Single Welt Sportswear Pocket

The sportswear style for a single welt pocket is used for all outerwear and most casual garments. The welt is placed into a precut "window frame" and then top-stitched. The topstitching around the welt gives the garment a sporty look and allows the sewer to accurately position the welt. A standard welt pocket has a 5½-inch opening, so the pocket bag is 6½ inches wide, allowing for a ½-inch seam allowance.

1 Cut a 6½ × 15¼-inch piece of self-fabric. Notch the long edges ¾ and 7¼ inches from the top. Fold the top to the wrong side at the first notches. Notch both long edges again ½ inch from the fold.

2 Mark the welt's window frame by piercing the fabric with an awl just inside the four corners of the window frame on your garment pattern piece. The frame for the pocket bag cut in Step 1 is 6½ inches wide and ½ inch deep.

3 On the wrong side of the fabric, mark the window frame lines of the window by connecting the four points, then mark the cutting line horizontally down the center. Be sure to mark these lines with a pencil or nonpermanent marker.

4 Slash open the window frame along the cutting line, cutting diagonally into the corners. Finger press the edges to the wrong side along the frame lines. You may press the sides back with your iron, but this isn't done in industrial production.

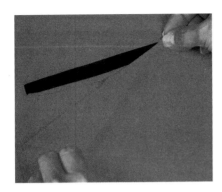

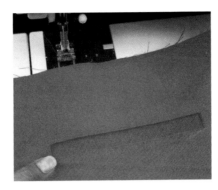

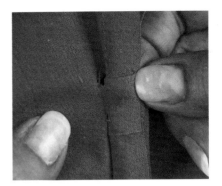

5 With the wrong sides of the pocket and garment together, place the welt edge of the pocket bag into the window frame. The side seam notches on the pocket should line up with the two sides of the window frame.

6 Topstitch across the bottom edge of the window frame through all thicknesses. Don't stitch past the ends of the frame because that makes it harder to stitch the "triangles" and the side seams in Step 7.

7 Fold the pocket bag along the bottom set of notches so that the right sides are together. Sew the side seams. Catch the triangle of fabric turned under on the outer edges of the window frame as you sew the side seams, but don't stitch through the garment.

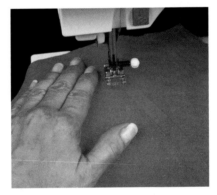

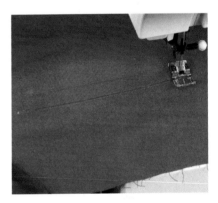

8 Fold the garment away from the pocket bag at one of the bag's side seams. Overlock this side seam edge of the pocket bag. Now overlock the bag's remaining side seam edge in the same manner.

9 From the right side, topstitch around the remaining three sides of the window frame by keeping the needle down in the fabric and pivoting at the corners without breaking the stitching line.

10 Bartack the two sides of the welt to strengthen the stress points at the ends of each side.

SHOP TALK

Some Pocket Bags Should Be Longer

IF THE WELT OPENING ON YOUR GARMENT IS JUST BELOW THE waistline or any type of seamline, you should extend the back edge of the pocket high enough above the window so that the edge will be caught in the waistline seam. In these situations, the length of the pocket piece may vary from the example on these pages.

Julia Linger

Traditional Single Welt Pocket

The pocket bag is sewn to the lower edge of the opening, then it's turned up to cover the slash. The breast pocket on a jacket and the waist pocket on a vest are typical examples of this treatment. Since it's small and on a slant, the pocket bag is usually cut from two pieces. Before proceeding with the steps below, interface and mark the area on the vest to be slashed for the pocket opening.

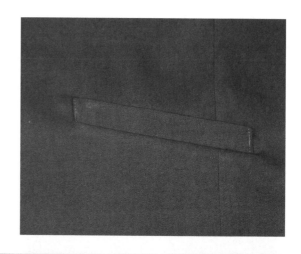

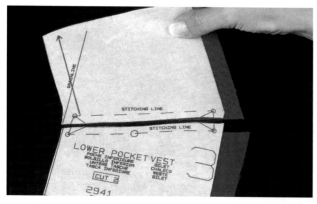

1 If you have a one-piece pocket pattern, cut it through the slash line to form two pieces. On the top portion, draw a new grainline parallel to the left edge. Use the top to cut one pocket piece from the self-fabric. Use the bottom to cut another pocket piece from the lining fabric.

2 Using your pattern instructions, cut, interface, sew, trim, turn, and press the welt. With right sides together and the welt on top, sew the cut edge of the welt to the top edge of the pocket lining, using a scant ¼-inch seam allowance. Don't stitch off the welt.

3 Draw placement markings on the interfacing: one horizontal line for the welt and two vertical lines. Extend each line 2 inches beyond the welt placement area. With a contrasting thread in the bobbin, baste over the markings to create thread tracings on the right side of the garment.

4 On the right side of the garment, position the cut edge of the welt facedown on the horizontal stitches, with the welt's finished edges between the vertical cross threads. Sew, keeping the previous stitches in the seam allowance. Backstitch. Pin the self-fabric pocket piece to the other side of the horizontal marking. Turn the garment to the wrong side. Backstitch and sew the pocket in place. Remove your basting threads.

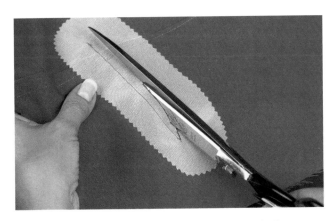

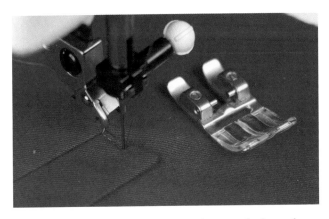

5 From the inside of the garment, cut evenly between the two rows of stitching, stopping about ¼ inch from each end. Diagonally clip into each corner to create a triangle at each end. Press to set the stitches. Fold and press the pocket lining toward the other pocket piece.

6 Following your pattern instructions, push the welt and pocket through the opening into the garment. Sew the triangles at the ends of the slash. Sew around the pocket. Press. On the right side, attach the short edges of the welt with slip stitching or topstitching.

Double Welt Pocket

*C*lotilde's sewing notions catalog offers an alternative for making a so-called buttonhole pocket. It is a Double Welt Pocket Maker. This device, originally presented at the 1939 World's Fair, allows you to create a double welt similar to the one that an industrial pocket welter produces. The instructions here provide an overview of how to use the Double Welt Pocket Maker. Complete instructions are included with the tool.

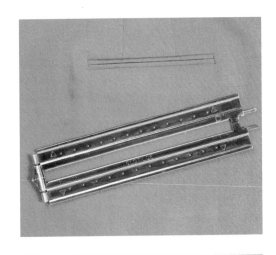

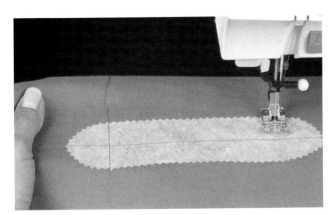

1 Cut a piece of lightweight fusible interfacing 2 inches wider and longer than the area to be slashed for the pocket opening. Pink the edges and curve the corners. On the wrong side of the garment, center and fuse the piece of interfacing over the area to be slashed. Sew placement markings on the interfacing.

2 For the welts, cut a fabric patch 4 inches deep and 1 inch wider than the pocket opening. (The opening cannot exceed 6 inches with the Double Welt Pocket Maker.) Fuse lightweight interfacing to the back. For the underlay, cut a strip of fabric 2 inches deep and the same width as the fabric patch.

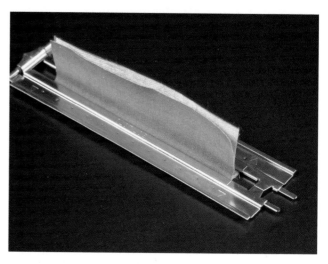

3 Cut a lining piece the width of the underlay and twice the pocket depth. Center the wrong side of the underlay on the right side at the top of the lining. Baste the top of the underlay with stitches ¼ inch from the edge. Turn the lower edge under ¼ inch and sew.

4 Insert the welt patch in the Double Welt Pocket Maker. Center the welt patch, and maneuver it so that the grain is even and the fabric between the prongs is taut. Line up the center markings of the tool with your horizontal and vertical placement stitches on the right side of your garment.

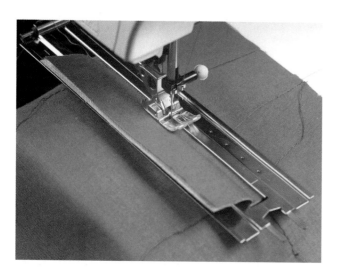

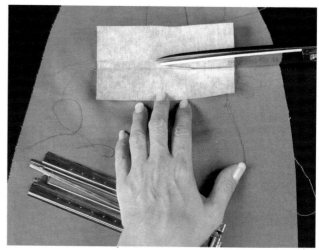

5 Position the Double Welt Pocket Maker under the presser foot, with the welt patch to the left. Sew the right side of the opening from one vertical stitching line to the other. Sew the other welt in the same manner.

6 Remove the Double Welt Pocket Maker and horizontal placement stitches. Cut through the center of the welt patch, diagonally clipping into each corner. Press. Proceed with the assembly as you would with any welt pocket. See Step 6 on page 159.

Pressing

During assembly, pressing is as important as sewing because it will influence the final appearance of your garment. Pressing is not a sliding activity like ironing. Rather, it's a three-step procedure: lower, hold, and then lift. Pressing sets the stitches, flattens the edges and seams, creases the folds, and shapes the garment. Since fabric can shrink or stretch in this process, you should learn the proper techniques. Your goal is to maintain the integrity of the fabric and give your work a professional look. Contrary to what some home sewers believe, pressing is an integral part of the assembly process in both a sample studio and a factory.

Pressing Points

After years of experience, Barbara Kelly assembled this list of guidelines for pressing. They apply to all but the most unusual situations.

- Preshrink and iron your fabric before you spread it out for cutting. Slide your iron with the grain of the fabric.
- Press a seam before crossing it with another.
- Smooth your pattern pieces with a warm, dry iron.
- Don't press over pins.
- Press from the inside as you sew.
- Take care not to stretch edges.
- Press in the direction you stitched.
- Press seams over a seam roll to avoid an impression of the seam allowance on the right side.

- After pressing, let the fabric cool and dry.
- Top press on the outside of your garment after you have finished sewing it.
- Fabrics like cotton and linen press best if they are damp.
- Press embroidered and lace fabrics facedown over a padded surface, like a terry cloth towel.
- Napped fabrics like velvet and corduroy need a needle board under them when they are pressed. Clotilde recommends the firm, large one that she buys from an industrial-equipment manufacturer. It's flexible and less expensive than a wood-base needle board.

Equipment

The proper equipment is essential for pressing. Shown here are tools found in most sample studios and small-production rooms where a variety of garments are made. Most of the items will be familiar to you because these same tools are available to home sewers. The essential pressing equipment for your sewing room includes (clockwise from top, left) a tailor board, a

ham and hamholder, a high-loft ironing board pad and board cover imprinted with a grid, a high-quality iron, a press cloth, a Velvaboard or needle board for piled fabrics, a point presser and clapper, a point turner, a variety of press cloths to suit your fabric, a seam roll, a sleeve board, strips of brown paper or legal size–letter envelopes, and a pressing mitt.

   Large manufacturers have specialized pressing equipment designed to efficiently handle the specific type of garments they make.

The important elements of pressing are heat, moisture, and pressure. You should always test combinations of these on your fashion fabric. Varying fabric types will alter the combinations. Each time you press you add to your experience and knowledge for achieving the best results on your fabric choices.

   Irons have temperature settings to guide you when ironing various types of fabrics. Start with the recommended setting for pressing. Next to your sewing machine, your iron is the most important piece of equipment for achieving professional results, so buy the best one you can afford.

   Moisture can come in the form of steam from the holes in

the sole plate, in the form of spray from the front of the iron, from a mister, or from a damp cloth. To produce steam, an iron needs to be at a high temperature. If you are concerned about the high temperature or about water marking your fabric, shield it with a press cloth.

   How moisture is applied to fabrics makes a difference. Some fabrics, such as gabardine, should not be steamed, but need moisture along with a press cloth to crease edges and flatten seams. Generally, thick materials require more pressure and the use of a clapper. Special press cloths can buffer the pressure needed to flatten seams and remove wrinkles.

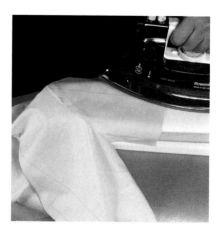

If you need to apply more heat, use a press cloth to prevent scorching or melting your fabric, which is what happened when this muslin sloper was pressed for too long with a very hot iron.

Straight Seam

You need to set stitches and open the seam allowances of all straight seams whether they will be later pressed to one side or enclosed. By opening the seam, you set a crease in the seam allowances and create ease for manipulating the fabric during another construction step. Creasing also prevents a tuck from forming when the seam allowances are pressed to one side.

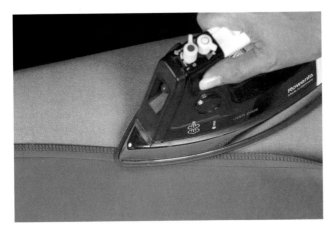

1 Place the closed seam on the ironing board. Check that the grainline and construction lines are straight. Press the seam flat to set the stitches.

2 Place the open seam over a seam roll so the seam allowances are up and spread open easily. Finger press the seam allowances open, then slide the tip of your iron over the stitching line to flatten it. If the seam needs additional flattening, use moisture and press it with the iron again, then press firmly with a clapper to set it. Continue this process along the entire seam.

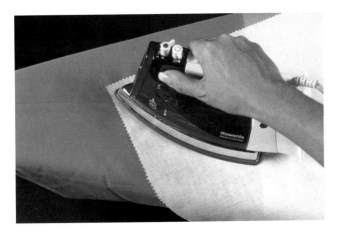

3 Turn the seam right side up and place it over the seam roll again. Cover the seam with a press cloth and top press.

SPINNING YARNS

The Midas Touch

LIGHTWEIGHT IRONS MAY BE GOOD FOR smoothing the wrinkles from your ready-to-wear clothes, but the pressing that takes place during the construction process needs an iron with some weight and heat-holding properties in the sole plate. When the iron isn't heavy enough, you will have to apply some pressure—but too much pressure gives fabric an old, worn appearance. It takes time to develop a "feel" for pressing. Because of the skill some pressers develop in the industry, they are paid more than sewers.

Barbara Kelly

Curved Seam

You may need to stretch or shrink the fabric along some curved seams. A princess seam is a good example. By pressing over a contoured ham, the seam is set, and the adjacent fabric is shaped. A few short snips in a concave seam allowance may also be necessary to obtain a smooth line.

1 Using a ham, press the seam closed, then open, explained in Steps 1 and 2 of "Straight Seam" on page 163. While pressing, check that the grain is straight and the curve is not stretched.

2 If the seam needs additional flattening, use moisture and press again, then press firmly with a clapper, using a rocking motion. Continue along the entire seam. Turn the seam right side up, place it over a seam roll, cover it with a press cloth, and top press.

Single Dart

Darts are pressed over a ham to preserve their shaping. Generally they are pressed toward either the center of the garment or the hem. When darts are deep or in heavy fabric, they are slashed through the center, stopped approximately ½ inch from the point, and pressed open. To avoid an impression when pressing, place a strip of brown paper under the dart.

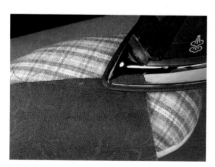

1 Place the dart with right sides together, as it was sewn, flat on the ironing board. Press the stitches to set them. Place the dart over a ham. Press the fabric in the dart to flatten it, and crease the folded edge.

2 Open the garment and place it facedown with the dart over the ham. Starting at the wide end, press the dart to one side. If the dart needs further flattening, use moisture and press it with the iron again, then press firmly with a clapper.

3 Turn the garment right side up and smooth the dart over the ham again. Cover with a press cloth and top press to achieve a nice curved shape.

Double Fisheye Dart

This contouring dart nips in fabric at the waist and releases it at the bust point and hips. Each half of the dart is pressed like a single dart, but the deep folded edge in the center needs to be stretched and clipped to prevent puckering.

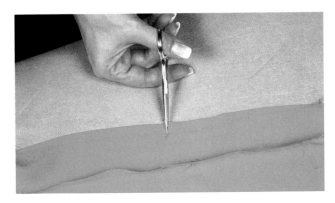

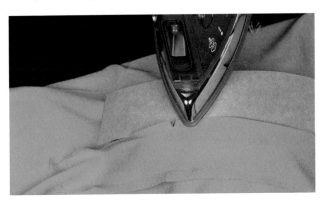

1 Press the dart flat, following Step 1 of "Single Dart" on the opposite page and handling each "leg" of the dart separately. Stretch and press the folded edge in the center, and clip the widest part of the dart to within ⅛ inch of the seam to release it and to form a contour.

2 Open the garment and place it facedown over the ham. Press the half of each dart over the ham, then turn the garment faceup and press, as explained in Steps 2 and 3 of "Single Dart."

Straight, Pointed Collar

Before a collar is topstitched or attached to a garment, it needs to be well pressed. Using either a point presser or a tailor board and a point turner will facilitate the process. When the seams have been completed, they will lie flat, and the points will be identical, without any bulk in the tips.

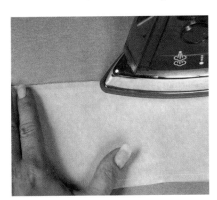

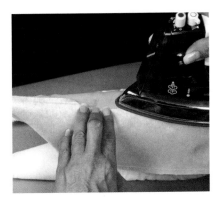

1 Place the seam that joins the upper collar and undercollar flat on the ironing board. Press the stitches to set them.

2 Place the same seam over the straight edge of a point presser or tailor board. Get the point of the wood into the point of your collar, and press the seam allowances open.

3 Rotate the collar, and place the short seam over the point presser or tailor board. Again, get the point of the wood into the point of your collar and press the seam open. Repeat on the other side.

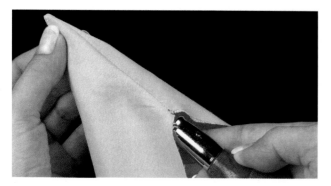

4 Clip the corners and trim or grade the seam allowances if it's necessary to eliminate bulk in order to turn the collar. Turn the collar right side out. Push out the points of the collar with a point turner, a creaser, or an awl.

5 Place the collar facedown on your ironing board, roll the long seam to the undercollar, and press so the seam is visible only on the underside along the edge. To flatten a stubborn seam, press with a clapper immediately after pressing with the iron.

Curved Collar

The various curved edges of a tailor board allow you to press open your collar seams with ease. Use any curve along the board that corresponds with the curve of your collar. In the final top pressing, the seam along the edge should have a nice smooth curve and be invisible from the front.

1 With right sides together, place the seam that joins the upper collar and undercollar pattern pieces flat on the ironing board. Press the stitches to set them.

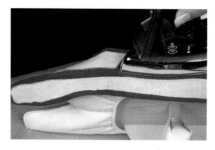

2 Starting at the center back of the collar, place one side of the long curved seam over the tailor board, and press the seam allowances open. Repeat on the other side.

3 Rotate the collar, and place the short front seam over the curve that corresponds with it; press the seam open. Repeat on the other side.

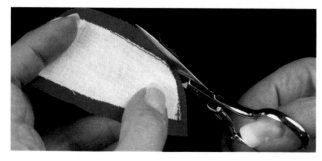

4 Trim, grade, or notch the seam allowances if necessary to eliminate bulk and to get the collar to lay flat when it's turned. Turn the collar right side out.

5 Place the collar facedown on the ironing board, roll the long seam to the undercollar, and press so the seam is visible only on the underside along the edge. To flatten a stubborn seam, press with a clapper immediately after pressing with the iron.

Set-In Sleeve

Simple, specialized equipment makes pressing sleeves easy. The sleeve seam readily slides over a sleeve board, and the sleeve cap fits over a press mitt and tailor board. You can slide the press mitt over the end of the sleeve board and set the cap while pressing horizontally. Or you can set the sleeve cap over the tailor board and press the cap vertically. Use steam or a damp press cloth to shrink out some of the fullness created by the gathers or easing.

1 Before sewing the sleeve to the garment, place the sleeve seam with right sides together as it was sewn. Position the sleeve flat on the ironing board and press the stitches to set them.

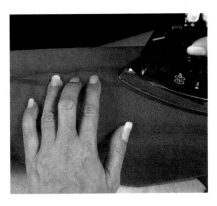

2 Slide the sleeve over a sleeve board and press the seam allowances open.

3 With a press mitt or curved section of a tailor board inside the sleeve cap, shrink out some of the fullness. Press the seam allowance with the tip of the iron.

4 Sew the sleeve into the garment. Then, with the tip of the iron, press the seam allowances toward the sleeve to set the stitches and flatten the seam allowance.

SPINNING YARNS

"Shampooing" Won't Clean Up a Mess

ONCE I WORKED WITH A PATTERNMAKER WHO WAS HAVING TROUBLE developing a particular dress. His boss rejected every sample even after numerous corrections were made to the drafted patterns. After the fourth failure, the worker was so frustrated that he steamed each section of the most recent sample until the entire garment was damp enough to cling to a dress form.

This technique is called "shampooing." It can make even a poorly constructed garment look good, but the effect is temporary and will not improve bad patterns. And the sample loses its shape as soon as it encounters humidity.

The next morning, the dress was dry, fit the form perfectly, and looked beautiful. It was hard to believe this was the same awful dress I saw the day before. The patternmaker wheeled the dress form, with the sample on it, into the boss' office for approval. The factory was immediately ordered to sew 500 garments. The dresses that came off the line a few days later were terrible because they weren't shampooed.

Laurel Hoffmann

Hems

Once your hem is marked, finished along the edge, and turned, it is ready for pressing. The fold is set with a crease, but to avoid a hem imprint, the cut edge is not pressed against the garment. A straight hem has an even grain along the sweep. A curved hem is uneven because of the variations in grain, and it needs to be marked and trimmed to an even depth before finishing.

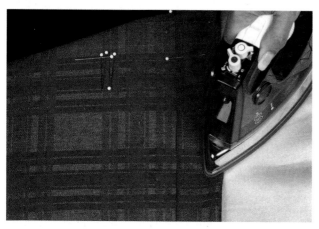

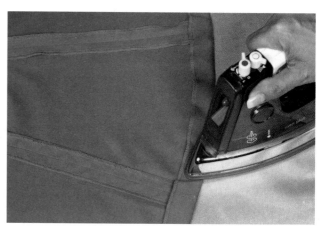

For a straight hem, measure, fold, and pin the fabric to the desired depth. Place the garment facedown on an ironing board. (Slide sleeves or pants legs over a sleeve board.) Remove the pins and press just inside the hem to set the fold. Replace the pins and rotate the garment, pressing the entire hem.

Mark a curved hem, then measure and trim it to the desired depth. Serge around the cut edge. Place the garment facedown on an ironing board. Fold and measure the hem. Press just inside the hem to set the fold and shrink out some of the fullness. Pin it to prepare for hemming.

There's More!

GARMENTS MADE OF SOFT, PLIable fabrics benefit from a bias strip of interfacing in the hem. This adds weight, prevents wrinkling, and acts as a buffer when the hem is pressed, thereby preventing the impression of the hem allowance from striking through. See "Interfacing a Garment's Hem" on page 121.

Seam Finishes Using a Sewing Machine

In an industrial setting, many seam finishes are performed by machines. A flat feller is a good example. Yet in a sample room and small studios, a variety of seam finishes are created by methods that you will find somewhat familiar and be able to duplicate. With this in mind, this chapter explains the steps for single binding, several types of flat felled seams, and French seams. "Serger Seam Finishes" is featured on page 174.

Single Binding

The Hong Kong finish described on the next page is the ultimate "designer" treatment for seam allowances, but it takes time to create. A less labor-intensive alternative is wrapping your seam allowances together with a length of bias binding.

1 Cut a 1-inch-wide bias strip that is equal to the distance around an armscye plus several inches. Fold back ½ inch at one end, and pin it to the armscye at the underarm seam so that the right side of the bias strip faces the wrong side of the garment's body and the raw edges are even. Baste if desired.

2 Sew, following the same seamline that attaches the sleeve to the garment. Upon completing the seam, when you have returned to the folded end of the bias strip positioned at the side seam, cut off the remaining end of the bias strip so that it overlaps the folded end. Stitch it down.

3 Fold the bias strip over the seam allowance, into the sleeve. Pin the bias strip to the seamline, rolling under ¼ inch of the remaining raw edge of the strip. Slip stitch or crack stitch in position.

Hong Kong Seam Finish

This is a traditional finish used by a handful of designers. A seam allowance is pressed open, and each raw edge is bound with a single fold of a bias strip of very lightweight fabric such as China silk or organza. This is an excellent treatment for handling hand wovens and other fabrics prone to raveling. When the Hong Kong finish is used on unlined or partially lined jackets, the facing and hem will also be wrapped.

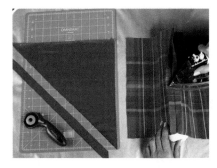

1 Sew, then press the seam open. Each seam allowance should be at least ½ inch wide. Cut enough 1-inch true bias strips of a lightweight fabric to cover the edge of each seam allowance.

2 With right sides together, match a cut edge of the bias strip to an edge of one seam allowance, and stitch with a ⅛-inch seam allowance. Don't stretch the bias as you sew. Repeat along the edge of the other seam allowance.

3 Place the seam of the garment facedown over a seam roll. Starting with one bias strip, press it back along the seamline so that the bias strip is covering the raw seam allowance. Repeat with the remaining seam allowance.

4 Wrap the bias strip around the cut edge, and place pins along the seam allowance to hold the bias strip underneath the seam allowance.

5 On the right side of the seam allowance, crack stitch along the seam that you made when you sewed the bias binding to the seam allowance in Step 2. No stitches will show on the right side of the garment. The presser foot was removed in this photograph for better visibility. Don't remove your presser foot when crack stitching.

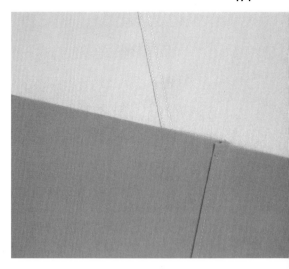

Flat Felled Seam

The traditional flat felled seam is produced on a multiple- needle industrial machine. Most sample makers modify their sewing to achieve similar results, two of which are described here. The turquoise fabric here shows one row of stitches, a nip-and-tuck technique, and works best in sheers and lightweight fabrics. The second technique, "Little Toughie Modified Flat Felled Seam" described on page 172, shown on the gold fabric, is sewn with a twin needle and works better on medium-weight fabrics.

Nip-and-Tuck Modified Flat Felled Seam

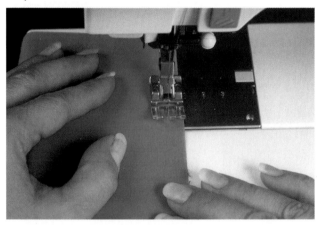

1 Cut out your fabric pattern pieces with ½-inch seam allowances. With the wrong sides of your fabric pattern pieces together, sew a seam, using a ¼-inch seam allowance. Press the seam allowances open, then press them closed.

2 Place your fabric pattern pieces right side up and open on an ironing board. Now fold the top pattern piece back only as far as the edge of the seam allowance, thereby leaving the seam allowance underneath to form a ¼-inch tuck. Press the tuck, then pin it in place.

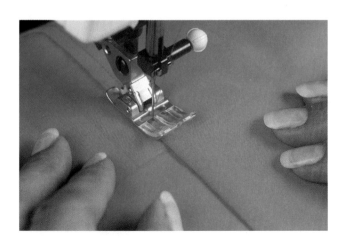

3 Position the fabric pattern pieces wrong side up under the presser foot, and insert your needle a generous ⅛ inch from the folded edge of the tuck. Sew alongside the fold for the entire length of the seam, ensuring that the stitching line is parallel to and an equal distance from the fold.

Fast Finish Flat Felled Seam

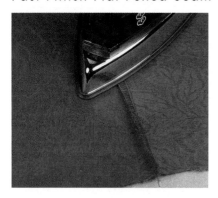

1 Cut out your fabric pattern pieces with ½-inch seam allowances. With the right sides of your pattern pieces together, sew, using a ½-inch seam allowance. Overlock the seam allowances together. Press the seam allowances toward the hem, so the tuck runs down, or to the center of, the garment.

2 Turn the garment right side up, and place it on the sewing machine needle plate with the seam allowance to the right of the seamline. From the right side, topstitch just beside the seamline, catching the seam allowance in the stitching.

3 Sew another row of topstitching beside the first row, placing the second row just less than ½ inch from the seamline.

Little Toughie Modified Flat Felled Seam

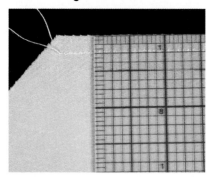

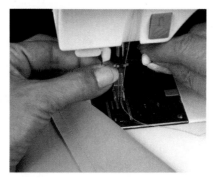

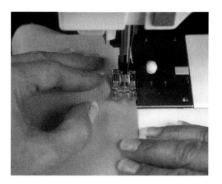

1 Wherever you plan to make this modified flat felled seam, cut your fabric pattern pieces with ½-inch seam allowances. With the wrong side of your pattern pieces together, sew your first seam, using a ¼-inch seam allowance.

2 Press the seam flat to set the stitches, then press the seam to one side. Change to a 4 mm/90 double needle. Check that you are also using a presser foot and throat plate with openings to accommodate the span of the needles. Thread your machine and the needles as recommended by your owner's manual.

3 Place the seam right side up on the machine's needle plate, with the seam allowance under the presser foot. Insert the needles so that one will edgestitch the folded seam. Backstitch, then sew along the seam, keeping the stitches even with the fold.

4 The needle threads will form one row of edge stitching and one row of topstitching. The bobbin thread will zigzag on the underside, thereby covering the seam allowance and preventing fraying.

French Seam

Quality garments made of sheer or fine fabrics are suitable for French seams. This classic finish isn't common in most ready-to-wear because it takes more time than overlocking the seam allowances. A completed French seam, which is no more than ¼ inch wide, encloses the raw seam allowances. Consider using this treatment for garments made of sheer fabrics such as organza, where the seam allowances are visible from the right side.

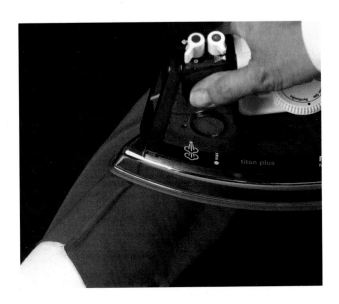

1 Don't overlock the raw edges of the seam allowances. With the wrong side of your pattern pieces together, sew your seam, using a ⅜-inch seam allowance. Trim the seam allowances to ⅛ inch. Press the seam allowances flat to set the stitches, then press the seam allowances open.

2 Fold along the seamline so that the right sides of the fabric pattern pieces are together. The seam allowances from Step 1 will be sandwiched inside. Sew ¼ inch from the fold, completely encasing the previous seam allowances. Press the seam flat and then press it toward the center front, the center back, or the hem.

There's More!

THERE'S AN EASY WAY TO FINISH a sleeve seam and a blouse side seam with one continuous French seam, which is suitable for sleeves with a less rounded cap. But before you get to the sewing machine, you have to "unlearn" the standard assembly procedure. Don't sew the sleeve or side seams first. Instead, sew the sleeve cap into the blouse armscye before sewing the sleeve and side seams. For complete instructions, see "Sleeves" on pages 177–180.

Serger Seam Finishes

Since home sewers gained access to a scaled-down version of the industrial serger in the early 1970s, the machine's popularity has grown steadily. The machine's popularity is understandable because the overlocked raw edges and seam finishes that it's capable of producing make home-sewn garments significantly more like ready-to-wear.

There is a bit of confusion, however, about the serger. Whether a three-, four-, or five-thread version, the home-sewing industry calls them all sergers. Yet only a five-thread serger, which produces an overlocked edge accompanied by a chain stitched seam, can accurately be called a serger. The three- and four-thread machines produce only an overlock stitch.

Home sewers have expanded the portfolio of applications for which a serger or overlocker can be used. But in the garment industry, the machines are basically used for six functions. An explanation of these follows.

Sample Room Guide to Overlocked and Serged Stitches

For guidance on setting the tension and threading your machine for individual applications, refer to your machine's owner's manual.

SHOP TALK

Taming the Wild with Woolly

THE PERFECT PEARL EDGE CAN BE elusive. Try using an extra fine stitch and woolly nylon thread. If you still aren't happy with the results, switch to your sewing machine and follow the steps on page 123.

Elissa Meyrich

The open pressed seam consists of a standard straight seam, made on a sewing machine, with raw edges finished by a two- or three-thread overlock stitch. This treatment is used on better-quality clothes and is the most effective finish for thick fabric, wools, cottons, silks, and some rayons and blends.

The stretch knit stitch is perfectly designed for sewing stretch fabrics, since it has the necessary "give" to prevent stitches from breaking. It's used on cotton Lycra, Spandex, jersey knits, polar fleece, sweatshirts, all swimwear knits, interlock knits, and microfiber knits.

The regular four-thread over-lock stitch, which has a smaller stitch length than the stretch knit stitch, is used when it is necessary to close the seam allowances, rather than overlocking the raw edges and pressing them open. The regular four-thread stitch is good for finishing stretch wovens and cotton or polyester microfibers.

A pearl edge, or rolled hem, is tightly stitched rows of two- or three-thread overlock stitches. It's suitable for lightweight fabrics like chiffon, satin, silk, and poly crepe de chine. The pearl edge also makes a beautiful hem on a bias skirt and a decorative finish on a polar fleece jacket.

SHOP TALK

Cleaning Up Loose Ends

When a garment is assembled in a designer's sample room, the first thing a sewer does is overlock all of the raw edges of the pattern pieces. You should do the same. By doing this prior to sewing any seams, you will avoid accidentally cutting a hole in the fabric with the knives on the serger. This finish is often referred to as a clean seam.

Elissa Meyrich

SHOP TALK

Skip Some Procedures

When you are overlocking a garment together, it isn't necessary to have any more than ¼-inch seam allowances. It's easiest to reduce your seam allowances when you're cutting your pattern pieces. Also, when you overlock your garment pattern pieces together, it isn't necessary to tie off your ending threads because the overlock stitch will not untie.

Elissa Meyrich

The five-thread chain and over-lock is the "serge" stitch in the garment industry. The effect created by using a three- or four-thread overlock machine can be duplicated by making a straight stitch on a sewing machine and then overlocking the seam allowances closed. It's used for jeans, work wear, and men's casual slacks. Loosely woven fabrics and seams subject to stress benefit from this finish.

A cover hem is a double-needle stitch that "covers" the hem as it is stitched. It's often used to finish the neckline of a T-shirt or sweatshirt. The stitch was popular in the early 1970s and is again appearing on sportswear and other garments as a decorative finish.

Sighting

You may not be familiar with the term sighting, but the day you began sewing on a machine, you started doing it. In fact, almost all sewing machines have a plate attached to the bed to the right and in front of the needle for this purpose. The plate has vertical lines, marking a variety of widths, to help you sight. When making a seamline, you guide your fabric through the presser foot while keeping the edge of the seam allowances aligned with one of these marks, which keeps your stitches an even distance from the raw edges. But as you know, there are many other parts around the needle that you can use for sighting.

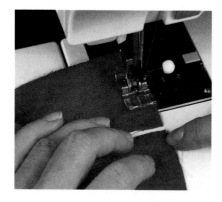

A presser foot is an obvious alternative tool. If you want to topstitch ¼ inch from a seamline or foldline, install a standard presser foot. Line up the seamline with an outer edge. You can measure the distance from the needle on wider presser feet and use them in the same manner.

The outer edge of your feed dogs is probably ¼ inch from your needle, so you can use it to align the edge of your fabric as you sew.

A quilter's guide-bar can be adjusted to a variety of distances from the needle. Both it and an edge stitching foot are suitable as guides.

SPINNING YARNS

Hi-Tech Layout

IN THE INDUSTRY, HIGHLY TRAINED OPERATORS PLAN layouts on computer screens. Paper "markers" are printed. The fabric is spread on tables, and the paper marker is pinned in place. The section of fabric with markers attached is loaded onto a computerized cutting machine. A vacuum is applied to compress the fabric, then cutting begins.

Lonny Noel

Sleeves

A *sleeve can be set into an armscye be-fore the side seam and sleeve seams are sewn. This will give you a nice smooth cap, and you'll find it easier to use French and flat felled seam finishes on these portions of your garment. If you choose not to use these seam finishes, you may want to apply bias binding to the armscye seam allowances after the sleeve is set in. The instructions follow the "Flat Assembly Method."*

Flat Assembly Method

The photographs for this method show a blouse created with French seams, al-though you can also overlock or flat fell the seam allowances. Specific instructions for the "Flat Sleeve Assembly with French Seams" are on pages 178–179. The flat assembly technique is most suitable for garments with a flatter sleeve cap. For this reason, the technique is more commonly used to install sleeves on men's shirts.

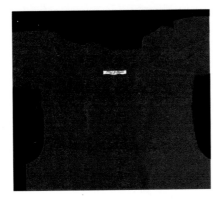

1 Cut out the fabric pattern pieces. Often with this method, the side seam, sleeve seam, armscye, and sleeve cap aren't overlocked until the seams are stitched. Don't clean-finish the aforementioned seam al-lowances if you are making French or flat felled seams. Don't ease stitch the sleeve cap.

2 Sew any darts and tucks in your blouse. If your pattern has a yoke, attach it now. With right sides together, sew the blouse fronts to the blouse back at the shoulders.

3 Sew the last 4 inches of the sleeve seam. Finish this section by overlocking, then either making another seam for a French seam or folding under and stitching the seam allowances for a flat felled seam. Sew the plackets to the sleeves, finish the cuffs, and sew the cuffs to the sleeves.

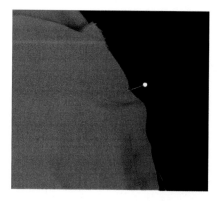

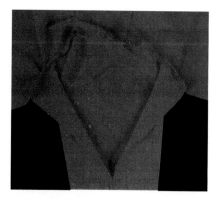

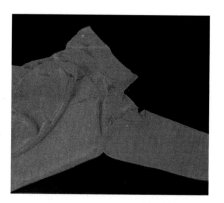

4 With right sides together, pin the center of the sleeve cap to the shoulder seam or the top of the armscye if the blouse has a yoke. Match one end of the sleeve cap to the corresponding start of the blouse's armscye. It isn't necessary to pin the entire sleeve cap into the armscye.

5 Sew with the seam allowance width suitable for your desired finish. Shift the sleeve cap seam allowance over to match the raw edges of the armscye seam allowance as the pattern pieces move under the presser foot. Overlock, encase, or overlap and stitch down the seam allowances, depending on your chosen seam finish.

6 Repeat Steps 3 through 5 on page 177 and this page for the remaining sleeve. Fold your blouse with right sides together, matching the side seams and the sleeve seams. Sew together in a continuous seamline, going up the side seam and down the sleeve seam to the bottom of the sleeve. Finish the seam by overlocking the seam allowances together or making a second row of stitching, depending on your chosen seam finish.

Flat Sleeve Assembly with French Seams

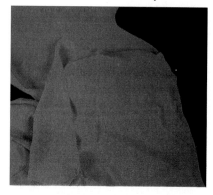

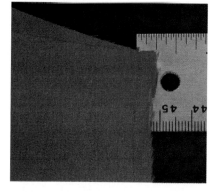

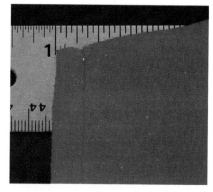

1 Follow Steps 1 through 3 of "Flat Assembly Method" on page 177. With wrong sides together, pin the center of the sleeve cap to the shoulder seam or the center of the armscye if the blouse has a yoke. Match one end of the sleeve cap to the corresponding start of the blouse's armscye. It isn't necessary to pin the entire sleeve cap into the armscye.

2 Insert the sleeve cap and armscye, sleeve side up, under the presser foot. Sew together, using a ³⁄₈-inch seam allowance. Trim to ⅛ inch. Shift the sleeve cap seam allowance over to match the raw edges of the armscye seam allowance as the pattern pieces move under the presser foot.

3 Fold along the seamline so that the pattern pieces are right sides together. The seam allowances from Step 2 on page 177 will be sandwiched inside. Sew ¼ inch from the fold, completely encasing the seam allowances from the previous step. Press the seam flat, then press the new seam allowance toward the sleeve.

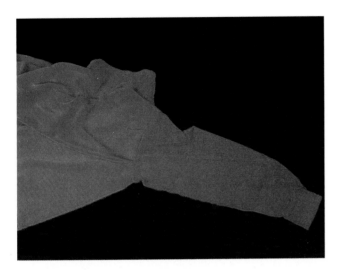

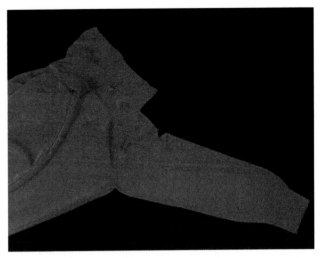

4 Repeat Steps 1 through 3 for the remaining sleeve. Fold your blouse with wrong sides together, matching the side seams. Match the sleeve seam allowances as well. Sew together in a continuous seamline, going up the side seam and down the sleeve seam to the bottom of the sleeve. Use a ⅜-inch seam allowance. Trim to ⅛ inch.

5 Fold along the seamline so that the pattern pieces are right sides together. The seam allowances from Step 4 will be sandwiched inside. Sew ¼ inch from the fold, completely encasing the seam allowances from the previous step. Press the seam flat, then press the new seam allowance to the back.

Bias-Bound Armscye

Most set-in sleeves are too fitted, hence too curved through the cap, for the flat assembly method. Yet it's still possible to produce nicely finished seam allowances in the armscye without resorting to overlocking, which would show unattractively from the right side of a sheer blouse. After the sleeve is sewn into the garment, a bias strip is wrapped around the seam allowances.

There's More!

You CAN SAVE TIME BY USING chain stitching to attach your continuous-lap sleeve plackets. See page 98.

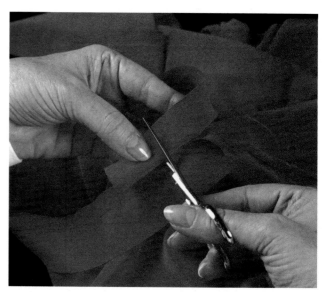

1 Cut a 1-inch-wide bias strip equal to the distance around an armscye plus several inches. Fold back ½ inch at one end, and pin it to the armscye at the underarm seam so that the right side of the bias strip faces the wrong side of the garment's body, rather than the wrong side of the sleeve, with raw edges even. Baste if desired.

2 Sew, following the same seamline that attaches the sleeve to the garment. Complete the seam, returning to the folded end of the bias strip positioned at the side seam. Cut off the remaining end of the bias strip so that it overlaps the folded end. Stitch it down.

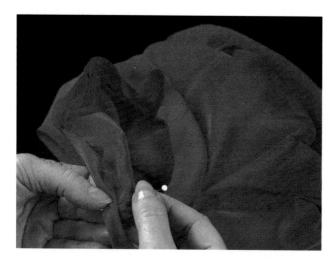

3 Fold the bias strip over the seam allowance, into the sleeve. Pin the bias strip to the seamline, rolling under ¼ inch of the remaining raw edge of the strip. Slip stitch or crack stitch in position.

Spaghetti Tubing

Spaghetti tubing is often used for straps on evening wear, Chinese button balls, closure replacements for buttonholes, bows and trims, and hanger loops. A sample maker in a small production room prepares a limited quantity of bias pieces and turns them with a loop turner or needle and thread tails. If many yards of spaghetti tubing are needed, a contractor makes the bias strips using an industrial serger with a spaghetti attachment. The strip is sewn, turned, pulled, and wound in one operation.

SHOP TALK

Use Your Noodle to Decide the Width of Your Spaghetti Tubing

THEORETICALLY, YOU CAN MAKE A narrow tube any length and turn it with a needle and thread tails, but eventually it becomes cumbersome and begins twisting, and your threads may break in the process. Thicker tubing and heavy fabrics require a wider bias strip, whereas very narrow tubing and lightweight fabrics can be constructed with a narrower strip. If you use a loop turner to turn your narrow tube right side out, your bias strip should not measure much beyond 2 feet in length.

I use a tape measure to determine the lengths for my project, add ½-inch seam allowances at each end, and then cut the bias strips 1¼ inches wide.

Barbara Kelly

Sewing Spaghetti Tubing

Make a test strip to determine the appropriate width for your fabric and the intended function of the tubing. The instructions that follow will set you up for any method you choose to turn your sewn tubing. The stitching can be done on a sewing machine or serger set with three threads or on a five-thread overlock without the chain stitch.

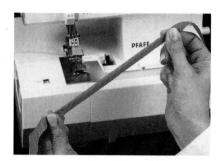

1 Set your sewing machine or serger for a fine stitch length. Cut a length of bias strip. Stretch the strip lengthwise. With right sides together, fold the strip in half lengthwise and stretch it farther. For instructions on making bias strips, see "Bias Binding" on pages 87–89.

2 Place the start of the strip under the presser foot. Align the strip so the seam is ⅛ inch from the fold. Hold the thread tails and lower the needle into the fabric. Continue to hold the thread tails with one hand as you pull a few inches of the bias strip taut with the other hand. Begin stitching.

3 Continue stretching the bias strip as you stitch consistently ⅛ inch from the folded edge. Stitching more than ⅛ inch from the fold will increase the circumference of the tubing; less will decrease its size. The seam allowance will become the filler when the tubing is turned right side out.

Turning Spaghetti Tubing

Once the tubing is sewn, it can be turned with a device or with a needle and thread. A loop turner is a popular tool that makes turning a snap once you get the process started. A needle and thread allows you to turn the narrowest of tubing.

Using a Loop Turner

1 After removing the tubing from the machine, cut one end of the strip on a diagonal. Open the hook of a loop turner, then insert the turner into, up through, and out the pointed end of the enclosed fabric tube.

2 Insert the sharp latch into the pointed end of the fabric and close it against the hook. With moistened fingers of one hand, begin manipulating fabric around the hook while pulling the ring of the loop turner with your hand to slide the fabric through the tube.

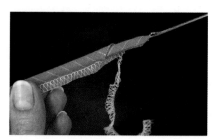

3 Continue to pull up the gathering fabric and coax it to roll into the tube while consistently pulling the ring. After the hook has passed through the tube, it can be unfastened, and the remainder of the spaghetti tubing can be pulled right side out by hand.

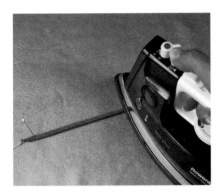

4 To take the stretch out of the tubing and make it as narrow as possible, pull it taut and pin it to your ironing board. Apply steam for a few seconds, let the tubing cool, and remove the pins. Then pull the tubing taut again and repin; leave it on the ironing board until it's dry.

Using a Needle and Thread

1 If you made your tubing on a serger, make a thread chain 9 or 10 inches long. Remove the tubing from the machine. Thread a large needle with the tail chain. If the tubing was stitched at the sewing machine, remove your work and clip the threads as usual. Thread a 10- or 12-inch length of heavy-duty thread onto a needle, and sew the end of the thread to one side of one end of the tubing.

2 Insert the needle, eye first, into the tube. Pull the needle through the tube with one hand, and manipulate the fabric with moistened fingers of your other hand to turn the tube into itself. Work the needle all the way through and out the other end, eventually turning the entire tube right side out.

Topstitching

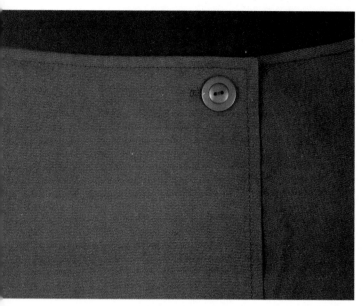

titches add definition to the outside of a garment. They can be functional, like those formed during the construction process of a flat felled seam, or they can emphasize a detail, as in the application of a patch pocket. Or the stitches might be decorative, with multiple and contrasting rows of stitches. In all cases, the stitches are formed neatly on the face and the back.

Sample Room Guidelines

Generally, the thread, needle size, and stitches per inch (spi) remain the same throughout the construction of garments, whether the stitches are showing on the outside or not. The common range of stitches per inch in the apparel industry is between 8 and 24. The exact number will vary depending on the garment. Some fine-quality men's shirts with exposed stitching may be sewn at 24 spi. Many sporty jackets with detailed topstitching will be sewn at 8 spi. The metric equivalents for these stitch lengths are in "Stitch Length" on page 66. The weight, density, and thread count of the fabric influence the type of thread, the stitches per inch, and, in turn, the needle size that is selected.

When the purpose of the topstitching is mainly decorative, don't limit your thread to the same type used in construction.

There is an infinite variety of colors, weights, and types to choose from. If you choose to vary the weight to make a bolder statement, you can double your construction thread or switch to a heavier variety. When you change to another type, ensure that it is compatible with your needle, fabric, and the laundering techniques you have planned. Always test on a sample.

Since topstitching is an eye-catcher, it's important that it be perfect. Even on inexpensive garments, topstitching is often exact because industrial machinery has guides and is designed to manipulate and sew the fabric according to rigid specifications. When it's not done well, topstitching is a tell-tale sign of a homemade garment.

When heavy-duty thread is used for topstitching, it is usually paired with a 90/14 or a 100/16

needle. This needle may also accommodate heavier topstitching and buttonhole twist threads, but it's better to use a needle designed for topstitching. The needle size should be appropriate for your fabric. The eye of the topstitching needle is elongated to accommodate the larger thread and to prevent it from fraying as it passes through the eye. You may need to loosen your machine tension. Check your owner's manual to see if you can use a larger thread in your bobbin as well. If you will often be using a heavier thread in your bobbin, sewing machine dealers recommend that you purchase an additional bobbin case that you adjust and reserve for the heavier thread. Frequently adjusting the small screw that regulates the bobbin thread tension will work away at the screw threads.

Topstitching Guides and Notions

Templates, adhesive-backed tapes, and other guides are designed to help you control your work and enhance your machine's capabilities. Search them out at your local fabric stores or in notion catalogs. The guides are designed to customize a sewing situation similar to an industrial operation and to make topstitching accurate and easy. Some bring instant results, and others take practice. Either way, your investment will prove especially beneficial if you frequently topstitch.

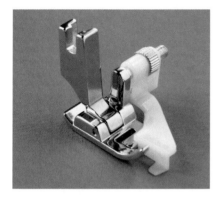

An edge stitching foot will help you keep your stitches close to, and parallel with, an edge.

A straight stitch foot, with its equal toes, stabilizes the fabric immediately around the needle and prevents broken and bent needles during topstitching. If you own a Bernina sewing machine, you may want to substitute the jeans foot for the straight stitch foot.

A walking foot, or an even feed foot, adapts the sewing operation so that it closely resembles that of an industrial lockstitch machine with a built-in walking foot. It feeds the top layer of fabric at the same time and in the same direction that the feed dogs move the lower layer.

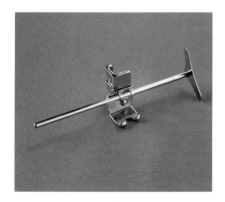

An adjustable topstitch foot and attached seam guide can be pivoted to provide you with an equal distance guide whether you are sewing straight or curved edges.

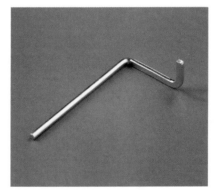

A quilter's guide-bar is positioned against the right edge of your presser foot. Keep your fabric under the foot and the seam edge against the guide as you stitch. This will keep your stitching an equal distance from the edge.

A Procedure for Top-Notch Topstitching

Whether strengthening or embellishing with topstitching, construction techniques are as helpful as specialized guides and feet. While testing, try a darker thread in the bobbin to see if you prefer the definition this will reveal. Or give the stitches a padded or quilted look by sandwiching a layer of flannel or fleece between your garment and the facing. Sew slowly and keep your fabric smooth. When topstitching, you may sew with the bulk of your fabric on either side of the presser foot.

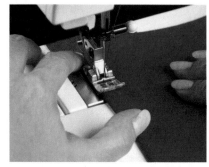

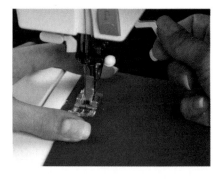

1 The presser foot must always be level. Position the edge of the garment under the presser foot. Fold a scrap of your garment fabric, and insert it under the back of the presser foot, beyond the needle.

2 Hold the thread tails as you begin sewing. Don't backstitch. Use the fingers of one hand to keep your fabric in front of and behind the needle smooth and taut. Use your other hand to steer the fabric.

3 Sew a few inches, stop with the needle in the fabric, and pick up the presser foot to release the fabric. Continue sewing in the same manner described previously.

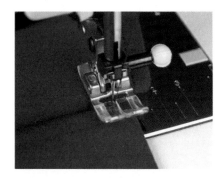

4 Don't stitch off the edge at a corner. Stop with the needle down when you reach a distance equal to the distance between your seam allowance and your top-stitching. Raise the presser foot, pivot your fabric, lower the presser foot, and resume stitching.

5 To prevent the stitches from get-ting smaller at bulky intersecting seams, the presser foot needs to be leveled. When the toes of the presser foot begin tilting upward, stop with the needle down.

6 Raise the presser foot. Fold over a section of the garment that is behind the presser foot and bring the fold under the rear of the foot. Lower the foot and resume stitching.

7 When you reach the end of your top-stitching, don't backstitch. Cut the thread, leaving 6-inch tails. Thread each tail into a hand-sewing needle, and bury 1 inch of the thread inside the fabric layers. Cut off the re-maining 5 inches.

Understitching

A *single line of stitching close to a seam-line prevents facings and linings from rolling to the outside of a garment. Some experts say that understitching is not done in a sample room or on a factory floor. However, examples can be found in ready-to-wear.*

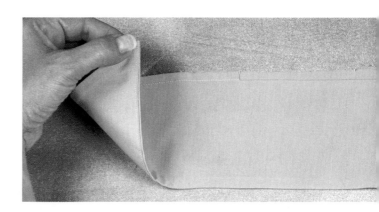

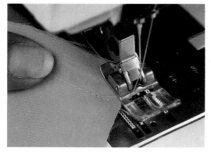

1 Sew the seam that attaches your lining or facing to your garment. Press the seam allowances flat to set the stitches, then finger press both seam allowances toward the facing or lining.

2 Set your sewing machine for a straight stitch with a length of 12 stitches per inch. Place your garment right side up under the presser foot with the facing and both seam allowances to the left. Insert your needle ⅛ inch to the left of the seamline.

3 Lower the presser foot and sew along the length of the seamline. As you sew, use your fingertips to feel along the seamline in front of the presser foot to ensure that the seam allowances are flat and to one side.

Applications

4 Remove your work from the sewing machine. Fold the facing to the wrong side of the garment. Press the garment from the wrong side, rolling the seamline slightly to the facing.

On the neckline of a lined vest, you may not be able to understitch as far as the center back if the armholes are already sewn together because fabric bunched up behind the needle will twist the lining and the seam allowances. Just end the understitching, turn the garment, and sew up the other side of the neckline as far as possible.

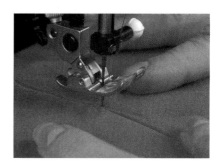

Understitching a lapel that rolls out at the breakpoint involves a trick. Understitch the seam allowance to the facing below the breakpoint. But understitch to the garment front above the breakpoint. An easy technique for accomplishing this with a single, unbroken line of stitching is described in "Lapel" on page 131.

Waistbands

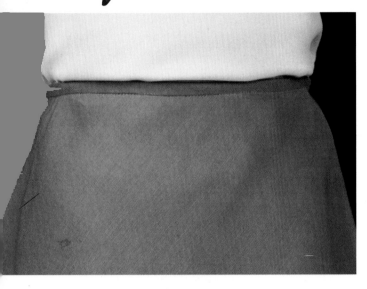

A vast array of waistband styles are used in the garment industry. Most emerged as a response to designers' needs to choose a treatment that works with the selected fabric and complements the desired look. Popular varieties that are presented in this chapter are the contoured and elasticized waistbands and faced waistbands with an interior tab closure. The contoured style is created by applying bias piping, grosgrain ribbon, or a self-fabric facing.

Figure-Flattering Piped Waistband

In 1993, a new waistband application emerged in designer sportswear. The traditional straight waistband was replaced with bias piping. You can apply piping to any waistline that calls for a straight waistband. But before applying it, insert an invisible zipper, sew the side seams, and machine baste the lining to the waistline seam.

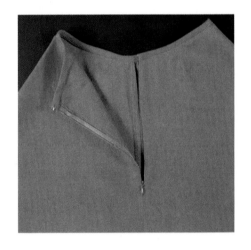

SPINNING YARNS

"Selvage" Some Extra Time

IN THE 1950S, MANY SKIRT WAISTBANDS were cut with one long edge along the selvage. This "finished" edge was placed inside the skirt to eliminate the need to overlock a raw edge. If you don't own a serger, you can adapt this idea for a quick-and-easy finish for your waistbands.

Cut the waistband as described on these pages. Pin the raw lengthwise edge to the skirt with right sides together. Sew on the waistband, starting at the underlap side. Finish the waistband by closing the 1-inch extension on the overlap side, then turn the waistband right side out. Now fold the waistband lengthwise into the skirt's interior, and pin it so that the selvage extends slightly past the waistline seam. Crack stitch from the right side.

Elissa Meyrich

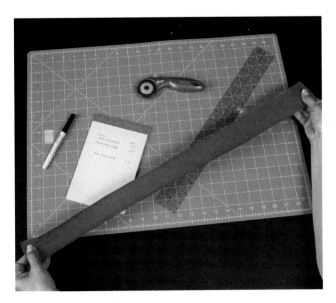

1 If your fabric is unstable, in other words, if it stretches, you must test it. Cut a 6-inch length of fabric on the bias. Measure it on a table in a relaxed state. Now measure how far it stretches. Deduct the amount that it stretches from your waist measurement.

2 The width of the bias strip depends on the finished width of your piping, either ½ or ⅝ inch. For ½-inch piping, cut a 2½-inch strip. A ⅝-inch finished piping needs a 3-inch strip. Cut the strip's length as determined in Step 1 plus 1 inch, unless your fabric isn't stable.

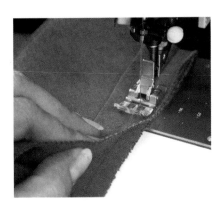

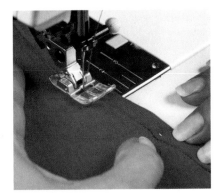

3 Fold the bias strip in half lengthwise with the wrong side together and raw edges even. Press. With raw edges even and ½ inch of the strip extending beyond both ends of the zipper, sew the strip to the right side of the waistband at the waist seam, easing the waistband by placing the skirt closest to the feed dogs.

4 Finger press the seam allowances toward the bias strip. Fold the bias strip toward the skirt's interior, and pin it so that the edge extends slightly beyond the waist seamline. Crack stitch from the right side. A ½-inch length of bias strip should still extend beyond both sides of the zipper.

5 Use an awl or large needle to push the ½-inch extensions at the zipper inside the piping. Slip stitch the ends, and sew a hook and eye to the ends of the piping.

Grosgrain Ribbon–Faced Waistband

A *contoured waist treatment made with grosgrain ribbon is a quick, effective finish for a skirt on which you don't want a waistband. You see this treatment in some Giorgio Armani skirts. It prevents a waistline from stretching and is applied after the zipper is inserted, the side seams are sewn, and the lining, which is optional, is machine basted to the waist seam. This treatment is suitable with any type of zipper treatment.*

1 Cut a length of 1-inch-wide grosgrain ribbon the same measurement as your waist plus 1 inch. Don't add any fitting ease. Shape the grosgrain by shrinking the waistline edge with an iron set on low heat and steam. Also stretch the opposite lengthwise edge of the grosgrain.

2 Overlap the grosgrain on the right side of the garment's waist, with the grosgrain extending ⅛ inch beyond the seamline and the remaining largest portion of the grosgrain extending off the garment. Allow for ½-inch extensions on both sides of the zipper opening. Sew the grosgrain to the skirt along the waistline seam. Don't clip the seam allowances.

3 At the zipper, fold both ends of the grosgrain extensions to the wrong side, so that the ribbon is flush with the zipper opening. Press. Sew the grosgrain to the zipper tape by following right on top of the stitching line used to attach the zipper to the skirt. Or slip stitch the grosgrain to the zipper tape by hand.

4 Tack down the grosgrain at the side seams and the darts. Sew a hook and eye to the ends of the grosgrain.

Designer Elasticized Waistbands

Elasticized waistbands or inserts allow more fitting ease and size tolerance; as a result, a garment fits more customers. But the issue of comfort cannot be overlooked. Elastic inserts in the back or on the sides offer added ease, yet allow the garment to maintain a tailored look. And you'll enjoy learning the allover elastic waistband technique because it's fast. A length of elastic is inserted into a waistband casing at the same time that it's sewn down.

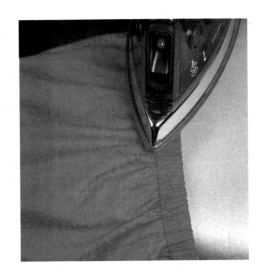

Allover Elastic Waistband

1 Your garment needs 2½ inches of fabric above the waistline to make a casing for 1-inch-wide elastic. Overlock the waistline's raw edge. Fold the top 1½ inches of the casing to the interior. Press a firm crease at the fold. Also press all of the garment's seam allowances open.

2 Pin a length of 1-inch, nonroll elastic snugly around your waist. Put a pencil mark on both ends of the elastic where they meet. Take off the elastic. Add 1 inch more to the length that went around your waist and cut it. Overlap the ends ½ inch. Sew the ends together.

3 Install a zipper foot on your sewing machine. This helps you to sew close to the elastic when you are making the casing. Slip the elastic over the wrong side of the garment's waistline, sandwiched inside the folded casing.

4 Place the garment wrong side up under the zipper foot, so that most of the casing is to the right of the needle and the elastic is not caught in the seam that you are about to sew. About ½ inch of the overlocked edge of the casing should be to the left of the needle.

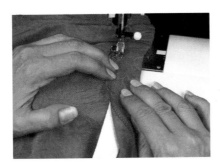

5 Sew around the casing through both layers of fabric. Keep your index finger on the edge of the elastic closest to the edge of the casing so that you don't sew onto the elastic. Continue until the fabric is too gathered for you to sew any further. Stop with the needle down.

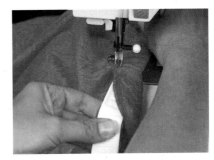

6 Lift the presser foot, pull the elastic toward you, and continue sewing to the end of the seam. Remove the garment from the sewing machine. Stretch the elastic to its fullest point to evenly distribute the gathers. Lightly steam the waistband to shrink the elastic and make it look flatter.

Partial Elastic Insertion

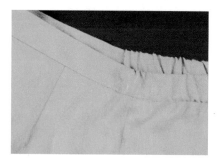

1 These instructions are for a 1-inch wide waistband with an elasticized back. If the waistband has a larger finished width, cut it back or use wider elastic. The darts on the back of the garment aren't sewn to allow a bit more fitting ease.

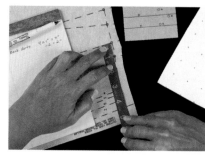

2 Measure the width of all of your back darts at the waistline. Generally speaking, this is about 4 to 5 inches. Add tissue or paper extensions equaling half of the total to each side of the waistband pattern piece. Cut out your pattern pieces.

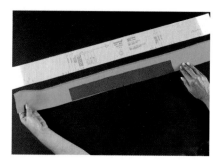

3 Notch the waistband at the side seams. Don't sew the back darts. Sew the center back, insert a zipper, and sew the side seams. Overlock all but the waist. Fuse interfacing to the front of the waistband between the notches for the side seams.

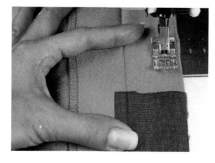

4 Fold the waistband in half lengthwise and press. Open out the waistband. With right sides together, raw edges even, and ½ inch of the waistband extending beyond both edges of the zipper opening, sew the waistband to the garment.

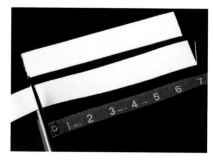

5 See "Body Measurements Workshop" on pages 17–21 to calculate your back waist measurement. Subtract 1 to 1½ inches from your measurement and divide this in half. Cut two lengths of 1-inch elastic to this final measurement.

6 Place one piece of elastic on the wrong side of the back (interior) portion of the waistband, with a short edge extending just past the side seam notch. Sew vertically through the elastic and waistband to secure.

7 With wrong sides together, fold the waistband in half. Place the other end of the elastic into the waistband's seam allowance at the zipper opening. Sew the edge of the extension at the zipper opening with the elastic caught in the seam. Repeat on the other side.

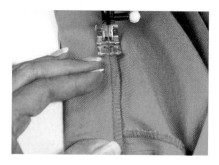

8 Turn the waistband right side out. Pin the seam allowance so it extends ½ inch beyond the waist seamline inside the garment. Crack stitch from the right side. You may find it easier to sew the waistband from the inside.

9 Remove the garment from the sewing machine. Stretch the elastic to its fullest point to evenly distribute the gathers. Lightly steam the waistband to shrink the elastic and make it look flatter.

Raised Waist with Facing and Interior Tab Closure

Inside support will prevent your fabric from stretching and will keep the facing flat. The facing is cut on the same grain as the pants or skirt—with the lengthwise grain running from top to bottom. The facing is bonded to an interfacing. Adding an inside tab with a button and buttonhole takes the pressure off of a zipper. This treatment works best with a centered zipper.

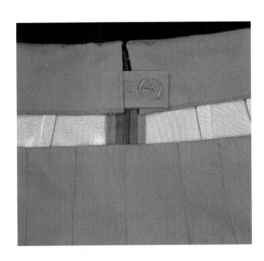

1 Cut a band of fusible interfacing the width of the front pattern piece and long enough to extend from the top of the pants to 3 inches below the waistline. Cut a 3-inch-wide band of interfacing for the back pattern piece. Pink the lower edge of the interfacing bands and fuse them.

2 Cut the front and back facing pieces and fuse interfacing to them. Sew the side seams and clean-finish (overlock) the bottom edge. Position a length of narrow stay tape on the seamline, so that it extends 1/16 inch into the seam allowance. Baste.

3 Overlock the raw edges on the remaining pattern pieces. Mark, sew, and press the darts and seams in the pants. Insert the zipper. With right sides together, pin the facing to the pants. Sew the seamline over the stay tape.

SHOP TALK

Attach the Lining Last

If YOUR GARMENT HAS A LINING, IT GETS ATTACHED AFTER THE elastic waistband has been completed. Sew the side and back seams, leaving an opening for the zipper. Install a zipper foot on your sewing machine. Fold back a portion of the garment's waistband along the waist seamline so the interior seam allowance is free. With right sides together and raw edges even, sew the top of the lining to this seam allowance. Work around the waistline in this manner, making sure that the side seams and center front match.

Elissa Meyrich

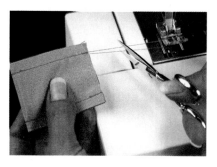

4 Grade the seam allowance of the facing and press the seams toward the facing. Understitch by sewing the seam allowances to the facing. Turn the facing to the inside and press in place. Turn under the facing on both sides of the zipper opening.

5 Cut a 2 × 5-inch scrap of fabric. Fuse interfacing to the back. Fold the scrap in half along the width. Sew ¼-inch seam allowances on the two longer cut edges, trim the corners, and turn right side out to form a tab. Machine stitch a buttonhole ½ inch from the fold.

6 Place ½ inch of the unfinished edge of the tab behind the fold of the facing at the waistline. Stitch the tab to the facing. Sew a flat button on the other side of the facing.

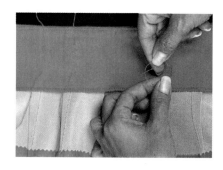

7 Hold the facings in place by stitching invisibly in the crack of the side and front seams. Backstitch at the beginning and end. Edgestitch along the folds of the dart seams. Don't backstitch. Pull the thread tails to the back, then knot and bury the tails.

SHOP TALK

Where Does the Interfacing Go?

FUSIBLE IS APPLIED TO THE ENTIRE WIDTH OF A WAISTBAND IF THE fashion fabric is thin or stretches. When the fabric is thick or stiff, it's necessary to fuse only to the front of the waistband. But remember, don't apply interfacing to the ½ inch of fabric along the lengthwise edge that is folded to the interior of the garment.

When fusing only the front of the waistband, cut the interfacing to half of the waistband's width plus an extra ½ inch. This bit of extra interfacing is folded to the interior of the garment to create a pleasing fold.

Elissa Meyrich

SPINNING YARNS

Designer Waistbands Are Narrower

THE AVERAGE WIDTH OF A STRAIGHT WAISTBAND IS 1 to 1½ inches. However, some designer waistbands are ⅞ inch wide.

Elissa Meyrich

Yoke

This treatment is suitable for a garment with a yoke that attaches to the fronts and the back. It's a nice way to encase seam allowances, using what Laurel Hoffman calls her "pull-through" technique. It appears to be complicated, but it isn't. There's no hand stitching. However, you need to prepare your pattern pieces by staystitching the neckline edges.

This procedure requires a yoke facing, cut to the same size and from the same fabric as the yoke. Use 1/2-inch seam allowances where the yoke attaches to the blouse front and back. To prepare, sew the darts and tucks and attach any pockets.

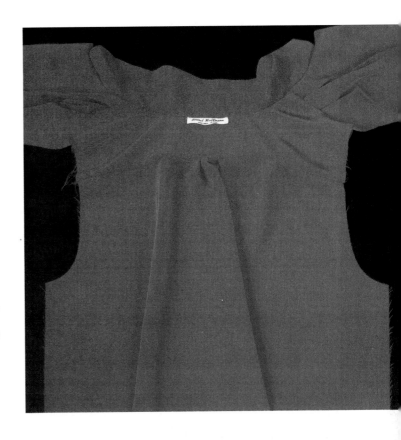

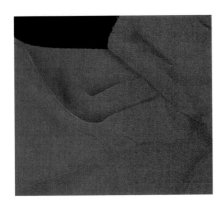

1 With right sides together, sew the yoke to the blouse fronts and the blouse back.

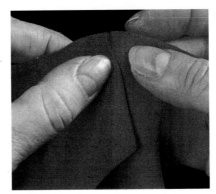

2 Attach the collar to the yoke facings and fronts. The edge of the collar will be positioned exactly at the notch on the front on both sides. With right sides together, sew the lapel facing to the yoke facing at the "shoulder." Press the seam allowances toward the yoke facing.

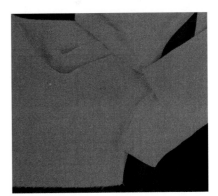

3 Make the "notched" portion of the blouse collar by sewing the top of the lapel and lapel facing together with right sides facing. Turn right side out.

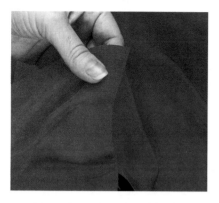

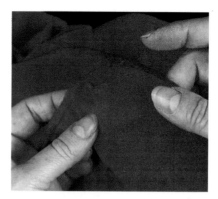

4 Place the right side of the left yoke facing on the wrong side of the left blouse front with raw edges even at the bottom of the yoke and the yoke facing. Sew over the previous stitching, catching the lapel facing in the new seamline. Attach the right yoke facing in the same manner.

5 Place the yoke and yoke facing right sides together with the collar in between. The undercollar will face the right side of the yoke. Sew together the collar, yoke facing, yoke, and lapel facing at the neckline. Trim the seam allowances in the two corners where the blouse front, collar, yoke, and yoke facing meet.

6 Grasp the bottom of the yoke facing in one hand and the seam allowances for the yoke and blouse back in your other hand. Tucking the blouse back between the yoke and yoke facing, match the bottom of the yoke facing to the seam allowances at the bottom of the yoke and blouse back.

7 The collar, blouse fronts, and blouse back will be sandwiched between the yoke and yoke facing. Pin the first few inches of this sandwich.

8 Sew the yoke facing to the yoke and blouse back by stitching along the seamline. As you move along the seamline, encase the other parts of the garment within the yoke and yoke facing. Don't let the other garment parts get caught in the seamline.

9 Sew as far as you can. With fine fabrics, you can completely join the yoke and yoke facing. But you may only be able to sew to the center back if the fabric is heavy. If the fabric is heavy, reverse the garment and start sewing the seamline at the opposite end of the yoke and yoke facing. Sew in to meet the previous stitching at the center back. Remove the work from the sewing machine, and pull the bulk of the garment out from between the yoke and yoke facing.

Zippers

From centered to lapped, separating, mock fly, and invisible, the zipper treatments in this chapter are used by sample makers throughout North America. The procedures will be familiar to you, but each is tweaked with timesaving or anxiety-reducing innovations. For example, the lapped and mock fly zipper insertions feature templates made from a postcard and adhesive labels. Sample makers create their own templates for a myriad of construction techniques, using anything on hand.

Pin-Free Centered Zipper

Sample makers don't baste the zipper opening closed or pin the zipper in position before installing it. Instead, they trust their experience and skill—aligning the edge of the opening as it is sewn to the zipper tape. This technique also prevents the zipper teeth from "peeking out" at the seam, which often occurs with the basted seam method. Zippers that are metal or have large teeth, hence more bulk, are the worst for "peaking" out from behind the zipper's plackets.

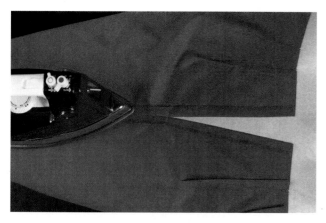

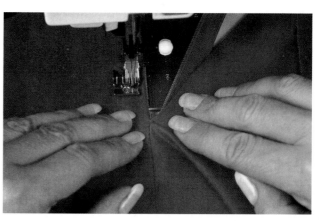

1 Cut your pattern pieces and notch the seam allowance at the bottom of the zipper opening. Clean-finish the raw edges. Sew the seam below the notch. Press the seam allowances open. Press back the seam allowances where the zipper will be inserted. Open the zipper and place the face of the right zipper tape on the back of the garment above the notch. The zipper coil should be even with the folded edge, the top of the zipper tape should extend ⅛ inch above the upper raw edge, and the staple at the bottom of the zipper should be below the garment opening.

2 Place the garment under the presser foot with the zipper closest to the feed dogs. Using the outer edge of the feed dogs as a guide, stitch the right side of the zipper. With the needle down in the fabric, stop 1½ inches from the staple. Lift the presser foot, slide the zipper head past the needle, and close the zipper. Continue stitching down the zipper until you reach the closed seam.

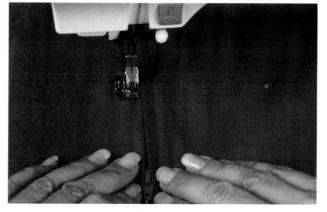

3 With the needle down, pivot the fabric and continue stitching across the bottom of the zipper just above the staple. Pivot again after crossing the coils.

4 Place the remaining, left folded edge against the opposite, loose zipper tape. Stop 1½ inches from the top and open the zipper. Finish stitching the side.

SHOP TALK

Stop before the Staple

A LWAYS BE SURE TO HAVE YOUR ZIPPER POSITIONED SO THAT you will be stitching across the zipper above the metal staple at its bottom. Doing this will give added protection to the end of the zipper and also prevent you from breaking a needle when you stitch across the zipper.

Julia Linger

Invisible Zipper

Though an invisible zipper foot adapter is available for industrial machines, production sewers use a right-hinged foot or a narrow straight stitch foot. A version of this installation technique is used by the sewers in the production room at San Francisco's Think Tank, owned by Lat Naylor, a Golden Sheers Award Winner. (Fashion veterans give this award to a Bay Area designer whose work exhibits creativity, marketability, and craftsmanship.)

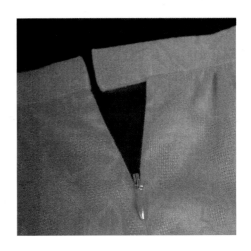

Invisible Zipper Application with a Sliding or Adjustable Zipper Foot

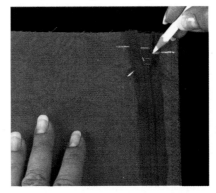

1 Finish the raw edges of the seam allowance unless the garment will be lined. With right sides together, place the closed zipper along the seamline. If no hook is planned at the waistline, place the top of the coils ⅛ inch below the seamline. Increase the distance by ¼ inch if a hook is planned.

2 At the seamline, mark 1 inch above the zipper's bottom stop and place another mark immediately above the zipper's top stop. Join the garment pieces by sewing the seam below the mark chalked at the bottom of the wrong side of the zipper. Backstitch at the beginning and the end of the seam.

3 Attach the zipper foot with the toe to the right of the needle. Place the open zipper tape facedown on the right side of the right garment piece. Position the zipper's top stop at the upper chalk mark. The zipper tape will be in the seam allowance with the coil on the seamline.

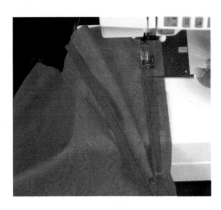

4 Place the garment under the presser foot. Lower the needle into the top of the tape close to the coil. Lower the presser foot and sew the length of the tape close to the coil. Keep a consistent distance from the edge of the seam allowance. Backstitch at the top of the slider.

5 Continue to hold the tape the same exact distance from the seam edge, and shift the garment slightly to the left to stitch around the slider. Backstitch at the end of the zipper tape. Close the zipper. Clip the threads and remove the work.

6 Place the unattached tape on the face of the left garment piece with the coil on the seamline and the edge an even distance from the seam allowance. Starting at the bottom of the zipper tape, sew along the coil. At the slider, raise the presser foot, move the slider, and resume stitching.

7 Clip the threads, remove your work, and close the zipper. From the right side, check that the stitches are as close to the coil on the right side as they are on the left. If not, open the zipper and restitch closer to the coil, forcing it aside with an awl as you sew.

Invisible Zipper Application with an Invisible Zipper Foot

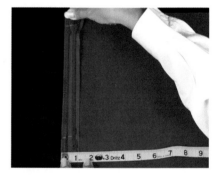

1 Finish the raw edges of the seam allowance unless the garment will be lined. Don't stitch the garment pieces together. Chalk the seam allowance above the bottom zipper stop where the zipper placket will end. On both the left and right garment pieces, staystitch along the seamline starting 1 inch above this chalk mark and ending 1 inch below it.

2 Attach the invisible zipper foot and align the center hole with the needle. Open the zipper. Place the zipper tape face down on the right side of the garment.

3 Position the left side of the zipper tape in the seam allowance with the coils on the seamline. If a waistband will be attached, the top of the coils should be $\frac{1}{8}$ inch below the waistline. Increase the distance by $\frac{1}{4}$ inch if the waist is faced or if a hook is planned above the slider.

4 Lower the needle a thread distance to the right of the foot's center. Lower the presser foot, so the right groove is over the coil. Maintain a consistent distance from the edge until you reach the slider. Backstitch. Clip the threads and remove your work.

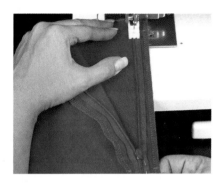

5 Close the zipper and match the face of the remaining half of the tape to the right side of the seam allowance of the matching garment piece. The coil will be on the seamline. Secure it with a few pins.

6 Open the zipper. Position the needle a thread distance to the left of the center marking on the foot. Lower the needle into the tape and fabric, then lower the presser foot, so the left groove is over the coil. Proceed as before, but sew slightly to the right of the seamline.

7 Close the zipper. From the right side, finger press along the stitches next to the zipper teeth. Continue the crease a few inches into the seamline below the zipper and along the staystitches. From the wrong side, insert a pin through the creases at the chalk mark at the bottom of the opening.

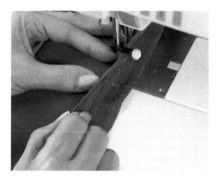

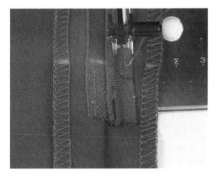

8 Replace the invisible zipper foot with a standard presser foot. Sew the garment pieces together along the seamline from the bottom to the chalk mark at the bottom of the zipper. Hold the fabric taut, push the zipper aside at the end of the seam, and backstitch. Remove your work from the machine.

9 Center the unattached zipper along the seamline. Sew only the lower portion of the right zipper tape and seam allowance together, using a conventional zipper foot and overlapping the last ½ inch of the previous seam. The presser foot in this photograph was removed for visibility. Don't remove your presser foot.

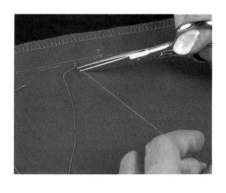

10 Repeat on the other side of the zipper. This photograph shows how the seams that you just made look underneath the seam allowance.

SHOP TALK

Getting a Grip

YOUR ZIPPER APPLICATION should look good, but there are several reasons why you may not accomplish an installation as quickly and efficiently as a sewer in a production room. The tension between the presser foot and the feed dogs is greater on an industrial machine than it is on a domestic machine, thus putting a firm hold between the tape and the garment. Production rooms often use customized presser feet to lift and/or guide during a sewing operation. Your conventional zipper foot can't hold the tape and push aside the teeth on the return row of stitches. For professional results, you can compensate by using an awl with your additional row of stitches.

Barbara Kelly

Fail-Safe Lapped Zipper

Two simple tricks make it easy to install a lapped zipper—using a slightly larger seam allowance on the lap, or right, side and improving your line of stitching by applying a guide to the right side of the garment before topstitching. Like sample makers, you can use just about anything to make a guide. In this instance, the edge of a postcard is effective.

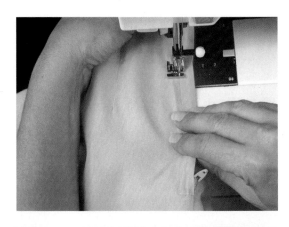

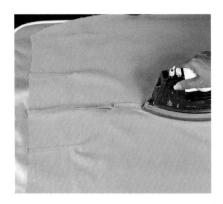

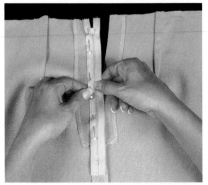

1 Add an extension to your garment piece, so the lengthwise edge of the zipper opening, the placket, is ¾ inch wide. Cut out your pattern pieces with extensions on both the right and left sides. Notch the bottom of the zipper placket. Overlock the raw edges. Sew the seam below the placket.

2 Press open the seam allowances. Turn under the ¾-inch extensions for the zipper placket. Roll out the fold on the left placket so that it extends ⅛ inch past the seamline. Press.

3 Pin the left side of the closed zipper tape facing to the wrong side of the zipper placket. The fold won't cover the coils, the tape will extend ⅛ inch above the upper raw edge, and the stop at the bottom of the zipper will be below the notch. Attach a zipper foot to your machine.

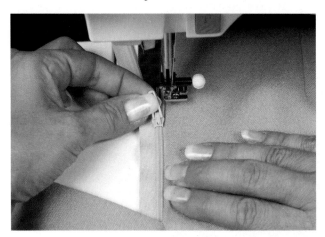

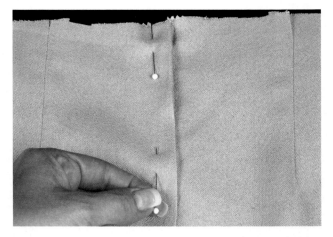

4 Open the zipper to the midpoint and sew the zipper tape ⅛ inch from the fold, stopping before the slider with the needle in the fabric. Raise your presser foot and close the zipper. Finish sewing the tape to the left side of the placket, backstitch, and end the seam.

5 Place the garment right side up on your worktable. Fold the right side of the placket over the left, covering the zipper coils and the pull. Pin in place at the waistline and the midpoint.

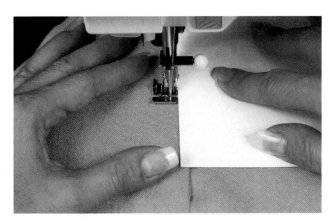

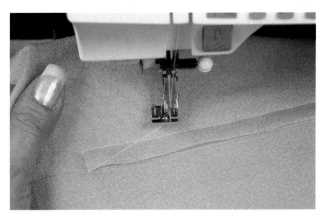

6 Using a zipper foot, place your placket right side up on the sewing machine bed to topstitch on the lap, or right side, of the placket through all thicknesses. Place the edge of a postcard or a piece of cardboard ½ inch to the left of the fold, and use this as a guide for the topstitching.

7 At the bottom of the zipper placket, stop with your needle in the fabric, lift the presser foot, and turn the garment at a right angle. Sew across the bottom of the zipper tape. Backstitch and break your threads.

Mock Fly Zipper with Template

The traditional fly zipper has separate pattern pieces that are sewn to the body pattern pieces. Generally speaking, this treatment isn't common in women's wear because it's labor intensive. Hence the "mock," or one-piece, fly is offered on most ready-to-wear garments and in home-sewing patterns. The facing juts out from the center front and is folded to the inside. In order to save on fabric, it's tempting to cut the facing off the left front pattern piece. Don't. Instead, fold this facing to the wrong side to give this area more stability.

The notable feature of the following instructions is the use of two adhesive address labels to create a template for the topstitching. This nonslip template doesn't stick permanently and won't mar a fabric's surface.

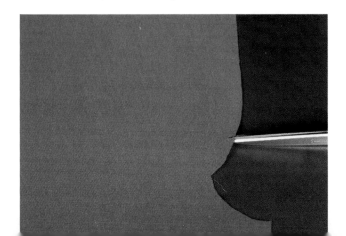

1 Cut out your pattern pieces. At the waistline, notch the foldline for the right front fly facing. Also notch the seam allowance across from the dot at the bottom of the facing. If your fabric is thin, bond a fusible to the facing. These instructions are for women's garment. In men's garments, the placket laps left over right.

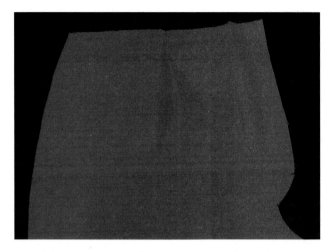

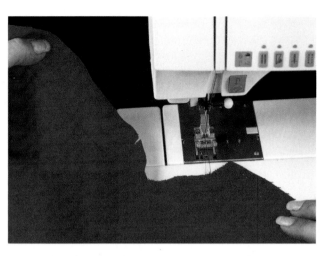

2 If the garment has front pleats, press down the one closest to the center front on both sides. Baste if desired. Fold the fly facing to the wrong side on both front pattern pieces. At the bottom of the facing on the left front, where you notched, slide the fabric out so that the fold is ⅛ inch past the center front, toward the right side. Press.

3 With right sides facing, sew the crotch of your pants fronts together from the bottom of the zipper to 1½ inches short of the end of the raw edge of the inner leg. Don't stitch the opening at the end of the seam; follow the pants "Assembly Procedure" on pages 220–225.

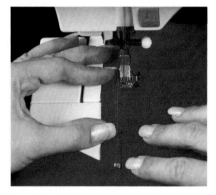

4 Pin the left side of the closed zipper tape behind the folded facing of the left garment front, with the bottom stop just below the notch. Extend the top of the zipper tape approximately ⅛ inch above the upper raw edge of the waistline.

5 Sew the zipper tape to the left front ¼ inch from the teeth. At the bottom the facing on the left front, where you notched, sew the fabric as it was pressed: Slide the fabric out so that the fold is ⅛ inch past the center front, toward the right side.

6 Lay the garment front right side up on your worktable. Lap the right front over the left at the center front, covering the zipper and the left vertical fold. Pin the right front to the left at the waistline and the zipper's midpoint.

7 Turn the garment wrong side up. Fold the right front away from the facing. Pin, then sew the right side of the zipper tape to the facing. Return the garment, wrong side up, to the worktable, and pin the facing to the garment's right front. Remove the pins that are holding the garment's right and left fronts together.

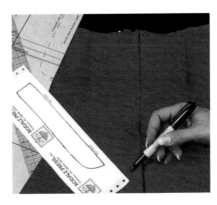

8 Overlap two 4 × 6-inch adhesive-backed address labels to make a template as long as the zipper, about 7⁄8 × 8 inches. Trace the shape of the fly, from the center front to the topstitching on the garment's right front pattern piece, onto the labels.

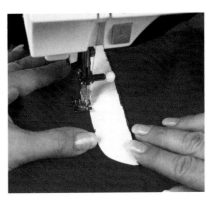

9 Place the template at the fly on the right front of the garment. Using a zipper foot or topstitching presser foot, sew along the curved edge of the template, through all thicknesses, starting at the top of the zipper. Peel off the template.

A Separating Zipper

The most common procedure for inserting a separating zipper can be frustrating. Using this industry technique will save your sanity because it's much simpler.

1 Open the zipper. Place its right side against the right side of the jacket front edge with the zipper teeth pointing toward the side seam. If you always remember to lay the right side of the zipper tape to the right side of the front, it will prevent you from attaching the zipper inside out.

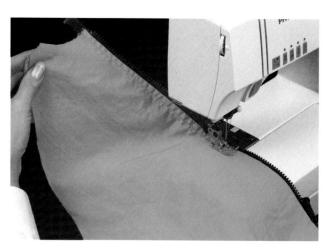

2 Place the right side of the facing on top of the right side of the jacket front. With the zipper now sandwiched between the jacket and the facing, sew down the front edge with ⅜-inch seam allowances, using a zipper foot so that you can stitch close to the zipper teeth.

3 Turn the garment right side out and finger press the seam allowance away from the zipper teeth. Using a regular presser foot, topstitch down the front on the folded edge of the fabric rather than on the zipper teeth, so that the line of topstitching is ¼ inch from the fabric's edge.

SHOP TALK

The Changing Colors of Fashion

THE EXAMPLES IN THE PHOTOGRAPHS for "A Separating Zipper" on page 205 and this page illustrate a common problem that home sewers face. I couldn't find colors to match, so the zipper on the finished jacket was custom dyed to match the fabric, but the previous samples illustrating the construction steps are different colors.

Almost every year, the color palate of the apparel industry changes. Trim and notion manufacturers follow suit, producing new, coordinating products. If a ready-to-wear manufacturer sources matching or complementary notions and finds them unavailable in a supplier's current inventory, it will have these items dyed to match.

Home sewers aren't so lucky. It's very important to realize how fre-

quently the color palate changes when you're considering buying notions for a garment that you are constructing with a recently purchased fabric. Only the most popular colors are available to consumers on the retail level, and what is considered a popular color will change from year to year.

I have learned the hard way not to wait when it comes to buying matching thread or notions for the piece of fabric that I buy today and sew...tomorrow. Many of my tomorrows have turned into next year, and the colors in my fabric no longer resemble anything that I can match. I have also learned to use complementary trims, as in the case of the black zipper with the teal fabric.

Julia Linger

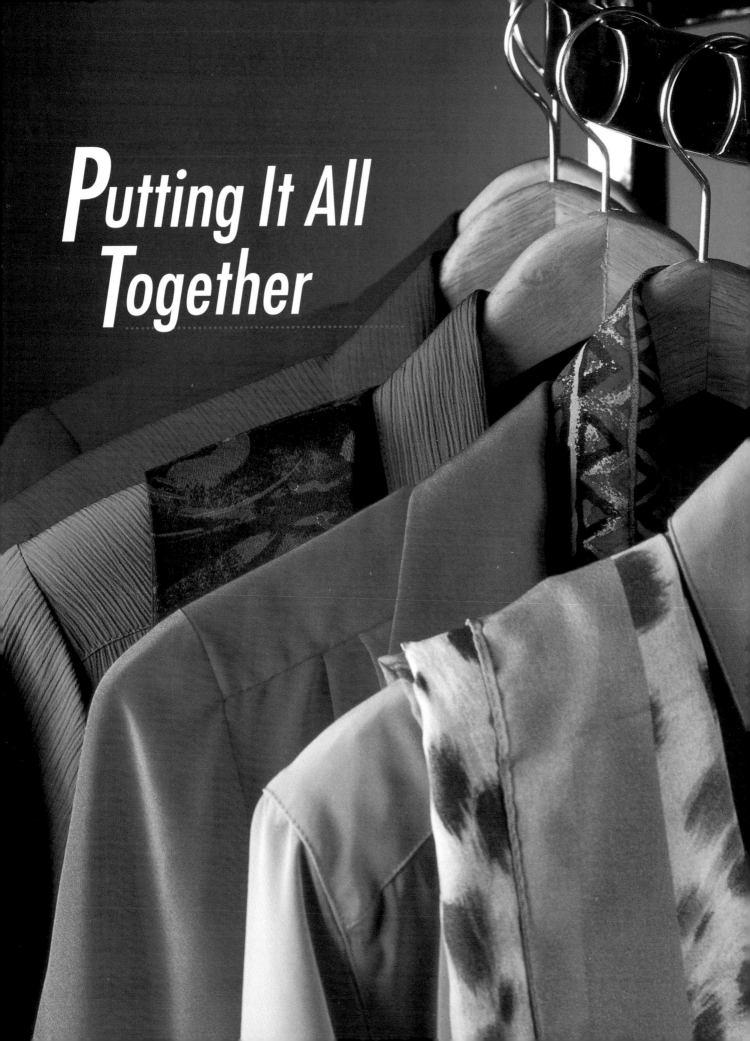

Putting It All Together

Hallmarks of a Quality Garment

To achieve the look of a professionally made garment, you would do well to consider integrating some of the current mass production techniques into the way you sew your own clothing. While some of these techniques may be viewed by the sewing elite as simply industrial shortcuts, speed and efficiency don't need to be sacrificed by those who strive to achieve the couture look. Using industry techniques, in place of the pattern guide sheet, will not diminish the final product. In most cases, it will enhance it.

For a home-sewn garment to achieve a professional look, the most important guideline is that none of the construction techniques be obvious. If anything that isn't a design detail stands out or calls attention to itself, it is usually a sign that something is wrong with the garment.

Interfacing should be chosen with care. Select a slightly lighter weight of fusible interfacing and bond it to both pieces of the cuff, collar, and neckband. Fusing to both pieces keeps the weight and amount of "give" uniform and eliminates unsightly shadows that are caused by bulky seams showing through the unfused fabric. Fusing the entire cuff piece instead of just to the fold prevents the folded edge from twisting or creating a ridge. Likewise, the facing rather than the garment should be bonded to the interfacing. This prevents a ridge where the interfacing ends. When using a sew-in interfacing, clean-finish the edge of the facing by attaching the interfacing to the facing with a narrow ¼-inch hem.

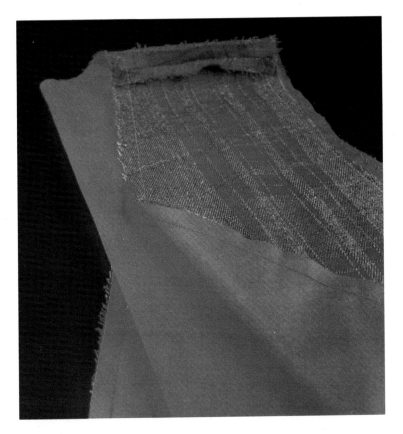

Seams should be smooth, not drawn or puckered. In an unlined garment, seam allowances that are ⅝ inch wide and pressed open are a dead giveaway that the garment is homemade. Ready-to-wear seam allowances are ¼, ⅜, and ½ inch; have an overlocked edge (unless the garment is lined); and are pressed to the back of the garment. See "Seam Allowances" on pages 42–49. Serged seams give a garment durability and a clean finish on the inside. When sewing a lined garment, especially one made from wool fabrics, press the seams open to reduce bulk.

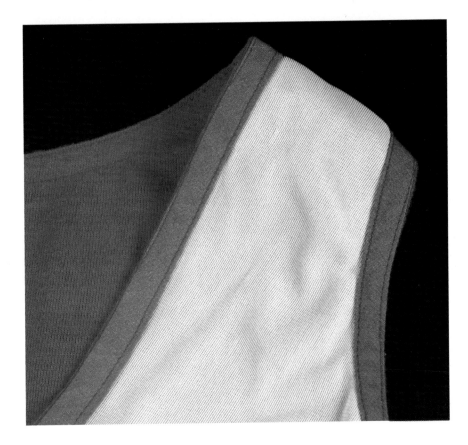

Facings, whenever possible, should be replaced with bias binding to create a stable and clean finished edge. See "Bias Binding" on pages 87–89. If you need a facing in the back of a garment with a wide or deep front neckline opening, lengthen the size of the facing piece so that it has enough weight not to flip to the outside. Be sure to understitch the facings to prevent them from rolling to the outside.

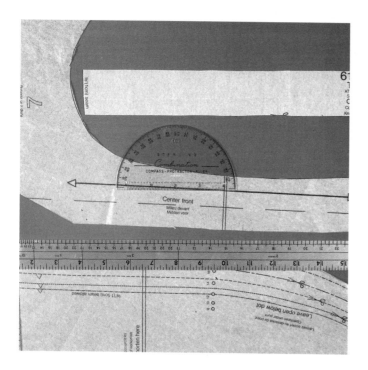

Grainlines marked on patterns are set to control the drape of the garment's style, so it is paramount that you always follow the markings on the pattern pieces. Tilting the pattern pieces off the grainline will alter the way a garment hangs and can even twist the garment. Tilting, or tipping, the grainline on pattern pieces causes the seams to twist. On pants, the side seam will shift around to the front of your leg, as you can see on many pairs of jeans currently on the market. See "Tilting Patterns" on page 69.

SHOP TALK

Another Place Where You Can "Cheat"

*W*HEN SETTING IN A SLEEVE, IT is more important that the grainline of the sleeve be square at the shoulder notch than it is for the underarm seam to intersect perfectly. While the sleeve will not hang properly if the grain is off, hopefully no one will want to inspect your underarms.

Julia Linger

Pressing should be integrated into the assembly process. Take the time to press all of your seams as you sew, and try to use the appropriate equipment. This not only "cures" the stitching line into the fabric but it also ensures a smooth intersection where all of the seams cross each other. See "Pressing" on pages 161–168 for information on techniques for handling a variety of seams as well as fabrics.

SHOP TALK

A Snug Fit Is Best

*T*O PREVENT A BUTTON FROM pulling open the buttonhole and popping out while you are wearing the garment, make sure the buttonhole length is only ⅛ inch more than the diameter of your button.

Julia Linger

Buttonholes are an important detail. If your sewing machine does not produce a neatly stitched buttonhole, you should consider other alternatives. Try using a bound or hand-stitched version. Or, on blouses, vests, and jackets, replace the buttonholes with loops of spaghetti tubing that are sewn into the garment when the facing is attached. Cut off the lappage on the right front pattern piece so that the loops extend from the center front.

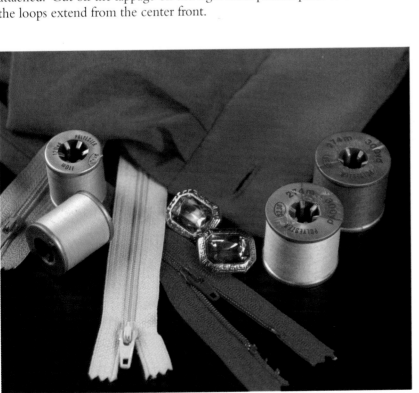

Thread, zippers, and notions should match or complement your fabric. If you cannot achieve an exact match, use a shade that is slightly darker. When topstitching, be sure your lines are straight and the stitches are not too small. Most sewing machines have a preprogrammed length of 10 stitches per inch (spi), but Julia Linger says topstitching should be done at 15 spi. The all-purpose presser foot on most machines can be used as a guide for topstitching that is ¼ inch from the edge. See "Topstitching" on pages 184–186.

Blouse

This chapter is a step-by-step guide to one of the many assembly procedures used in the garment industry to construct a blouse. After reading "Getting Started," beginning on page 1, and "Tips and Techniques," beginning on page 83, you can use the following instructions as you would those found in a home-sewing pattern. Since seam allowances aren't ⅝ inch in the industry, the instructions start with advice on recommended seam allowances, followed by an "at-a-glance" summary of the assembly of each step. The blouse shown in this chapter has a notched collar, yoke, patch pocket, and tucks rather than darts.

Tips for Professional Results

It's very important to pay special attention to the focal points on a blouse. The two main areas are usually the front placket, which contains the buttons and buttonholes, and the collar. Also consider the following:

• Professionally made buttonholes are neat and clean, without excess threads or interfacing peaking out and no blank spots in the stitching. For a sharp, clean cut, use a block and chisel to open up your buttonholes.

• A properly constructed and fused collar attractively frames your face. When the blouse has a traditional stand collar, the neckband stands crisply around the neckline, which supports a firm, smooth collar. The way to achieve balanced support in a collar and neckline is to use interfacing on both pieces of the collar and the neckband. Select a slightly lighter weight of fusible than you would use if you were only bonding in-

terfacing to one side of the collar. Fusing both sides of a flat collar will keep the upper collar smooth and prevent the shadowing of the seam allowance that is often seen in lightweight fabrics.

• For a smooth, balanced look, fuse cuffs in the same manner as collars. Topstitching close to all of the edges gives cuffs a flat and finished look. And it's just as important to have neat buttonholes on the cuffs as it is on the center front of the blouse, so use the same care.

• Continuous-lap sleeve plackets usually provide function but little style. Unless your placket is intended as part of a special design, it should definitely not be seen.

212

Recommended Seam Allowances

You will be well on your way to achieving the look of ready-to-wear by adjusting seam allowances before cutting out the pattern pieces for your garment. For detailed instructions, see "Seam Allowances" on pages 42–49.

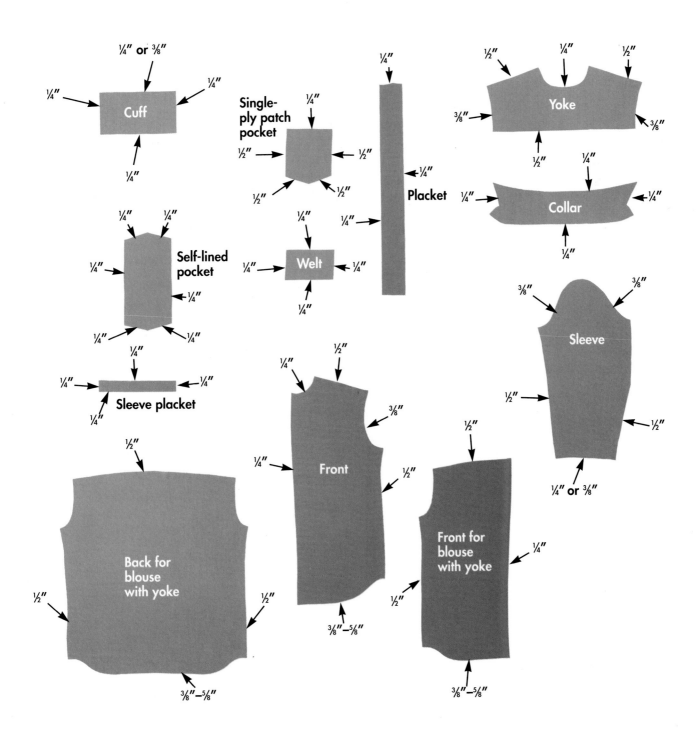

Assembly Procedure

The following pages don't offer specific instructions for each procedure that is part of assembling a blouse. For example, you are told at what point the collar should be attached but not given the exact procedure. As in the industry, you have many choices and should choose a technique that is most suited to your available time, skill level, and equipment. Several options are described in detail in "Collars" on pages 99–107. From chain stitching to yokes, you can select the techniques that you will use to make your garment.

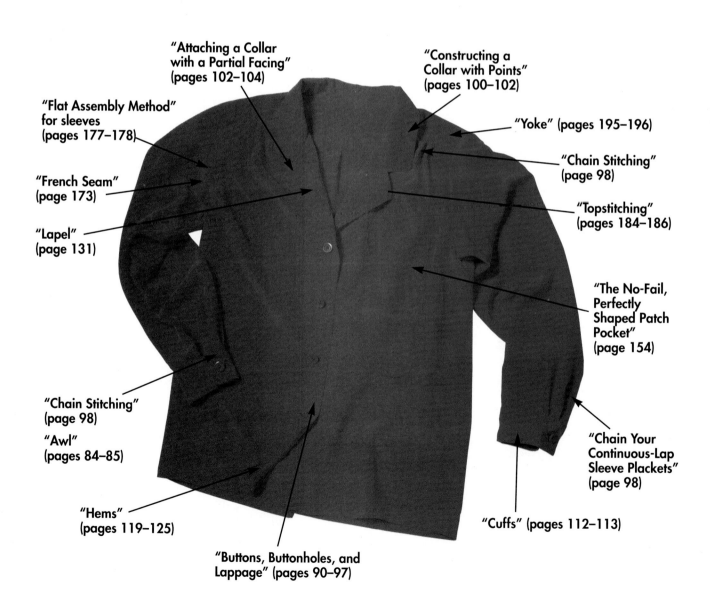

"Attaching a Collar with a Partial Facing" (pages 102–104)

"Constructing a Collar with Points" (pages 100–102)

"Flat Assembly Method" for sleeves (pages 177–178)

"Yoke" (pages 195–196)

"Chain Stitching" (page 98)

"French Seam" (page 173)

"Topstitching" (pages 184–186)

"Lapel" (page 131)

"The No-Fail, Perfectly Shaped Patch Pocket" (page 154)

"Chain Stitching" (page 98)

"Awl" (pages 84–85)

"Chain Your Continuous-Lap Sleeve Plackets" (page 98)

"Hems" (pages 119–125)

"Cuffs" (pages 112–113)

"Buttons, Buttonholes, and Lappage" (pages 90–97)

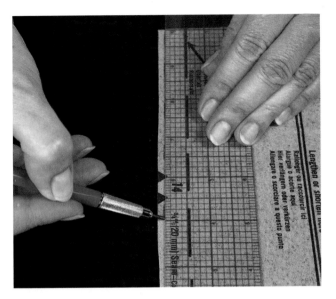

1 Test your fabric. See "Shrinkage Tests" on page 51 and "Crocking Test" on page 52. Reduce the seam allowances on your pattern pieces, referring to "Seam Allowances" on pages 42–49. If you want a lined patch pocket, and your commercial pattern offers one that is hemmed at the top, draft a new pattern. See "The No-Fail, Perfectly Shaped Patch Pocket" on page 154.

2 Alter your pattern pieces. See "Alterations for Patterns and Blocks" on pages 28–38. You may also want to adjust your self-facing pattern for more neckline shaping. See "Attaching a Collar with a Partial Facing" on pages 102–104. If you aren't using the button size recommended by your pattern, or if you plan vertical rather than horizontal buttonholes, then you must alter your blouse front. See "Lappage" on page 91.

3 Cut out your fabric. See "Laying Up and Cutting Out Fabric" on pages 65–82. Notch the center back on the appropriate pattern pieces. Notch the foldline for the front self-facing and tucks, the lapel's break point at the lower end of the roll line, the side seams on the front and the back at the midpoint, and any other notches indicated on the pattern pieces. See "Notches" on pages 71–73.

4 Interface the collar, lapel, and cuff pattern pieces. A sew-in organza is used for this blouse. To apply the organza and finish the long, unnotched edge of the facing, simultaneously sew the organza to the facing, with right sides together, then understitch the seam allowances to the organza. Now fold the organza back to the facing with wrong sides together, and baste the raw edges together.

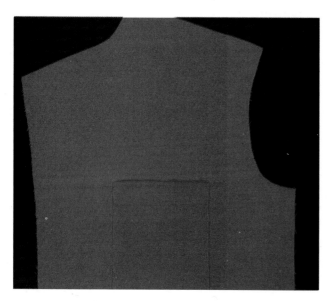

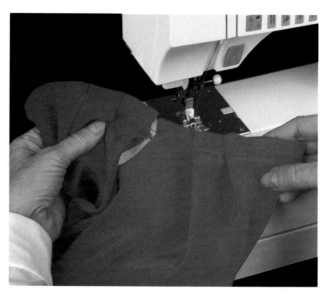

5 Overlock all of the raw edges except the ones that will be enclosed in upcoming procedures: collar, cuffs, and yoke. If you plan to use French seams for the sides, don't overlock the side seams. If your blouse has darts, sew them now. See "Single Tapered Dart" on page 117, "Single Dart" on page 164, and "Double Fisheye Dart" on page 165. Make and attach the patch pocket. See "The No-Fail, Perfectly Shaped Patch Pocket" on page 154.

6 Baste all of the tucks in the blouse fronts, back, and sleeves at the same time. See "Chain Stitching" on page 98.

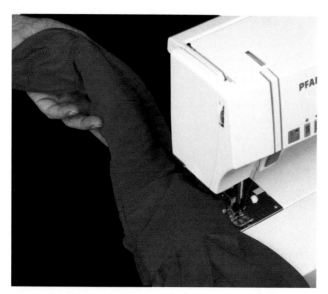

7 Assemble the collar, yoke, and facings. This involves sewing together the upper collar and undercollar, plus attaching the lapel facing to the front, the yoke to the fronts and back, the yoke facing to the lapel facing, and the collar to the facings. See "Yoke" on pages 195–196 for detailed instructions. Understitch the lapel. See "Lapel" on page 131.

SHOP TALK

Collar Detail

ACCORDING TO LINA LUK, A sewer and cutter who works in New York, the most important detail on any shirt, blouse, or dress is the collar. She says this is the first thing people notice, so great care must be taken. Your cutting must be exact and your sewing precise.

Elissa Meyrich

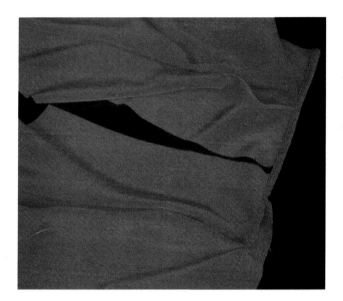

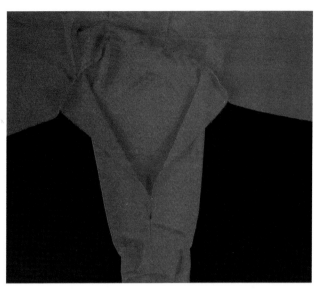

8 Make and attach the continuous-lap sleeve plackets and the cuffs. Chain stitching and crack stitching will streamline both of these processes. See pages 98 and 110. Sew the last 4 inches of the seams on both sleeves before attaching the cuffs. See "Cuffs" on pages 112–113.

9 Sew the sleeve cap into the armscye, then sew the side seam. See "Flat Assembly Method" on pages 177–178 and "French Seam" on page 173. For a nicely finished interior, wrap bias binding around the armscye seam allowances. See pages 179–180.

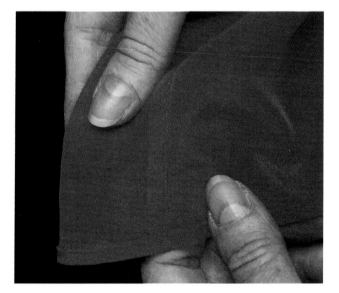

10 Open out the lapel facing and narrow hem the blouse. Fold the lapel facing back with the wrong sides of the facing and blouse front together. Secure the facing by sewing on top of the stitching for the narrow hem. Add buttonholes to the right front and sew buttons to the left front. See "Lappage" on page 91.

SHOP TALK

On a Roll

A COLLAR WILL ROLL NICELY AT THE SEAMLINE IF you make the undercollar a bit smaller. After sewing the outer edges together, understitch the seam allowances to the undercollar, and press so that the seamline rolls to the undercollar. Before joining the collar to the garment, it helps to baste together the loose edges of the upper collar and undercollar. At the machine, it helps to position the garment piece undercollar up and roll the outer edge of the collar to keep the pattern pieces edge to edge.

Laurel Hoffman

Pants

Assembling a pair of pants involves many of the ideas and techniques that are described in Parts 1 and 2 of this book. This chapter is a step-by-step summary of an assembly procedure. By following it, you can make choices about how you will assemble your pants. The chapter is set up to reflect the guiding principle that exists in many sample rooms—there is no "right" way to assemble a garment, only choices that fit the allotted time and budget.

Tips for Professional Results

Pants are one of those tricky garments for which the fit can be as crucial a hallmark as the construction itself. Unless you are making Lycra/Spandex pants, don't forget to allow the necessary ease for pants to drape attractively on the body. The key points of construction that need special care are the waistband, pockets, pleats, fly, and hem. In well-made pants, only the decorative features or the figure of the wearer should stand out.

- Pants should be hemmed with a slight angle to the back and no more than a ½- to 1-inch hem.
- Seams shouldn't ripple or pucker, and the inseam shouldn't draw up toward the crotch.
- Pleats should be pressed flat only above the crotch. If the crease runs the entire length of the leg, it should merge with the crease of the pleat.
- Pocket openings should be smooth, not stretched out, and lay flat against the body.

- Pants should drape smoothly from the waistband to the hem with no ripples or puckers along the seamline. The most crucial element to the drape of pants is the position of the grainline on the leg of the garment. Take care when laying out the pattern and cutting the fabric to ensure that the grainline of the pattern matches that of the fabric. Rippled seams can easily be avoided by applying slight pressure to the seam on either side of the needle when stitching.

Recommended Seam Allowances

You will be well on your way to achieving the look of ready-to-wear by adjusting seam allowances before cutting out the pattern pieces for your garment. See "Seam Allowances" on pages 42–49 for complete instructions.

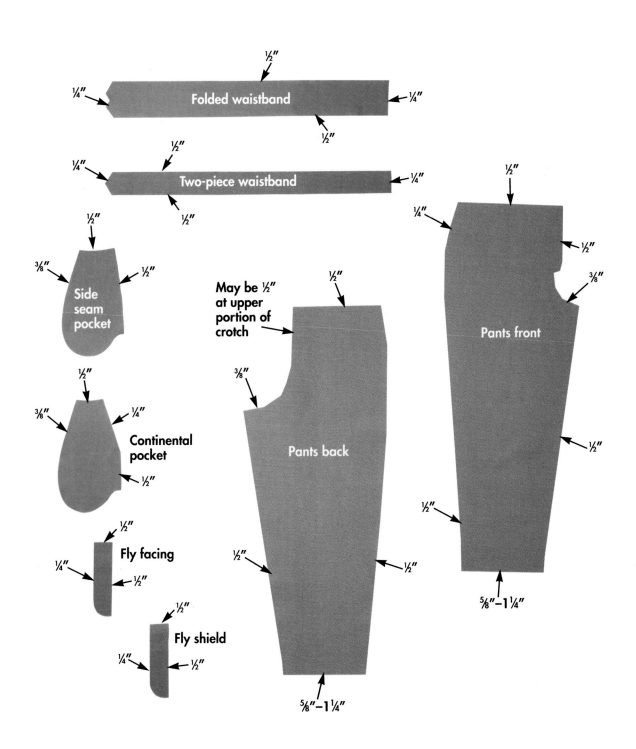

Assembly Procedure

The instructions that follow are a summary of an assembly procedure that will take you through the process of cutting out and sewing together a pair of pants. The featured instructions are as general as possible, but they do refer to pleated pants with cutaway (angled) side pockets and a fly front. Like the instructions in a home-sewing pattern, the step-by-step procedure described on the following pages will take you from cutting out your fabric to finishing the hem. Since it is a summary, you can refer to the referenced pages for specific information on techniques.

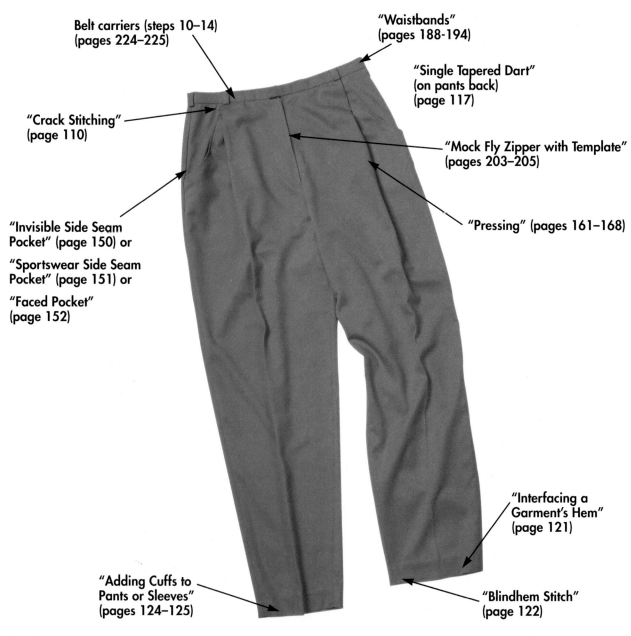

Belt carriers (steps 10–14)
(pages 224–225)

"Waistbands"
(pages 188-194)

"Single Tapered Dart"
(on pants back)
(page 117)

"Crack Stitching"
(page 110)

"Mock Fly Zipper with Template"
(pages 203–205)

"Invisible Side Seam
Pocket" (page 150) or

"Sportswear Side Seam
Pocket" (page 151) or

"Faced Pocket"
(page 152)

"Pressing" (pages 161–168)

"Interfacing a
Garment's Hem"
(page 121)

"Adding Cuffs to
Pants or Sleeves"
(pages 124–125)

"Blindhem Stitch"
(page 122)

One Size Doesn't Fit All

....

$\mathcal{E}$ACH PATTERN COMPANY DESIGNS FOR A DIFFERENT body shape, as is obvious when you compare two pants pattern pieces that are the same size but have different labels. Most American pattern companies design for a rectangle-shaped body and a B bra cup. The rectangle-shaped body is slightly to moderately curved, and the fat is distributed fairly evenly. Also, a person may be wide or slim, but the body shape remains the same, without exaggerated curves at the bust or hip. Keeping this in mind, a body type with less curve can often handle a closer fit. This means that sometimes there might be a bit less design ease. For this person, a Vogue pants pattern might be a good choice because the crotch has a small crotch extension (the curved areas on the front and back pattern pieces, which extend to connect between the legs) to accommodate for a less curved derriere.

European companies such as Burda design for a fuller figure. Usually a person with this type of figure has a more defined shape and body fat that is distributed in the bust, upper arms, hips, and upper thighs. Burda pants patterns have longer, more exaggerated back crotch extensions that fit around the curve of a fuller derriere and more design ease to accommodate the roundness.

The same principle applies in the bust area. I recommend testing a similar pattern from each company to see which fits you best. Very often, you may wear a jacket from one company and a pants pattern from another, just as you would in ready-to-wear.

Shermane Fouché

patternmaker, dressmaker, and owner of Shermane Fouché Pattern Collection

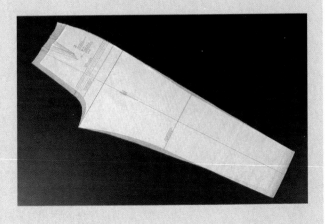

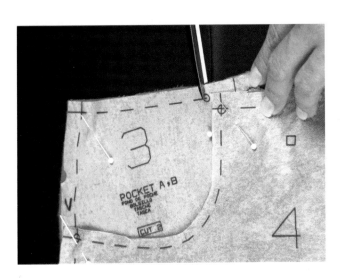

1 Test your fabric and interfacing to determine if they require pretreatment, adjust the seam allowances on your pattern pieces, proceed with the layout, and cut out the pattern pieces. See "Fabric" on pages 50–56, "Interfacings" on pages 57–64, and "Laying Up and Cutting Out Fabric" on pages 65–82. Make sure you notch the placement of the angle pocket and the center front closure. Overlock all raw edges on the pattern pieces, except the waist. Don't overlock the pocket and pocket facing until these pattern pieces are sewn together. If your fabric is prone to seam slippage, fuse a strip of interfacing to the crotch seamline. See "Fusible Tape" on pages 62–63.

2 Press the crease into both pants front pattern pieces, extending it from the hem into the first pleat in the pants. Now press the remaining pleat. On traditional pants, the pleats are folded toward the center front. But you will see pleats folded toward the side seams in some ready-to-wear. The direction your pleats lay is your choice; in fact, you may find that one direction is more flattering to your figure. Finally, press the fly opening for the zipper at the front of your pants.

3 Sew the back darts. See "Transferring Pattern Markings to Darts" on page 114 and "Single Tapered Dart" on page 117. If the dart on the pants pattern isn't contoured, refer to "Custom Fitting with Contoured Darts" on pages 116–117 before marking the darts. Baste the pleats to hold them in place at the waistline. Topstitch the pleats, if desired, as a design detail. If you won't be top-stitching the pleats, omit the basting. When attaching the waistband, use an awl to position the pleats, which are already marked because they were pressed in the last step.

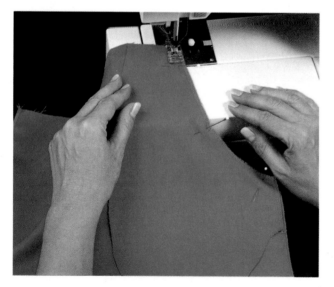

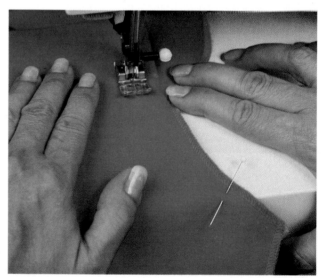

4 Install the pockets in the pants fronts. See "Pockets" on pages 149–160 for instructions on a variety of pocket treatments. Machine tack each pocket in place at the waistline and the side seam. If you are working with a fabric that has a lot of stretch or is thin, such as rayon and lightweight wool, apply a ¾-inch-wide length of fusible interfacing to the seamline before attaching the pocket bag to prevent stretching.

5 The crotch is sewn in two sections that are joined later. This two-step procedure is used on better-quality pants because the crotch will hang better. First sew the left and right fronts together along the crotch seam, starting 8 inches below the waist, which leaves an opening for the zipper insertion. Stop 1½ inches before the raw edges at the end of the pattern pieces at the center of the crotch, marked above with a pin.

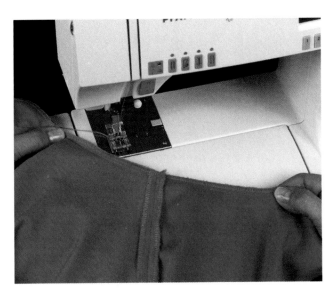

6 Join the left and right back pattern pieces, starting at the waist and stopping 1½ inches before the raw edges of the inner leg seam, as done in Step 5 to the fronts. When the pants front and pants back sections are later sewn together, there will be a 3-inch opening at the center of the crotch, as shown.

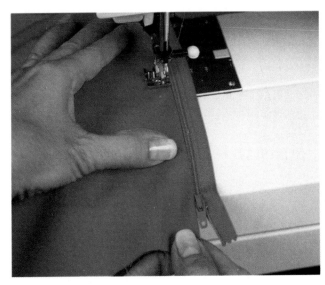

7 Sew the fly zipper into the 8-inch opening in the pants front. Complete instructions for this procedure are found in "Mock Fly Zipper with Template" on pages 203–205. You will find that it is easier to apply the zipper if you have notched and pressed the fly front foldline and notched or chalk marked where the zipper stop ends.

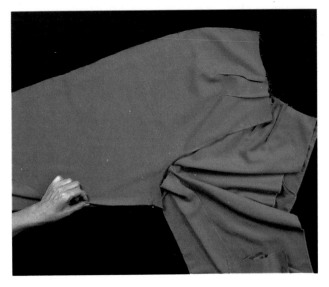

8 The side seams of the legs are sewn together next. The pants front and pants back sections are not joined at the crotch yet. Press the seams open and flat. Now sew together the inner leg seams by joining the left front to the left back and the right front to the right back. Press open and flat.

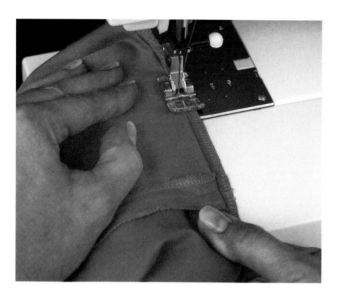

9 Sew together the remaining open portion of the crotch seam, thus joining the pants front and pants back sections. Reinforce the entire crotch seam with a second row of stitching, starting below the bottom of the zipper and ending at the waist at the center back.

10 The belt loops are prepared before the waistband is attached. Cut a piece of fabric that is five times as long as one belt loop, with the grainline running lengthwise. Some dressmakers cut the fabric on the bias so the loops have some give, thus reducing the possibility that they will pull out of the seam when a belt is inserted. Each belt loop length needs to be the width of the waistband plus ½ inch for ease and 1 inch for two ½-inch seam allowances. See "Uh-Oh! Not Spaghetti-Os" on the opposite page.

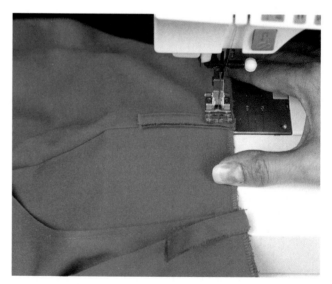

11 Prepare the waistband by serging the raw edges and applying interfacing. If the fabric is thin or stretchy, iron the fusible to the entire width of the waistband. With fabric that is thick or stiff, it is only necessary to fuse the front part of the waistband plus an extra ½ inch that extends past the foldline. The extra ½ inch is folded to the back of the waistband.

12 Determine the position of each belt loop along the waist. For this pair of pants, the loops are positioned at the side seams, center back, and above the pleats on both sides of the center front. Baste one edge of each belt loop to the waist with right sides together and raw edges matching.

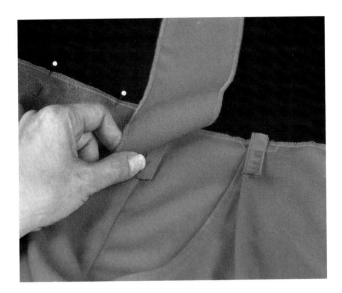

13 Staystitch the waist of the pants to prevent stretching. Pin, then sew the waistband to the pants waist with right sides facing, edges even, and the belt loops sandwiched between. Remember to leave a 1-inch extension on the left side. Several alternative treatments, such as a faced waistband, are explained in "Waistbands" on pages 188–194.

14 Fold the waistband to the inside of the pants. Let the waistband seam allowance extend below the seamline. From the right side, crack stitch the waistband to the pants. See "Crack Stitching" on page 110. Now turn up the belt loops and fold under the raw edges. Machine tack the loops in place at the top of the waistband.

15 Hem the pants or trousers or add a cuff. See "Hems" on pages 119–125 and "Adding Cuffs to Pants or Sleeves" on pages 124–125.

SPINNING YARNS

Uh-Oh! Not Spaghetti-Os

BELT LOOPS MADE FROM SPAGHETTI TUBING scream homemade. Instead, cut a "running strip" for five belt loops. In this case, the running strip is cut along the fabric's selvage. It is three times as wide as the finished width of the belt loop. The length is five times the finished length of one belt loop plus ten times the seam allowance width. In other words, the running strip is 12½ inches long and 1¼ inches wide for a 1-inch-wide waistband. Overlock one long edge of the strip, or cut it out with one long edge on the selvage. Fold the running strip in thirds lengthwise with the selvage on top. Topstitch the length of the strip ⅛ inch from both folded edges. Cut the running strip into five belt loops. Remember to add two ½-inch seam allowances, plus ½ inch of ease, to every loop, so the strip is cut into five lengths, each 2½ inches long.

Elissa Meyrich

Skirt

Assembling a skirt involves many of the ideas and techniques that are described in Parts 1 and 2. This chapter guides you through cutting out and sewing a skirt by summarizing a garment industry procedure and technique. The assembly method applies to a lined or unlined skirt, and it's the same procedure used by many sample makers.

Tips for Professional Results

The most crucial focal point in the construction is the drape of the garment. The grainline of a skirt will dictate style and function and must be followed as the pattern directs. Though secondary to the grainline, care must also be taken in hemming, zipper insertion, waistband closures, and seams. Poor technique in any of these areas will become the focus of attention and detract from the harmony of a well-made skirt.

- The hem should hang evenly and be in proportion to the skirt's fullness. A straight skirt hem should be no more than 2 inches wide, while a full skirt hem should be 1 inch or less. See "Hems" on pages 119–125.

- Bias-cut skirts are notorious for the way the hem dips unevenly, and they will look unprofessional if hemmed too soon. Let the skirt hang for at least one night before evening off the lower edge and sewing the hem.

- Waistband fasteners should be attached with small, neat stitches. It's preferable to attach fasteners by machine.

- In a well-made skirt, the seams blend into the fabric and aren't even noticed. Applying slight pressure to the seam on either side of the needle while stitching will ensure that the seams lay smooth without puckers when pressed. If sewing a bias-cut skirt, do not apply extra pressure to the seams.

Recommended Seam Allowances

These illustrations detail the recommended seam allowances for your skirt. For the best results, reduce them prior to cutting out your pattern pieces. See "Seam Allowances" on pages 42–49 for step-by-step instructions.

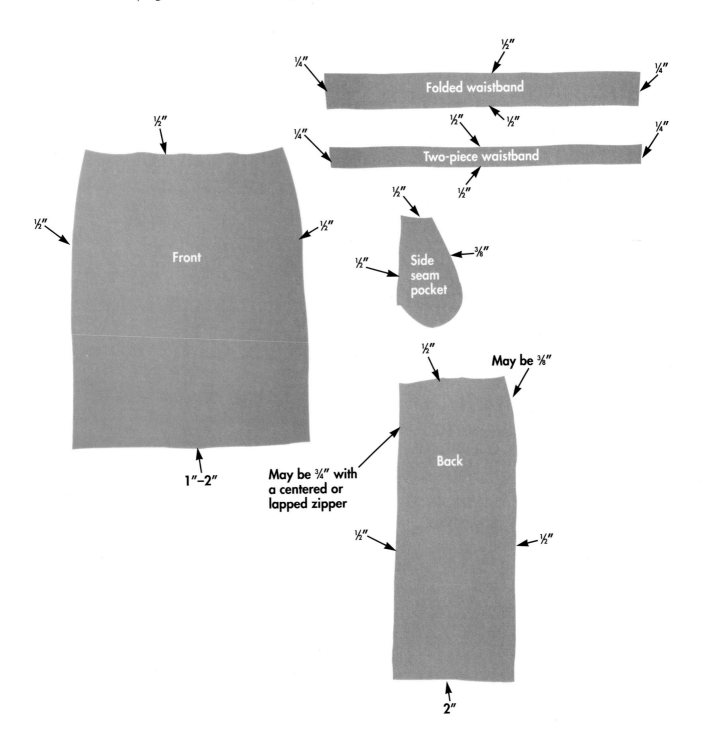

½"
¼" Folded waistband ¼"

½" ½"

½" ¼"
¼" Two-piece waistband ¼"
½" ½"

½"
Front

½" ½"

½"
Side seam pocket ⅜"
½"

½" May be ⅜"
Back

May be ¾" with a centered or lapped zipper

½" ½"

1"–2"

2"

Assembly Procedure

This skirt has an invisible zipper and a box pleat at the center back. Refer to Part 2, beginning on page 83, for step-by-step instructions for a particular procedure. For example, this skirt doesn't have pockets. But if you wanted to add these to your garment, you can select a style from "Pockets" on pages 149–160, adjust the pattern pieces, and sew them into your skirt following the instructions, and then continue assembling the skirt with the steps in this chapter.

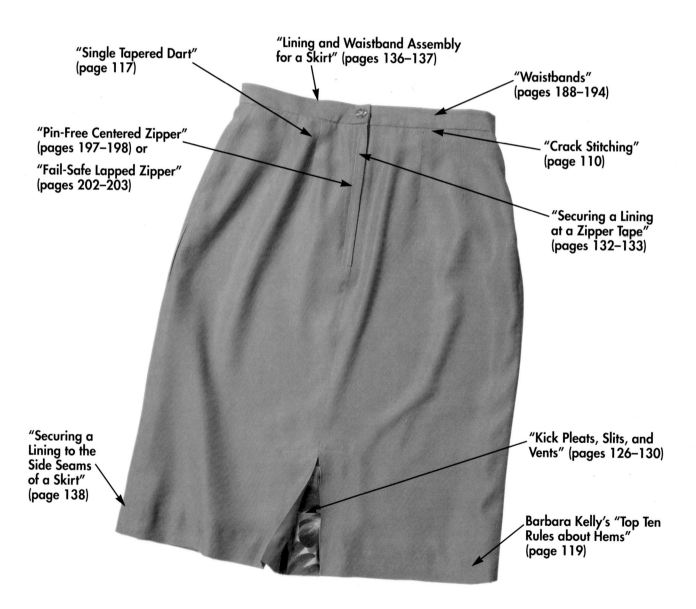

"Single Tapered Dart" (page 117)

"Lining and Waistband Assembly for a Skirt" (pages 136–137)

"Waistbands" (pages 188–194)

"Pin-Free Centered Zipper" (pages 197–198) or

"Fail-Safe Lapped Zipper" (pages 202–203)

"Crack Stitching" (page 110)

"Securing a Lining at a Zipper Tape" (pages 132–133)

"Securing a Lining to the Side Seams of a Skirt" (page 138)

"Kick Pleats, Slits, and Vents" (pages 126–130)

Barbara Kelly's "Top Ten Rules about Hems" (page 119)

A Place of Experimentation and Design

THE WAY WE WORK IN A DESIGNER'S sample room is based on an orderly method of assembly. When a sewer gets a style to sew, all she receives from the patternmaker is a tied-up bundle with a sketch of the garment. The sketch shows the sewer how the garment should look plus details the topstitching, trim, and notions. Looking at the illustration, the sample maker decides which assembly method to use.

There isn't an instruction sheet. Sometimes the sample maker and the patternmaker discuss the approach to an unusual garment. Then, when the garment is joined together, the sample maker mounts the garment on a dress form and the designer and the patternmaker evaluate the fabric, fit, and, of course, design features.

Elissa Meyrich

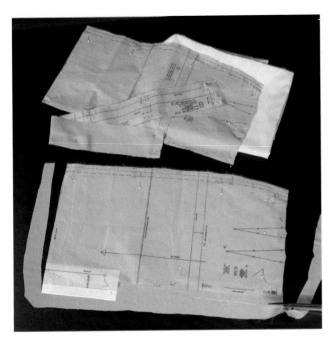

1 Test your fabric. See "Shrinkage Tests" on page 51 and "Crocking Test" on page 52. If you are not making a box pleat, vent, or lapped zipper, your lining will be identical to the skirt, so cut all of your yardage simultaneously. See "Multi'ply' Productivity" on page 68. Adjust, if necessary, and cut out your pattern pieces.

2 Notch the ends of the dart legs at the waist and mark all of the dart points with chalk or tailor's tacks. Also notch the center front and center back at the waistline and the hem on all pattern pieces and at the foldlines for the zipper and the pleat. The waistband needs notches on the left side for the extension. If your skirt has tucks at the waist, notch at the foldlines and placement lines.

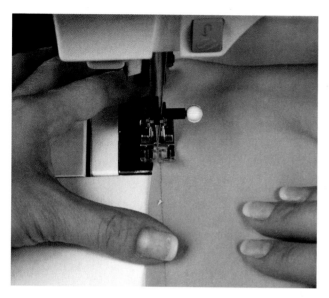

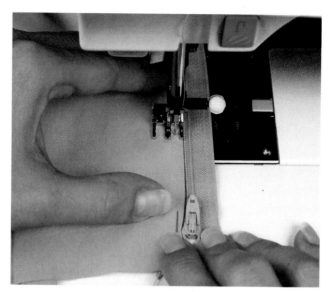

3 Overlock all of the raw edges except for the waistline and hem. Don't overlock the skirt side seams if you are adding an invisible side seam pocket. And don't overlock any seams if your skirt is lined. Sew the darts on the front and back pattern pieces for the skirt and lining and press them toward the center front. See "Single Tapered Dart" on page 117 and "Pressing" on pages 161–168.

4 Sew the center back from the pleat's release point to the bottom of the zipper opening. Press open the seam allowances. Install your zipper, using the notches at the center back waistline as guides for folding back the extensions. See "Zippers" on pages 197–206 for instructions and tips for inserting a variety of zipper treatments. Sew the skirt backs to the front at the side seams.

5 Finish the pleat, vent, or slit at the center back. In this example, a box pleat with a contrasting backing is added. See pages 126–130 for step-by-step instructions on sewing a kick pleat, vent, or slit. If your skirt pattern has a slit, you can fine-tune it with "Wonder Tapes," as explained on page 128, or convert it into a vent or slit.

6 Overlock a three-thread narrow hem on the right and left back lining pattern pieces below the release point for the slit and above the notch at the bottom of the zipper. If you don't have a serger, narrow hem the identified spots. Sew the lining back pattern pieces together from the release point to the bottom of the zipper opening. Sew the lining side seams together, starting at the hem.

"Waist"ing Your Fusible

*T*HERE IS A GARMENT INDUSTRY method for quickly calculating the size of the strip of fusible interfacing to cut for your waistband. Fold the waistband pattern piece in half lengthwise and pin it to the fusible. Draw a line on the fusible ½ inch from the fold and parallel to it. Cut along this line and around the remaining three sides of the pattern piece.

Elissa Meyrich

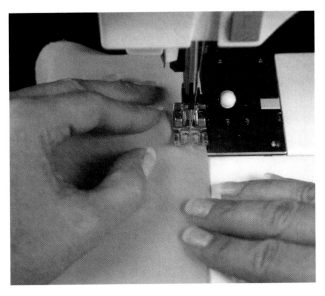

7 Staystitch the waist on both the skirt and the lining. Slip the lining into the skirt with the wrong side of the lining facing the wrong side of the skirt. Make sure the side seams and darts match. Baste at the waist. Turn the garment right side out.

8 Sew the lining to the zipper tape. Like the bagged lining for a vest, attaching the lining to the zipper tape involves pulling a portion of the skirt inside out and sewing from the wrong side with the right sides together. For step-by-step instructions and photographs of this procedure, see "Securing a Lining at a Zipper Tape" on pages 132–133.

9 Apply interfacing to the front of the waistband if desired. See "Interfacings" on pages 57–64. Sew the waistband to the skirt, starting at the center back on the left side of the skirt and allowing a 1-inch extension at the center back on the left side.

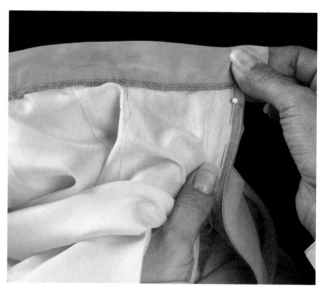

10 With right sides together, fold the waistband in half lengthwise, encasing the skirt lining, skirt, and zipper inside the waistband. Sew the short end of the extension through all thicknesses, starting at the fold. Then sew along the lengthwise edge as far as possible, making sure the fabric encased in the waistband isn't caught in the seam. Trim the corners diagonally and turn the end right side out.

11 Fold the waistband to the wrong side of the skirt, pin, and crack stitch from the right side. Sew a buttonhole and button or a hook and eye to the waistband. This same technique is used to sew a cuff. See pages 112–113 for step-by-step instructions and photographs.

SHOP TALK

Sew Professional

SEW HEM TAPE TO THE RAW edge of the skirt bottom to give your hem a clean, professional finish. The seam tape covers ¼ inch of the skirt's raw edge. Don't pull or ease the tape while stitching. The hem of your lining should face the hem of your skirt.

Elissa Meyrich

12 Even out the hem on the skirt and the lining. The hemline of the lining should be 1 inch above the skirt's hemline. Overlock and sew the lining hem. Overlock the skirt hem, unless you plan to attach hem tape. Hem depth varies, so see "Professional Hem Depths and Stitches" on page 120 before finishing the hem. In this example, the skirt hem is 2 inches and the lining hem is 1¼ inches.

Assembly Methods for Alternate Skirt Silhouettes

Sample makers assemble garments in a logical manner, joining smaller pieces then attaching them to build bigger pieces. For example, if a skirt has four gores in the front and four in the back, you join together all of the front pieces and then all of the back pieces. When you have a front and a back, you join them. This prevents the pieces from getting mixed up. A selection of skirts and their assembly methods follow.

Gored skirts are joined by first sewing the side fronts to the center front panel. Then the side backs are sewn to the center back. Finally the side seams are joined, then the zipper is inserted, the waistband is added, and the garment is hemmed.

A skirt with pockets is handled in much the same way as a pocketless skirt with similar design details. The only difference is that the pockets are attached before any other seams are sewn.

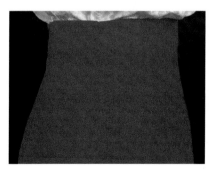

Soft pleats are easier to position by notching the waist's seam allowances. With the help of an awl, position the pleats as you attach the waistband. If you want to topstitch the first inch of each pleat prior to assembling the pattern pieces, fold and press the pleats. The creases are good stitching guides. Now sew the skirt together following the procedure for a straight skirt.

Wrap skirts are made by first sewing all of the darts or pleats. Hem or face the vertical edge of the wrap front that won't be joined in a seam. Next join the side seams and attach the waistband. Replacing a waistband with piping or grosgrain ribbon makes a handsome treatment for a wrap skirt. For instructions on these procedures, see "Figure-Flattering Piped Waistband" on pages 188–189 and "Grosgrain Ribbon–Faced Waistband" on page 190. The hem is last.

High waist skirts and skirts without waistbands are made with a shaped facing. Cut the facing pattern pieces from self-fabric or grosgrain ribbon. If the skirt is lined, attach the lining to the facing pattern pieces, then join the facing/lining pattern pieces. Sew the center back, then install the zipper and slit, vent, or kick pleat. Insert pockets, if desired. Join the facing to the skirt waist, understitch, and press.

Vest

This assembly method for a vest was taught to Elissa Meyrich by sample maker May Fong, who works in the garment district in New York City. Both high-quality factories and some studios use the procedure, which involves only a few inches of hand stitching at the center back.

Tips for Professional Results

Vests are often considered an accessory item in clothing and are worn to enhance the other garments in the ensemble. Great care should be taken on even the smallest of details in a vest so that nothing will detract from its overall beauty. Neat and clean buttonholes become even more important in vests because they are often worn unbuttoned. Linings and facings, while only functional in other garments, can also become a decorative feature when part of a vest.

• Edgestitch around all outer edges of the vest to prevent the lining from rolling to the outside. Many better ready-to-wear vests are edge stitched around all of the outer edges, preventing the lining from rolling to the outside.

• Clip notches at all key locations on both the vest and the lining pattern pieces. When properly matched, these notches ensure that your seams will match and that the lining will fit into the vest. Notches also help you sew the vest to the lining in an efficient manner.

• Carefully stitch all details such as buttonholes and welts or pockets with smooth, unbroken lines of stitching.

• Cut open buttonholes with a block and chisel to prevent loose strings and jagged edges.

• Reduce your seam allowances so that you don't need to trim them as you sew.

Recommended Seam Allowances

You will be well on your way to achieving the look of ready-to-wear by adjusting seam allowances before cutting out the pattern pieces for your garment. See "Seam Allowances" on pages 42–49 for detailed instructions.

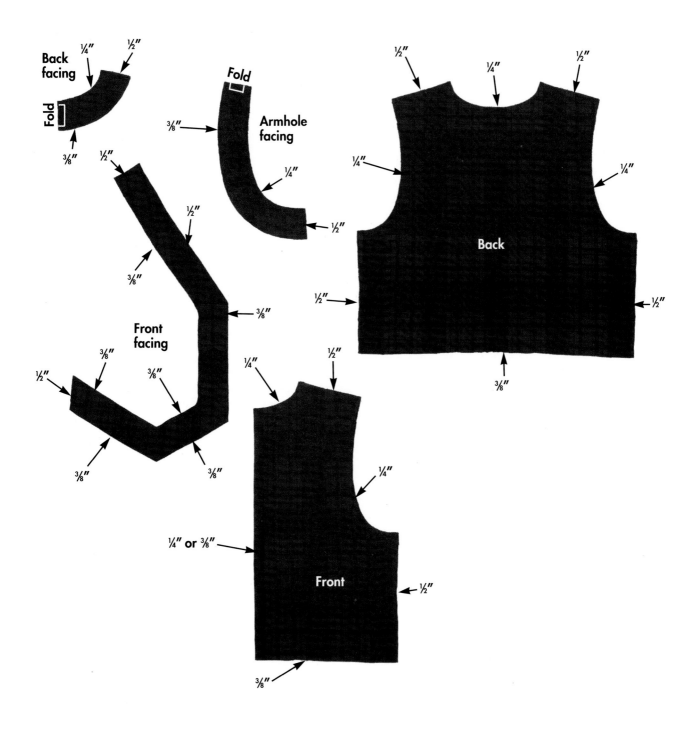

Assembly Procedure

May Fong's assembly method is different than the instructions you find in most home-sewing patterns. Additional notches are added to the pattern pieces so that the lining sews in easily. And prior to cutting out the pattern pieces, seam allowances are trimmed to ½ inch, or smaller, from the home-sewing standard of ⅝ inch. Eliminating bulk in the cutting stage is very important to a garment-industry sewer.

"Understitching" (page 187)

"Matching Plaids" (page 11)

"Single Welt Sportswear Pocket" (pages 156–157) or

"Faced Single Welt Pocket" (page 155) or

"Double Welt Pocket" (pages 159–160)

"Buttons, Buttonholes, and Lappage" (pages 90–97)

"Bagged Lining For a Vest" (pages 134–135) or

May Fong's assembly method in this chapter (pages 237–239)

1 Test your fabric and interfacing to determine if they require pretreatment. Then adjust the seam allowances on your pattern pieces, proceed with the layout, and cut out the pattern pieces. If the vest and lining pattern pieces are identical, you can cut the pattern pieces from both the fashion fabric and lining at the same time. See "Fabric" on pages 50–56, "Interfacings" on pages 57–64, and "Laying Up and Cutting Out Fabric" on pages 65–82. Don't overlock the pattern pieces because they are encased in the interior of the garment.

2 Notch the center back on the fabric and lining pattern pieces at the neck and the hem. Notch both sides of the front neckline at the midpoint between the shoulder seam and the top of the center front. Also notch the armscye on the front and back pattern pieces in the lower third of the armscye and at the midpoint on the side seams. If desired, fuse interfacing to the pattern pieces and install welt pockets on the fronts. This vest will have single welt sportswear pockets (featured on pages 156–157).

3 With right sides facing, sew the shoulder seams of the vest fronts and vest back together. Press the seam allowances open. Prepare the lining pieces in the same manner.

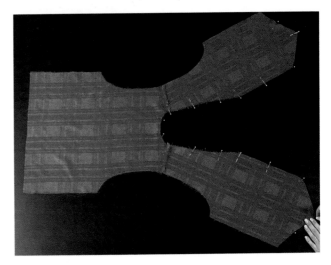

4 Pin the vest and lining front pattern pieces together with right sides facing and notches matching. Join the vest and lining along the hem, front edge, and neckline. Don't pin the side seams together yet. These will be joined later in the assembly procedure.

5 Sew the lining and vest together as pinned, but stop about 4 inches short of the side seam at the hem. Trim the seam allowances to ⅛ inch at the points. Reach into the vest and turn the points right side out. Don't turn the rest of the vest right side out yet. Tips for sewing, trimming, and turning points are featured in "Corners" on pages 108–109.

6 Understitch the lining. This will hold the seam allowances in position and prevent the lining from rolling to the outside of the garment. Your vest should be understitched unless you plan to topstitch it. Understitch from the hem to the neckline, excluding the points at the hem and sewing as far up the front of the vest as possible.

7 Sew the lining to the vest at one armhole, with the right sides still facing. The best way to sew this seam in the armscye is to start at the front and end at the back. If desired, trim the armhole seam allowances. Now sew the remaining armhole.

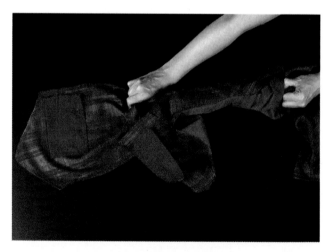

8 Reach into the vest through the open side seam of one of the fronts. Your hand and arm go between the front vest and front vest lining and up through the shoulder. Grasp the vest back. If you find this awkward, use both hands.

9 Start pulling the back of the vest through the shoulder. Gently pull it completely through the shoulder and out the open side seam of the vest front. Continue pulling fabric through the shoulder seam until the second front also emerges from the open side seam. The garment is now right side out. Press the front and armhole seams carefully, making sure the lining fabric is not rolling to the outside of the garment.

10 At one side seam, pin the front to the back with right sides facing and notches and seams matching. The fashion fabric front and back will be joined, and the lining front and back will be joined. Sew one side seam together. Don't sew the hem opening closed. Repeat on the other side seam. Press the side seams to the back of the garment.

11 Turn the vest wrong side out. Don't turn the points on the vest front. Pin the bottom of the vest together, leaving approximately 4 inches open at the center back. This opening is needed to turn the vest right side out again. Sew the vest back at the hem on both sides of the opening. Press the seamline.

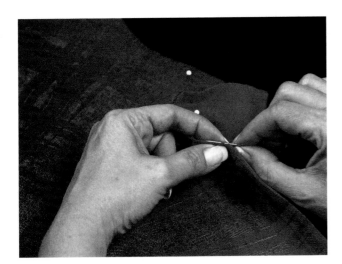

12 Turn the vest right side out by pulling it through the opening at the center back. Hand sew the opening shut. Add buttonholes to the right front and buttons to the left front. See "Buttons, Buttonholes, and Lappage" on pages 90–97 for guidelines on buttonhole size and placement and lappage and for instructions for sewing on buttons by machine.

SHOP TALK

Consider Blocking Lightweight Fabrics

THIN FABRICS, SUCH AS RAYON, SILK, AND SOME cottons need a lightweight interfacing that is designed to be fused to the fiber content of your fabric. These thin fabrics sometimes look better if the entire front of the vest is backed with an interfacing. This procedure is explained in "Block-Fusing Procedure for Slippery Fabrics" on page 76. Heavy fabrics, such as wool, denim, corduroy, and some stiff or thick cottons, need only minimal interfacing. The vest front neckline and the armholes are reinforced with interfacing that is cut 1½ to 2 inches wide and that follows the shape of the front neckline and armholes.

Elissa Meyrich

Buyer's Guide

Allentown Sewing Machine Outlet
725 North 15th Street
Allentown, PA 18102

This company sells Pfaff sewing machines and brand-specific and universal presser feet.

Apparel City Sewing Machine Company Inc.
1330 Howard Street
San Francisco, CA 94103

Alpha-Numeric Marking Paper used for pattern alterations can be purchased by the roll from this company.

Clotilde, Inc.
2 Sew Smart Way B8031
Stevens Point, WI 54481-8031
(800) 772-2891

This is a mail-order source for many sewing notions, including Invisible 0.004 Nylon Wonder Thread by Sew-Art, the pressing equipment shown in the photographs in this book, and a T-square ruler.

Fashion Fabrics Club
10490 Baur Boulevard
St. Louis, MO 63132
(800) 468-0602

Fashion Fabrics Club has been in the fabric mail-order business since 1956 and features fabric from the clothing lines of top designers such as Liz Claiborne, Jones of New York, and Leslie Fay at a fraction of comparable retail cost. A warehouse outlet is open to the public.

HTC-Handler Textile Corporation
24 Empire Boulevard
Dept. RP
Moonachie, NJ 07074
(800) 666-9683

HTC interfacing products are widely available. Write to the company for the name of a store near you or to obtain the name of a mail-order source.

Pfaff American Sales Corporation
610 Winters Avenue
Paramus, NJ 07653-0566

Write for the name of your local Pfaff dealer.

Sew Fast/Sew Easy
147 West 57th Street, 2nd Floor
New York, NY 10019

This company sells Super Curve Curved Petersham, which is recommended for facing contoured waists on skirts and pants.

Unique Techniques
3840 136th Avenue NE
Bellevue, WA 98005
(800) 557-5563

Fusible tape, which this company calls fusible roll line tape, is sold by the roll in black or white. You can order tape that is on the straight of grain or bias cut.

lossary

Apex. The point, or tip, of a dart where the dart legs intersect.

Baby hem. A garment industry term for a rolled hem.

Baby hem foot. A rolled hem presser foot.

Break point. The location where the roll on a faced collar, shawl collar, or lapel changes direction above the top button and buttonhole. This spot is the start of the roll line.

Chain stitch. This stitch is formed on a machine that has needle threads but no bobbin threads, such as a serger. Thread from a needle passes through fabric that is under the presser foot, forming stitches on the top of the fabric and "locked" loops on the underside.

Clean-finish. To overlock or pink a raw edge.

Condition. To let a piece of fabric or interfacing dry and cool thoroughly. It's best not to move an item as it conditions.

Crack stitch. The garment industry term for stitch in the ditch.

Crowding. Using a finger to bunch the fabric behind the presser foot as a line of stitching is created.

Dart leg. One of the two sides of a dart.

Fill. In a woven fabric, the yarn running from selvage to selvage at right angles to the warp.

Fuse tape. Also called fusible tape. A strip of fusible interfacing. Sewers can make their own or purchase it by the roll.

Lay up. A garment industry term for laid-out fabric and pattern pieces.

Lockstitches. Stitches formed when even amounts of thread are drawn from the top and bottom of the fabric under the presser foot and "locked" together.

Needle plate. The piece of metal mounted on the bed of a sewing machine or serger under the presser foot.

Oak tag. Lighter than cardboard, this is strong, pliable paper that is used to make slopers.

Off-grain. When the design stamped on a fabric, or the pattern pieces cut from a fabric, doesn't follow the fabric's warp or fill, it is off-grain.

Pearl edge. Another name for a rolled hem.

Pocket bag. A pocket and pocket facing.

Release point. The location at the top of a slit, vent, and kick pleat where the stitching stops and the garment splits.

Right- or left-hinged zipper foot. A single-toe presser foot that can be positioned to the right or left of a needle.

Rolled hem. A home-sewing term for a baby hem. This ⅛- to ¼-inch-wide hem is used for fine, delicate fabrics. It's created by hand sewing, by using a specialized machine, or with a special presser foot.

Roll line. The place a finished faced collar or lapel changes direction and rolls to the outside of a garment, usually above the top button.

Sliding zipper foot. Also called an adjustable zipper foot. A single-toe presser foot attached to a horizontal sliding bar, this foot can be positioned to the right or left of a needle.

Sloper. A pattern, often made on oak tag, without seam allowances or style lines that acts as a template for new patterns. A sloper is also a basic pattern that can be compared to new patterns for fit.

spi. The abbreviation for stitches per inch.

Stitch in the ditch. To crack stitch. To stitch in the ditch, secure part of a pattern piece to the wrong side of a garment by extending the loose section past the seamline on the wrong side of the garment, then sewing it in place from the right side with a line of stitching in the previous seamline.

Strike-through. The result when the bonding agent on interfacing shows through to the right side of the fabric to which it's fused. The term also refers to anything that shows through to the right side of a garment, for example, a hemline that is visible on the front of a garment because it wasn't ironed with a press cloth.

Top press. To press from the right side.

True bias. A perfect 90 degree angle from the straight grain of a fabric forms the true bias.

Warp. In woven fabrics, this is the set of yarns that runs lengthwise and parallel to the selvage and is interwoven with the fill.

Webbing. A strip of fabric coated with a heat-activated resin. Placed between two pieces of fabric, it bonds them together when pressed.

Weft. Another name for the fill yarns in a fabric. The weft runs perpendicular to the selvages.

Authors' Contributions

Laurel Hoffman

Equipment: *Introduction*
Seam Allowances
Buttons, Buttonholes, and Lappage: *The entire chapter, except Bound Buttonholes*
Chain Stitching
Crack Stitching
Lapel
Lining a Skirt or Vest: *Securing a Lining to the Side Seams of a Skirt*
Seam Finishes Using a Sewing Machine: *Single Binding* and *French Seam*
Sleeves
Understitching
Yoke
Blouse, Pants, Skirt, and Vest: *Recommended Seam Allowances*
Blouse: *Assembly Procedure*

Barbara Kelly

Equipment: *Why Buy an Industrial Sewing Machine?, Stitch Length,* and *Successful Combinations*
Fit
Slopers
Alterations for Patterns and Blocks: *The entire chapter, except the material on altering the bust*
The Sloper Shortcut to Fast Pattern Alterations
Making a Muslin
Backstitching
Buttons, Buttonholes, and Lappage: *Bound Buttonholes*
Collars: *Flat Collar, Convertible Collar, Attaching a Collar with a Partial Facing,* and *Popular Edge Stitched Standing Collar*
Corners: *Making a Point*
Crowding
Darts
Hems: *The Top Ten Rules about Hems, Interfacing a Garment's Hem, Blindhem Stitch,* and *Adding Cuffs to Pants or Sleeves*
Matching Seams
Mitered Corners
Pintucks
Pockets: *The No-Fail, Perfectly Shaped Patch Pocket, Traditional Single Welt Pocket,* and *Double Welt Pocket*
Pressing
Seam Finishes Using a Sewing Machine: *Hong Kong Seam Finish* and *Flat Felled Seam*

Spaghetti Tubing
Topstitching
Waistbands: *Raised Waist with Facing and Interior Tab Closure*
Zippers: *Invisible Zipper*

Julia Reidy Linger

Equipment: *Feed Dogs*
Bias Binding: *Replacing Facings with Bias Binding*
Collars: *The Ten-Minute Collar with Stand*
Cuffs
Lining a Skirt or Vest: *Bagged Lining for a Vest* and *Lining and Waistband Assembly for a Skirt*
Plackets
Pockets: *Invisible Side Seam Pocket, Sportswear Side Seam Pocket, Faced Pocket, Inside Patch Pocket, Single Welt Sportswear Pocket,* and *Faced Single Welt Pocket*
Zippers: *Pin-Free Centered Zipper* and *A Separating Zipper*
Hallmarks of a Quality Garment
Blouse, Pants, Skirt, and Vest: *Tips for Professional Results*

Elissa Meyrich

Equipment: *Presser Feet* and *Seam Guides*
Laying Up and Cutting Out Fabric: *Notches*
Awl
Bias Binding: *Making Bias Strips*
Corners: *Turning a Corner*
Hems: *Rolled Hem*
Kick Pleats, Slits, and Vents
Lining a Skirt or Vest: *Securing a Lining at a Zipper Tape*
Seam Finishes Using a Sewing Machine: *Serger Seam Finishes*
Waistbands: *Figure-Flattering Piped Waistband, Grosgrain Ribbon–Faced Waistband,* and *Designer Elasticized Waistbands*
Zippers: *Fail-Safe Lapped Zipper* and *Mock Fly Zipper with Template*
Pants, Skirt, and Vest: *Assembly Procedure*
Skirt: *Assembly Methods for Alternate Skirt Silhouettes*

Lonny Noel

Fabric
Interfacings
Laying Up and Cutting Out Fabric: *The entire chapter, except Notches*

Index